BEYOND THE BOOK
EXTENDING MARC FOR
SUBJECT ACCESS

BEYOND THE BOOK
EXTENDING MARC FOR
SUBJECT ACCESS

edited by TONI PETERSEN & PAT MOLHOLT

G.K. HALL & CO · BOSTON · MASSACHUSETTS

First published 1990
by G.K. Hall & Co.
70 Lincoln Street
Boston, Massachusetts 02111

10 9 8 7 6 5 4 3 2 1

Library of Congress Cataloging-in-Publication Data

Beyond the book: extending MARC for subject access /
   edited by Toni Petersen and Pat Molholt.
      p. cm.
  Includes bibliographical references and index.
  ISBN 0-8161-1924-4. – ISBN 0-8161-1925-2 (pbk.)
  1. MARC System.
  2. Cataloging of nonbook materials – Data
processing. I. Petersen, Toni. II. Molholt, Pat.
Z699.4.M2E96   1990
025.3'4 – dc20   90-40717
                                                      CIP

The paper used in this publication meets the minimum requirements of
American National Standard for Information Sciences – Permanence of
Paper for Printed Library Materials. ANSI Z39.48-1984   ∞™
MANUFACTURED IN THE UNITED STATES OF AMERICA

I dedicate this book to those in my family who,
in the race to obtain ISBNs,
allowed me to come in third.

–T.P.

I dedicate this book to my daughters,
Rebecca and Stephanie,
for their support and patience.

–P.M.

■ Contents

■ Acknowledgments

We wish to acknowledge our colleagues in the Art Libraries Society of North America, the Visual Resources Association, and the Society of American Archivists, who over the past decade have shared their efforts to bring their collection data into the MARC environment. The librarians, archivists, and visual resources curators represented in this volume have methodically stretched the bounds of MARC, expanding its usefulness as a communications format.

We would also like to thank our editor, Carol Chin, and development editor, India Koopman, whose puzzlement over subfield tags and daggers never deterred them from a consistently kind attempt to guide us in pulling this book together.

■ Introduction

Toni Petersen

The purpose of this collection of essays is to sample the current thinking of those new constituencies who are turning to MARC to provide the vessel for their data collections. MARC has been the successful communications format for book and serial materials for the last two decades. It has provided the container or vehicle in which reside millions of bibliographic records and has been a model for their control in machine-readable form. In the last few years, however, a growing number of newcomers has signed on as actual or potential passengers. These new constituencies recognize the needs of their end users as paramount in the development of access systems. While they look to MARC to carry their data baggage, they also press new requirements on the old vessel, driven by the ways in which their users access collections.

In drawing together this collection, we have found it interesting that much of the work being done to investigate the use of the MARC format is occurring in fields within the humanities, especially in art, architecture, photography, and other visual arts. It is not often that the humanities take the lead in new developments in information handling and retrieval. These fields and the field of archival work that overlaps many of them have long histories of maintaining files of manual cataloging records. As these fields begin to automate their catalogs, they encounter two important needs: (1) a common format for data collection and exchange and (2) new controlled vocabularies that provide enhanced subject access. In their desire for more precise and sophisticated retrieval of information, they are examining not only whether MARC can be extended to accommodate new fields for their data but also how subject access can be enhanced beyond the subject fields currently available in the MARC format.

Book library catalogers recognize that they too must stretch beyond the confines of their old format structures in order to meet the demands of their users. There is a growing body of literature on the impact of online public access catalogs and on user expectations. Librarians and other information managers are raising access issues at conferences and meetings nationwide. Stressed the most is the necessity to consider how data in MARC records might be manipulated and displayed in order to provide enhanced access to online catalogs. System builders will have to be aware of two important areas: They will have to acquire knowledge of what users need and how user queries are made; and they must acquire the technical expertise to build the automated systems to meet those needs. Such systems will require the merging and presentation of diverse subject vocabularies in an easily retrieved manner.

For outsiders approaching MARC for the first time, two of the great challenges are the intricacy and rigidity of MARC coding and the inflexibility of its structure. These basic problems are being addressed on several fronts. Traveling workshops organized by the Society of American Archivists have been extraordinarily successful in training archivists in the use of the MARC Archives and Manuscripts Control Format (AMC), breaking down the barriers against the use of MARC coding in particular. Similar workshops have been held by other groups on the use of special thesauri in MARC, and a group within the Art Libraries Society of North America (ARLIS) is working toward a compendium of practice for visual images. This follows an earlier compendium produced at the Chicago Historical Society, which described use of the then new Visual Materials Format.

A highly problematic attendant concern has been the widespread feeling that *Library of Congress Subject Headings* (*LCSH*) is inadequate for providing subject coverage in specialized fields. Without a large body of extant records already in the MARC format and with high expectations for powerful subject retrieval capabilities in local online catalog systems, these catalogers of nontraditional materials are faced with a double dilemma: how to avoid *LCSH* when it does not provide vocabulary adequate to their needs and where to get adequate, controlled vocabularies acceptable for use in MARC. With new thesauri proliferating for use in MARC fields other than the traditional 650 Topical Subject Field, problems of authority control of multiple vocabularies and of information retrieval must be addressed.

Despite the raising of these dangers, our new MARC passengers, represented by the writers of the essays in this volume, seem to want to proceed. What do they think of their chosen or hoped-for mode of transportation? What do they want from it? Some of the answers to these questions will emerge in this volume.

The first group of essays discusses some of the practical steps that have already been taken and describes ongoing cataloging projects that make use of the MARC format in new ways. The first essay, by Patricia Barnett and Toni Petersen, describes the development of the *Art and Architecture*

Thesaurus (*AAT*) as a new controlled vocabulary with a faceted classification of terms in separate hierarchies. The *AAT* is designed for the description of art literature, images, and objects. Its implementation in the MARC format has led to some changes in MARC, including the addition of a new topical subject field to accommodate faceted thesauri. This new 654 field is described, and examples of how it might be used are shown. Following this is a description by Jeanne Keefe of Rensselaer Polytechnic Institute of a project that integrates a collection of slide records with traditional bibliographic records in an online public access catalog. Students and faculty interested in architecture at Rensselaer can, from the same online source, find books on a building or other structures and slides portraying images of them. Subject access to the slides, previously unavailable in the manual catalog, is achieved through use of the *AAT*.

Other catalogers of nonbook materials have begun to use MARC beyond the 650 topical subject field for subject access. Jackie Dooley and Helena Zinkham's essay is a thorough review of the fields that enhance description and access, especially the 655 Form/Genre Field and the 755 Physical Characteristics Field, and of the various subject lists and thesauri that are being developed to provide the data content for these fields. The authors conclude with the warning that thesaurus developers must work together to prevent a lack of consistency at the term level in these new thesauri. Such inconsistency would add to the confusion already being felt among those who must choose from this growing number of controlled vocabularies.

Cathleen Whitehead's essay on the mapping of *LCSH* into the *AAT* is instructive in pointing out the differences between *LCSH* and *AAT* and provides a first step in resolving the problem of the use of multiple thesauri in MARC. The *AAT*, realizing the importance of maintaining compatibility with *LCSH* and aware of the problems that would surface whenever online would access point to more than one controlled vocabulary or subject authority file in MARC, took on the task of mapping its developing vocabulary into *LCSH*. By tracking *LCSH* headings in *AAT* MARC authority records, they hope that these links will be of help as librarians using *LCSH* and others using *AAT* for art materials merge their MARC records in commonly held databases on utilities like the Research Libraries Information Network (RLIN).

Martha Yee describes the work of the National Moving Image Database Standards Committee to provide a national standard list of form and genre terms in the 655 field, *Moving Image Materials: Genre Terms*. She enumerates several serious problems encountered by those who are aware of issues of searching and retrieval based on current use of the MARC format. Yee stresses the importance of taking users' needs into account in the design of subject access systems – for instance, in needs for differences in depth and exhaustivity of indexing. Another issue raised by Yee is the problems in retrieval that emerge from postcoordinated use of single terms in the 655 and 755 fields and is one that is covered in other essays that discuss the use of these fields (notably, Jackie Dooley and Helena Zinkham, and Linda Evans). She also raises the issue, along with Snow and Evans, of the problems inherent in the confusion as to whether a subject term refers to the item itself being described or cataloged or to its *aboutness* – that is, its subject content.

Although it has come late to automated cataloging and its use of the MARC format is still in dispute, the museum field is in a period of intensive examination of systems and formats to put its object records online. Deirdre C. Stam's essay provides an overview of a twenty-year effort to develop a code for the description and cataloging of art objects. Stam's discussion ranges across Europe and the United States, identifying the principal organizations active in this quest and detailing both the failures to achieve a code and the new attempts that are being made.

The Inventory of American Sculpture at the National Museum of American Art, a groundbreaking project that uses the MARC format to catalog realia, has been using a modified MARC Visual Materials Format to catalog works of sculpture. Christine Hennessey describes this project, which will give impetus to other museums that are looking for guidance in attempts to translate their manual object records into machine-readable catalogs. A whole range of realia, hitherto dealt with in MARC only by bibliographic references to literary sources, may now join other nonbook materials in the MARC format.

Another set of essays is grounded on the theme of a call for new advances in the field. One of the essential elements needed by users of archival material is information that provides an understanding of the context in which the records were created. Applying terms that describe the *function* – the reason the records were brought together by the creating agency – allows archivists and researchers access to records that would not normally come together in searches on topical subjects or personal and corporate names. Through the Research Libraries Group's (RLG) Government Records Project, in which a number of state archives have joined with the National Archive to add records to the RLIN database, Alden Monroe and Kathleen Roe propose the creation of a new controlled vocabulary to be used in the 657 Function Term Field, a field that was added to the MARC format at the request of the archival community.

Brad Young, in enumerating recent trends in access to music materials, also calls for a new music thesaurus to aid in providing access to users of these materials. He raises the importance of classification research for subject access, especially the development of classification schemes that use faceting to allow flexibility in the representation of complex topics. Such flexibility holds the most promise for better online postcoordinate searching. The MARC Music Format, which provides unique codes for medium of performance, form of composition or musical genre, and format of score, and notes the presence of parts, is given as an example of the potential to be realized within the MARC format for access to multiple aspects of a topic. Originally prepared as a paper presented at an ALA conference program on 28 June 1986, entitled "New Directions in Subject Access to Nonbook Materials," Young's essay has been updated to take into account work done in this area through 1989. The contribution it makes to this collection—it differs from the other essays in its recommendations for seeking new ways of encoding data—lies in the fact that Young is pointing to the importance of making use of electronic information retrieval techniques to draw data from MARC records in a way that will enhance user satisfaction. His recommendations, drawn from classification theory, may differ from traditional subject cataloging but nonetheless may demonstrate ways in which the traditional means of providing subject access may be broadened.

Linda J. Evans is interested in the cataloging of artifacts, especially in a museum setting. She points out the new requirements for MARC if it is to be accepted by museum curators, who traditionally have prepared catalog entries for the objects in their collections. She speculates about what fields in the MARC format might be used to provide access to museum artifacts. For example, book catalogers have applied topical subject headings in one MARC field, the 650, with some confusion between the identity of the object being cataloged and its subject content. Evans urges that such melding of physical characteristics and aboutness must be sorted out before the MARC format can be used successfully to describe unique items.

The final group of essays calls for new parameters for access to nontraditional materials. Howard Besser and Maryly Snow at the University of California at Berkeley (UCB) describe the prototype Image Database Project, which is designed as a retrieval system for the display of both bibliographic and image records and the actual images themselves, across the range of the university's library and museum collections. The aim of the project is to provide a single easy-to-use online catalog, incorporating both text and image information, that is accessible from any workstation on the campus network. The problems of implementing such a visionary system, which combines text and image, are exposed, including the reluctance of museum curators and computer technologists to use the MARC format. Yet the authors contend that mapping to MARC from diverse collection records is technically feasible and should be undertaken for the common goal of sharing information. Maryly Snow then goes on, in a follow-up essay, to give one slide librarian's vision of the building of a national visual index through the addition to the bibliographic utilities of slide records with citations to illustrations in monographs and journals.

David Bearman challenges the MARC format to grow and evolve to accommodate the requirements of archival information systems, where identification of the provenance of a set of records is critical, and of museum systems, which go beyond archival requirements into areas of description of unique items and networks of associations with like objects. Having helped to shepherd the AMC format through its development process, he is well equipped to note the political and technical issues that call for resolution if the MARC format is to continue to be adapted to the needs of new constituents. Finally, Pat Molholt points to the need for new access techniques, undergirded with artificial intelligence, that will require a reexamination of our traditional tools such as thesauri, syndetic structures, and classification techniques.

As we have seen, the pressure to extend MARC comes from many directions. This collection does not pretend to represent all of them. For example, we would like to have included descriptions of the work being done at the National Library of Medicine to map the *Medical Subject Headings* (*MeSH*) thesaurus into *LCSH* and to explore the potential use of the MARC format in some of the special databases on RLIN. Another area of discussion might be the integration of journal indexing databases with library online public access catalogs. The *Avery Index to Architectural Periodicals* currently uses a modified MARC structure, one of the only journal indexes to do so, and it might provide a model for such integration. There are surely other instances of pertinent work that extend the use of MARC outside the book library field.

It has been a pleasure to bring together this strong group of articulate and challenging proponents of extension and change to the MARC format in order to meet a new and diverse constituency. Those of us who have watched the progress MARC has made in the last two decades have no doubt that it can be done. All aboard!

Publisher's note: Throughout the book dollar signs ($) have been used to represent double daggers (‡) in MARC codes.

■ Extending MARC to Accommodate Faceted Thesauri: The AAT Model

Patricia J. Barnett
Toni Petersen

SUBJECT CONTENT OF NONTRADITIONAL MATERIALS

Those involved in the documentation of art bring a new dimension to the conceptualization of the subject of an item to be cataloged. Whereas bibliographic catalogers define *subject* primarily as the object being described, following parameters set by the *Library of Congress Subject Cataloging Manual,*[1] art documentalists, including art object catalogers and visual materials catalogers, add the dimension of subject as the iconographic content of the artwork. A clear distinction is made between identifying the object type, for example, ISOMETRIC DRAWINGS, and the object depicted, for example, SKYSCRAPERS. Although the distinction seems obvious, there has been confusion in applying subject terms in the MARC format.

Library of Congress Subject Headings (*LCSH*) is a list of topical subject headings; we may presume that it provides us with the topics to be used in the description of the document we are reading or the object at which we are looking. *Topical*, as defined by *Webster's Third New International Dictionary*, means "of, relating to, or arranged by topics,"[2] yet *LCSH* can be used inconsistently in the headings it presents as topics. Until recently – and still evident in book cataloging – works with the subject of, for instance, "drawings" were indexed in a way similar to books of drawings because there was but one slot traditionally used in the MARC format (the 650 field) for all topical subjects, whether they were topical, iconographic, genre type, or physical descriptions.

In the mid-1980s, the MARC format began to allow a clearer distinction by promoting the use of the 655 and 755 fields in the Archival and Manuscripts Control (AMC) and Visual Materials (VM) formats. These fields for genre type (655) and physical description of the cataloged item (755), if used properly, would go far toward ameliorating the current confusion caused by the blurring of the distinctions among catalogers who are treating these materials inconsistently.

Despite these problems, the MARC formats have proven their ability to carry bibliographic data. Nearly all library-associated catalogs use them, and they hold promise to accommodate a growing number of organizations wishing to use changing and emerging MARC formats for documents other than books: archival materials, architectural drawings, photographs, other graphic materials, and even museum objects, or realia. These nontraditional MARC users bring a fresh approach to the problems of formatting and retrieving subject content. Their insistence upon making a distinction between the subject content of a work and the physical or genre nature of the work itself was instrumental in bringing about the establishment of the 655 and 755 fields, for example.

There is also activity among catalogers of nontraditional materials to produce authoritative lists of terms to be used for different kinds of subject access.[3] These lists sometimes draw terms from *LCSH* and expand on them to provide more intensive coverage for their fields while clearly defining whether they are topical, iconographic, genre, or physical description terms.

SUBJECT CATALOGING AND CLASSIFICATION

"The purpose of visual resources classification and cataloging is to establish a precise and predictable place for each slide or photo[graph] within a logical system."[4] Although this is also the purpose of bibliographic classification – to place one book in one location – it is not the purpose of bibliographic subject cataloging. For bibliographic catalogers, classification and subject cataloging serve different purposes.[5] Subject cataloging provides *subject* access to the object or document's information, which can mean access from multiple points.

Catalogers of nontraditional materials are just beginning to expand access to their materials via subject cataloging, thanks to the capabilities of computerized catalogs. Until slide libraries began to automate, the most common cataloging situation called for each slide physically to occupy its place in the classification scheme and even to hold, on a card preceding the slide, whatever cataloging information was given. Some slide libraries had card catalogs as well, but most often such catalogs contained only one card per slide, allowing one point of access, usually the name of artist when known. To add to this picture of lack of subject access, art documentalists have been blocked from providing full subject coverage not only because they have come late to automation but also because there was no comprehensive vocabulary available in the field of art.

AAT: ITS HISTORY AND DEVELOPMENT

The *Art and Architecture Thesaurus* (*AAT*) developed out of a need to provide better subject access in the field of art and architecture. The art bibliographic and library world was dissatisfied with its de facto subject authority standard, *LCSH*, and the art documentation community was dissatisfied with the lack of their own standard.[6] The founders of the *AAT* project wanted to fill the needs of these communities by building a standard and controlled vocabulary of art and architecture terms for both indexing and retrieval in an art information database, whether it was bibliographic, visual, or object oriented.[7]

The *AAT* is being developed as a faceted, or postcoordinated, hierarchically structured vocabulary (Figure 1). The majority of terms in the *AAT* describes object types and modifying concepts such as style or material. Terminology is warranted by use in current literary sources and is validated by the scholarly community. Where possible, it incorporates already existing authority lists, such as *LCSH*, which may then be enhanced or modified.

The vocabulary in the thesaurus covers the following areas in the visual arts:

> Built Environment: built works and the human elaboration of the natural environment.
> Furnishings and Equipment: artifacts with a primarily utilitarian purpose, often embellished.
> Visual and Verbal Communication: primarily nonutilitarian forms created according to aesthetic, conceptual, or symbolic principles.

Iconographical terminology, that is, terminology describing the visual content or subject of works of art, is not within the scope of the *AAT*. Other subject lists, such as the *LC Thesaurus for Graphic Materials*, have been developed to handle this type of terminology.

Figure 1   Sample Hierarchy Section

<single built works by specific type>
  <single built works by function>
    <recreation structures>
      <winter sports structures>

**SINGLE BUILT WORKS
AND OPEN SPACES (RK)**

RK.1079	ski jumps
RK.1080	ski lifts
RK.1081	toboggan runs
RK.1082	*<religious structures>*
RK.1083	*<freestanding altars>*
RK.1084	arae
RK.1085	bomoi
RK.1086	fire altars
RK.1087	thymeles
RK.1088	holy wells
RK.1089	idgahs
RK.1090	martyria
RK.1091	minarets
RK.1092	religious buildings
RK.1093	baptisteries
RK.1094	churches
RK.1095	*<churches by form>*
RK.1096	double churches
RK.1097	hall churches
RK.1098	rock-cut churches
RK.1099	stave churches
RK.1100	*<churches by function>*
RK.1101	chapels of ease
RK.1102	pilgrimage churches
RK.1103	procathedrals
RK.1104	*<churches by location or context>*
RK.1105	abbey churches
RK.1106	cathedrals
RK.1107	cave churches
RK.1108	collegiate churches
RK.1109	minsters
RK.1110	mission churches
RK.1111	monastic churches
RK.1112	parish churches
RK.1113	domus ecclesiae
RK.1114	kivas
RK.1115	meeting houses
RK.1116	Quaker meeting houses
RK.1117	mosques
RK.1118	*<mosques by form>*
RK.1119	four-iwan mosques
RK.1120	hypostyle mosques
RK.1121	*<mosques by function>*
RK.1122	jamis
RK.1123	masjids
RK.1124	pagodas
RK.1125	synagogues
RK.1126	temples
RK.1127	*<temples by form>*

May be used in combination with other descriptors (e.g., **fieldstone** + **cottages**; **prefabricated** + **ranch houses**; **three-story** + **parking garages**; **Georgian** + **saltbox houses**; **temple** + **porticoes**).

<religious structures>
religious buildings
temples
<temples by form>

RK.1128	hypaethral temples
RK.1129	rock-cut temples
RK.1130	speoses
RK.1131	wats
RK.1132	*<temples by function>*
RK.1133	aedes
RK.1134	fire temples
RK.1135	chahar taqs
RK.1136	mortuary temples
RK.1137	*<temples by location or context>*
RK.1138	cave temples
RK.1139	shrines
RK.1140	chaityas
RK.1141	heroa
RK.1142	jinjas
RK.1143	mashhads
RK.1144	mithraea
RK.1145	naiskoi
RK.1146	sacella
RK.1147	t'ai miao
RK.1148	stupas
RK.1149	chortens
RK.1150	dagobas
RK.1151	prachedis
RK.1152	sukkahs
RK.1153	ziggurats
RK.1154	*<research structures>*
RK.1155	particle accelerators
RK.1156	cyclotrons
RK.1157	linear accelerators
RK.1158	research buildings
RK.1159	laboratories
RK.1160	aerodynamical laboratories
RK.1161	aeronautical laboratories
RK.1162	agricultural laboratories
RK.1163	biological laboratories
RK.1164	chemical laboratories
RK.1165	conservation laboratories
RK.1166	crime laboratories
RK.1167	electronics laboratories
RK.1168	environmental laboratories
RK.1169	experiment stations
RK.1170	research laboratories
RK.1171	veterinary laboratories
RK.1172	observatories
RK.1173	astronomical observatories
RK.1174	research stations
RK.1175	ice stations
RK.1176	meteorological stations

May be used in combination with other descriptors (e.g., **fieldstone** + **cottages**; **prefabricated** + **ranch houses**; **three-story** + **parking garages**; **Georgian** + **saltbox houses**; **temple** + **porticoes**).

AAT terminology is prepared by an editorial staff according to American National Standards Institute (ANSI) and British Standards Institute (BSI) standards,[8] using the National Library of Medicine's Medical Subject Headings (MeSH) thesaurus as a model.[9] Initial work on the *AAT* was funded by the Council on Library Resources, the National Endowment for the Humanities, and the Andrew W. Mellon Foundation. In 1983, the *AAT* became an operating unit within the Art History Information Program of the J. Paul Getty Trust. The *AAT* has been endorsed by the Art Libraries Society of North America, the College Art Association of America, the Society of Architectural Historians, the American Institute of Architects, and the International Conference of Architecture Museums.

Figure 2 *AAT* Facets and Hierarchies

ASSOCIATED CONCEPTS FACET
   Associated Concepts

PHYSICAL ATTRIBUTES FACET
   Design Attributes
   Design Elements
   Colors

STYLES AND PERIODS FACET
   Styles and Periods

AGENTS FACET
   People and Organizations

ACTIVITIES FACET
   Disciplines
   Functions
   Events
   Processes and Techniques

MATERIALS FACET
   Materials

OBJECTS FACET
   Built Environment
   Settlements, Systems and Landscapes
   Built Complexes and Districts
   Single Built Works and Open Spaces
   Building Divisions and Site Elements
   Built Works Components

Furnishings and Equipment
   Tools and Equipment
   Measuring Devices
   Hardware and Joints
   Furniture
   Furnishings
   Personal Artifacts
   Containers
   Culinary Artifacts
   Musical Instruments
   Recreational Artifacts
   Armament
   Transportation Artifacts
   Communication Artifacts

Visual and Verbal Communication
   Image and Object Genres
   Drawings
   Paintings
   Prints
   Photographs
   Sculpture
   Multi-Media Art Forms
   Communication Design
   Exchange Media
   Book Arts
   Document Types

The *AAT* is currently a compilation of more than thirty-five thousand terms gathered, researched, and arranged conceptually into forty hierarchies and is halfway toward completion. The terms in the *AAT* are drawn from existing subject lists – for example, *LCSH*, the *Avery Index to Architectural Periodicals*, *RILA*, *RIBA Architectural Periodicals Index*, and *Nomenclature: A System for Classifying Man-Made Objects* – augmented by terms from reference works and authoritative monographs. As each section is completed, it is reviewed and validated by advisory teams of scholars.

The forty hierarchies are clustered into seven broad categories, called *facets*. (See Figure 2 for a list of *AAT* facets and hierarchies.) These facets, representing mutually exclusive categories of information or categories of knowledge, are meant to work in combination with such non-*AAT* facets as chronology, geography, personal or corporate names, art work or structure names, and iconographic subjects. Individual terms may be selected from hierarchies within the *AAT* facets, or more complex subject headings may be constructed by combining terms from different facets. Current research in the field of subject access indicates that a faceted vocabulary is most suitable to the organization and integration of knowledge databases.[10] The *AAT* developers recognize that numerous art history information databases beginning to emerge contain records that are surrogates for many different media (art objects, textual information, slides, photographs, etc.). It is expected that a faceted vocabulary can serve the requirements of each of these databases and, at the same time, prepare for their compatible integration.

A set of architectural terminology and support hierarchies is now ready for application; a number of test sites are participating in its use and providing feedback. These model projects include slide collections, photograph collections, architectural drawing collections, archives, periodical indexes, trade catalogs, and vertical file materials (Figure 3).

Ironically, the art library community that first voiced dissatisfaction with its de facto standard, *LCSH*, may have the most difficulty in adopting the *AAT*. Bibliographic libraries have undergone enormous changes in response to revised cataloging standards brought about by *AACR 2* and the transition from manual to online cataloging. Additional change brought about by adoption of new standards would not be welcomed at this time.[11] In the meantime, catalogers of nontraditional materials can move forward rapidly because they are not bound by long use of *LCSH*. The onetime hindrance of a lack of standardization may now be viewed as an asset, especially with the prospect that the *AAT* may be accommodated in an expanded MARC format that will allow for the faceting of subject information.

Figure 3   Selected *AAT* Users, 1990

Archives of American Art
Archives of the District of Columbia
Arkansas Arts Center, Decorative Arts Museum
Art Bibliographies Modern
Avery Index to Architectural Periodicals
AVIADOR Project of the Avery Library
Boston Museum of Fine Arts
British Architectural Library
Brooklyn Museum Planning Office
Canadian Centre for Architecture
Chicago Historical Society
Cleveland Museum of Art Slide Library
Cornell University Slide Library
Fogg Museum Slide Library
Getty Conservation Institute
Glossarium Artis
Graduate School of Design Library, Harvard University
Library of Congress, National Union Catalog of Manuscript Collections
Library of Congress, Prints and Photographs Department
Marburger Index
Massachusetts Institute of Technology, Rotch Slide Library
McGill University, School of Architecture Slide Library
McGraw-Hill Encyclopedia of Architecture
Metropolitan Museum of Art, Clearinghouse of Art Documentation and Computerization
National Gallery of Art, Photo Archive
New York Historical Society
New York State College of Ceramics Slide Library
Program for Art on Film
Rensselaer Polytechnic Institute Slide Library and Archive
SN/G, Scuola Normale Superiore
State University New York – Cortland Slide Library
University of California at Berkeley, Architecture Department Slide Library
University of California at San Diego, Slide and Photograph Library
University of Iowa, School of Art and Art History, Slide Library
University of Maryland Libraries
University of Massachusetts at Amherst Slide Library
University of Nebraska-Lincoln, Architecture Slide Library
University of Pennsylvania, Slide Library
University of Texas at Austin, Slide Library
WaveHill, Catalogue of Landscape Records in the United States

FACETED INDEXING

Facets refer to unique categories of subject information. This concept is similar to that developed by Derek Austin in Preserved Context Indexing System (PRECIS),[12] the indexing system developed principally for the British Library that has spawned a number of other syntactic string indexing systems.[13] In such systems, the indexer "atomizes" the different parts of the concepts to be indexed into pieces based on syntactic categories such as material used, object type, geographic locale, technique or process, and chronology. The strings contain codes, or *operators*, allowing various permutations to be generated and displayed.

Example of PRECIS coding:

        (z) (o) Italy
        (z) (p) Padua $d 1400-1500
        (x) (1) painting
        (x) (2) iconography $21 Christian
    Strings generated:
    Italy
    Padua, *1400-1500.* Painting
    Italy
    Padua, *1400-1500.* Christian iconography
    Padua. Italy,
    1400-1500. Painting
    Padua. Italy,
    1400-1500. Christian iconography
    Painting, Padua, *1400-1500.* Italy
    Iconography. Padua, *1400-1500.* Italy
    Christian iconography
    Christian iconography. Padua, *1400-1500.* Italy

On the other hand, bibliographic subject cataloging relies on strings of terms, sometimes long and including subheadings, consisting of different concepts bound together to describe an item. No attempt is made to differentiate among single concepts, except for the place and date, which are subfielded separately in *LCSH*, and the *topical subdivisions*, a vague designation covering both form and genre *and* modifying elements. For example:

        Canvas embroidery, Victorian
        Cities and towns, Ruined, extinct, etc. – Greece
        Bronze pitchers, Etruscan – Rome
        Housing – Sociological aspects

In contrast, catalogers of archival and visual materials have tended to use each term representing a concept independently, making no attempt to create syntactic expressions.

> Canvas
> Embroidery
> Victorian

> Cities and towns
> Ruined
> Greece

As noted above, *LCSH* is a syntactic indexing system of sorts, in that different characteristics of a topic are often combined into one heading, or precoordinated. *LCSH* strings often contain the same facets, or categories of information, used for subject indexing by catalogers of nontraditional materials, but they are not clearly identified. For example, although date and place are clearly separated into the $y and $z subfields common to *LCSH* strings, the main part of the heading, $a, contains in one undifferentiated expression several different categories of information. For example, in the heading BRONZE PITCHERS, ETRUSCAN, ETRUSCAN is a style that may be applied to a wide variety of objects and concepts; PITCHERS is an object type; BRONZE is a material. In addition, $x, the topical subdivision, may contain form and genre terms, such as BIBLIOGRAPHIES, as well as topical concepts, such as CONSERVATION AND RESTORATION. This system of undifferentiated headings causes problems for those outside the bibliographic cataloging field.

In a simple example of three facets: technique, chronology, and geography, a nonbibliographic indexing format might arrange them as follows:

> Technique: Drawing
> Chronology: 19th century
> Geography: France

In a MARC-based bibliographic indexing string, however, the facets are expressed as follows:

DRAWING – 19TH CENTURY – FRANCE

Rather than labeling each facet, the bibliographic model embeds MARC codes in the string that signal the system to index one term as a *topical subject*, in this case, DRAWING (which is actually a *technique*); another, 19TH CENTURY, as a *chronological period*; and another, FRANCE, as a *geographic location*.

$aDRAWING$y19TH CENTURY$zFRANCE

In the Etruscan bronze pitchers example, the facets relating to style and material are lost within the LC coding:

$aBRONZE PITCHERS,ETRUSCAN$zROME

LCSH developed over the years with the indexing needs of one constituency in mind, the bibliographic cataloger, and from a base of manual catalogs. Although warnings have been posted concerning the structure of *LCSH* headings,[14] the number of records using *LCSH* in our bibliographic databases is now so massive that any suggestion for making changes, even to a single heading, is cause for consternation. A revolution equal to the change to *AACR 2* in 1981 would be required, and there is a sense that the library field is not ready for another such upheaval, at least not yet. Therefore, we may assume that the basic structure of *LCSH* headings will remain as they are.

The *AAT*, on the other hand, has developed over the last decade with automated cataloging databases firmly established and with the requirements of a diverse group of constituents in mind, not the least of whom are art librarians. Many of the art librarians are cataloging bibliographical materials, so the *AAT* has been progressing toward a goal of providing a faceted vocabulary for computerized indexing systems while at the same time accommodating current MARC cataloging procedures. However, MARC will also need to evolve, to some degree, in two important areas: the first, in its *authority format*, which has already undergone changes to accommodate newer syndetic structures of hierarchical vocabularies and a growing number of subject-specific thesauri;[15] and the second, in its *record format*, which needs to accommodate more precise indexing by adopting faceted categories of subject access.

MARC AS A FACETED FORMAT FOR SUBJECT CATALOGING

The *AAT* was the first specialized subject thesaurus to maintain its authority records in the *USMARC Format for Authority Control*. This has facilitated its use online in bibliographic utilities and national online database services in which MARC is the common communication format. In 1985, representatives of the *AAT* and MeSH, which at that time also began planning to convert its authority file into MARC, approached the Library of Congress to request MARC fields and codes for hierarchically structured thesauri. These requests have been incorporated into the *USMARC Authority Format*, making it possible to load a hierarchically arranged thesaurus into a MARC formatted online system. The *AAT* also received a special thesaurus code that both permits *AAT* terms to be used in MARC subject fields and identifies these terms as coming from the *AAT*.

Some institutions are already inputting *AAT* terms into their MARC records, using indicator 7 in the 650 field, and subfield 2 followed by the code "aat" (Figure 4). Effective use of the powerful capabilities of the *AAT* for subject indexing, however, is based on the classification of the terminology into facets with the ability to track these separate elements and to combine terms in ways that increase precision in retrieval. In order to do this, the facets, or separate elements of an indexing string, need to be identified within the MARC subject field structure. Until now, subject catalogers of art materials have been left with the problem that *AAT* terms cannot be applied as postcoordinated subject headings because of the lack of an approved set of application rules.

Figure 4 Sample RLIN Record

ID:NYDA87-F95		RTYP:c	ST:s		FRN:	MS:	EL:		AD:03-06-87
CC:9554	BLT:km	DCF:a	CSC:d		MOD:	SNR:	ATC:		UD:03-06-87
CPR:xx	L:eng		INT:?			TEQ:?	TYPE:k	MEI:1	
PC:q		PD:1943/1953			RUN:???	GPC:?		ACMP:?????	
MMD:	OR:	POL:	DM:	RR:	COL:	EML:	GEN:	BSE:	
COM:g	FMD:	OR:	CL:	PRS:	SEP:	MDS:	WD:	SSP:	
COM:k	FMD:	OR:	CL:	PRS:	SSN:				
COM:m	FMD:	OR:	CL:	PR:	SEP:	MDS:	WD:	KS:	ARV:
COM:v	FMD:	OR:	CL:	VF:	SEP:	MDS:	WD:	KS:	
RMD:	OR:	SPD:	SND:	GRV:	DIM:	WID:	TC:	KD:	KM:
KC:	RC:								
COM:a	SMD:	OR:	CLR:	MPHY:	TREP:	PRD:	PL:		
COM:d	SMD:	OR:	CLR:	MPHY:	TREP:				

040	NNC$cNNC$egihc
043	n-us-az$an-us-nv
100 1	Ferriss, Hugh, $d1889-
240 10	Hoover Dam (Ariz. and Nev.)
245 10	Crest of Boulder.$h[graphic]
260	$cSep 14.
300	1 drawing :$bcharcoal on tracing paper on board ;$c50.8 x 38.0 cm. (20 x 15 in.) 30.7 x 23.3 cm. (12 1/8 x 9 1/8 in.)
500	Preliminary for "Hoover Dam, Arizona-Nevada Line" #49, Power in buildings / by Hugh Ferriss, 1953.
650 7	Architectural drawings$xAmerican.$2aat
655 7	Perspective drawings.$2aat
655 7	One-point perspectives.$2aat
691 4	Arizona.
691 4	Nevada.
697 24	Hoover Dam (Ariz. and Nev.)
755	Charcoal drawings.$2aat
799 43	The Hugh Ferriss collection.
789	$iNYDA.1000.001.00010.

Since 1984, a Research Libraries Group (RLG) task force has been working to solve the problems that hamper the use of the *AAT* in MARC-based systems. It is composed of five members of the Art and Architecture Program Committee (AAPC), plus Toni Petersen, *AAT* director, and it is chaired by Nancy Allen, director of the Boston Museum of Fine Arts Library. Its first task was to prepare an application protocol based on the faceted structure of the *AAT*. The protocol proposes the combination of terms from *AAT* facets into expressions and strings that resemble *LCSH* headings. However, when the group examined the possibility of putting *AAT* headings into the current structure of the 650 field, the limitations of the field became immediately apparent: Subfield "a," for main terms, and subfield "x," for topical subdivisions, are not defined clearly or specifically enough.

James Anderson, in a paper describing the bilingual art history database for the *International Repertory of the Literature of Art* (*RILA*) and the *Répertoire d'art et d'archéologie*, states that bibliographic database design provides extensive structure and definition to elements of document description while "knowledge description is frequently relegated to a few, relatively unstructured fields. . . . The MARC Format exemplifies this practice, devoting the major part of its structure to bibliographic details of documents."[16] The important distinction made here is between *document* retrieval and *knowledge* or *subject content* retrieval.

Outside the MARC world, among information scientists building online retrieval databases, there is an enormous amount of activity centered on research into the building of knowledge databases, the possible contribution of artificial intelligence methodology, the effect of indexing techniques on data retrieval, the ratio between recall and precision as a result of types of indexing, and so on. (For relevant examples of this work, see the programs presented at the annual conference of the American Society of Information Science (ASIS) in Boston, October 1987, and the midyear meeting of ASIS in Ann Arbor, May 1988.) In contrast, the library world and its associated disciplines that are adopting the MARC formats are just beginning to carry out the necessary research to acquire information about the needs of their users and the kinds of subject access required to meet those needs.

As the RLG task force struggled to solve how the *AAT* might be used within the MARC format subject fields and yet maintain the precision of its faceted structure, a new look at the subject fields began to emerge. The 650 field already contains subfields that operate like very simple *AAT* facets. They denote various characteristics of a subject:

subfield a = main term (e.g., bronze pitchers)
subfield x = topical subdivision (e.g., conservation and restoration)
or form subdivision (e.g., bibliographies)
subfield y = time (e.g., 3d century)
subfield z = geography (e.g., Rome)

In the 650 field, the major elements of a subject heading are combined in the "a," or main term, subfield. However, as was noted earlier, an examination of many *LCSH* main terms shows that they are actually precoordinated terms containing compound concepts. For example,

    wooden doors

    painting, Renaissance

Because of the *AAT*'s faceted structure, these same terms would be expressed through combining the individual concepts from different *AAT* facets and hierarchies:

    wood (from the Materials hierarchy)

    doors (from the Architectural Components hierarchy)

    painting (from the Processes and Techniques hierarchy)

    renaissance (from the Styles and Periods hierarchy)

In an attempt to combine the idea of *AAT* expressions and strings with the necessity to input headings into the MARC format, the RLG task force conceived of a way to structure MARC subject fields that would preserve the clean faceting structure of the *AAT*. The task force proposed adding a subfield to allow special thesauri to denote different facets of information about a topic in a single subject heading. In the *AAT*, these facets are:

1.   Associated Concepts

2.   Physical Attributes

3.   Styles and Periods

4.   Agents

5.   Activities

6.   Materials

7.   Objects

By linking these subfields to the indicator and code assigned to each thesaurus by LC, each thesaurus potentially could draw up its own list of facet categories. This would allow greater flexibility in the ordering of headings into strings according to different practices because each element of a heading would be broken down into its basic content characteristics.

The task force also proposed the use of a *focus code*, which would identify the key element (main term) in a heading; for example, the focus code could be used to emphasize the major element in a heading (e.g., PITCHERS) versus elements that modify it (e.g., BRONZE) and could become the pivotal point around which displays or printed strings are generated.

The result of the task force's work was summarized by the LC Network Development and MARC Standards Office and presented to the MARBI Committee as discussion paper no. 19 at its January 1988 meetings in San Antonio. LC expanded on the idea prepared by the task force and proposed the addition of a new field to the MARC format, 654, to be entitled Subject Added Entry–Faceted Topical Heading. To quote from Proposal 88-10, the proposal that grew out of the original discussion paper and that was voted on at the July 1988 MARBI meeting in New Orleans: "Such a field would enable users (such as those using the *Art and Architecture Thesaurus*) to label the facet or hierarchy from which each term found in a topical subject expression on a bibliographic record came from and to also specify which term is the focus term of the expression."

The 654 field contains two indicators and the following subfields:

$a Focus term
$b Nonfocus term
$c Facet designation
$2 Thesaurus code

It is understood that a special delimiter (noted in the samples below as a slash) would be needed to mark the beginning of each new expression in a string.

The following examples are drawn from possible *AAT* indexing strings and use *AAT* facet codes, plus $y and $z as date and geography facet codes. Each piece of the heading is preceded by either $a, to indicate it is the focus term, or $b, to indicate it is not a focus term. Each term is then followed by $c and a facet designator code.

Examples:

$bcharcoal$cMT$adrawings$COb$zGreat Britain$y 18th
    century$2aat
charcoal drawings – Great Britain – 18th century
$alimestone$cMT$2aat
limestone
$ahousing$cOB$zUnited States/$asociological aspectscDO2aat
housing – United States – sociological aspects
$BFrench colonial$cSP$alandscapes$cSL$zUnited States
    $zNew Jersey/$bfrenchcSPainfluencescCP2aat
French colonial landscapes – United States – New Jersey –
    French influences

EPILOGUE

Those of us involved in bibliographic documentation need to acknowledge the long lag between research and actuality. The *AAT*, beyond the halfway mark of its development, has reached a usable application stage, but art library systems have not yet applied it. Art research libraries are only now preparing for local online catalogs. National bibliographic utilities have only recently begun to load the machine-readable file of *LCSH* but have not yet reached the point of being able to accommodate multiple thesauri or hierarchical thesauri. The MARC format remains the primary tool for making information transportable from system to system, from the bibliographic utilities to the local online public access catalogs, and vice versa, but it should transport its data in the most precise manner possible and in a manner that eliminates so-called electronic noise.

MARC was designed originally as a bibliographic format and then adapted to accommodate other media – serials, maps, visual materials, archives, and manuscripts. Just as MARC has successfully expanded to accommodate newer media and their descriptions, it now needs to grow to accommodate the finer categories of knowledge in its subject fields. If it can accomplish this, by allowing the specific definition of subject facets, it will go a long way toward closing the gap between subject cataloging of the past and sophisticated, efficient, automated subject access of the near future.

NOTES

1. Library of Congress, Subject Cataloging Division, *Subject Cataloging Manual* (Washington, D.C.: Library of Congress, 1985).

2. *Webster's Third New International Dictionary of the English Language*, S. V. "topical."

3. *AAT: Art and Architecture Thesaurus* (New York: Oxford University Press, 1990; *Descriptive Terms for Graphic Materials: Genre and Physical Characteristic Headings* (to be used in fields 655 and 755) (Washington, D.C.: Library of Congress, 1986); *Genre Terms: A Thesaurus for Use in Rare Book and Special Collections Cataloging* (Chicago: Association of College and Research Libraries, 1983); Thomas Hickerson and Elaine Engst, comps., *Form Terms for Archival and Manuscripts Control* (Stanford, Calif.: Research Libraries Group, 1985); *Moving Image Materials: Genre Terms*, comp. Martha M. Yee for the National Moving Image Database Standards Committee, National Center for Film and Video Preservation at the American Film Institute (Washington, D.C.: Motion Picture Broadcasting and Recorded Sound Division, Library of Congress, 1988); Elizabeth Betz Parker, comp., *LC Thesaurus for Graphic Materials: Topical Terms for Subject Access* (Washington, D.C.: Library of Congress, 1987).

4. Nancy DeLaurier, "Some General Principles and Basics," *International Bulletin for Photographic Documentation of the Visual Arts* 12, no. 4 (Winter 1985): 9-10.

5. Patricia J. Barnett, "The Art and Architecture Thesaurus as a Faceted Marc Format," *Visual Resources* 4, no. 3:247-59.

6. Dora Crouch, Pat Molholt, and Toni Petersen, *Indexing in Art and Architecture: An Investigation and Analysis* (Report to the Council on Library Resources) (Washington, D.C.: Council on Library Resources, 1981).

7. Toni Petersen, "The AAT: A Model for the Restructing of LCSH," *Journal of Academic Librarianship* 9, no. 4 (September 1983): 207-10.

8. American National Standards Institute, *Guidelines for Thesaurus Structure, Construction and Use: Approved June 30, 1980* (ANSI-Z39.19-1980) (New York: ANSI, 1980); British Standards Institution, *Guidelines for the Establishment and Development of Monolingual Thesauri* (BS 5723) (London: BSI, 1979).

9. National Library of Medicine, *Medical Subject Headings*, 2 vols. (Bethesda, Md.: National Library of Medicine, 1986).

10. James D. Anderson, *Knowledge Structure Representation: Planning and Design for a Bilingual French-English Art History Database.* (Paper based on the *RILA* and *Répertoire d'art et d'archéologie* (*RAA*) merger) (January 1986).

11. Pauline A. Cochrane, Brian Aveney, and Charles Hildreth, "Modern Subject Access in the Online Age," in *Redesign of Catalogs and Indexes for Improved Online Subject Access: Selected Papers of Pauline A. Cochrane* (Phoenix, Ariz.: ORYX, 1985) 269-74.

12. Derek Austin, *PRECIS: A Manual of Concept Analysis and Subject Indexing* (London: Council of the British National Bibliography, 1974).

13. Timothy C. Craven, *String Indexing* (Orlando, Fla.: Academic Press, 1986).

14. Mary Dykstra, "LC Subject Headings Disguised as a Thesaurus," *Library Journal* 113, no. 4 (1 March 1988): 42-46.

15. Library of Congress, Network Development and MARC Standards Office, *USMARC Format for Authority Control* (Washington, D.C.: Library of Congress, 1987).

16. Anderson, *Knowledge Structure Representation*, 1.

■ The Use of the Visual Materials Format for a Slide Library Integrated into an OPAC

JEANNE M. KEEFE

In 1985, the Rensselaer Polytechnic Institute Architecture Library's slide curator used funding from the National Endowment for the Arts to test the applicability of the *Art and Architecture Thesaurus* (*AAT*) within the context of a working slide library. This coincided with the administration's determination to reorganize and convert the library card catalog to an online public access system and to integrate the slide catalog. Several of the questions we were asked to consider during the conversion process were:

- Is *AAT* terminology useful for catalogers and patrons?

- What problems are encountered when *AAT* terminology is applied to an established collection?

- What level of expertise is necessary for an indexer or cataloger to use the *AAT* to its fullest extent?

- How much time would be involved in converting a small part of a collection to the online catalog format?

- How much time would it take to convert an entire collection of approximately fifty thousand slides?

In addition to these questions, we had several more of our own. This is an account of an evolutionary process and the many problems encountered before final implementation of the system. It is hoped that this account will be of use to others who might be planning to computerize their cataloging systems.

BACKGROUND INFORMATION

The Rensselaer Architecture Library's slide collection was established in 1932 and at the time of the project contained approximately fifty thousand slides. The collection has increased at an average rate of six thousand slides per year for the past few years, and that rate increased to nearly ten thousand in 1987. Nearly one-third of the collection consists of 3 1/4-by-4-inch glass lantern slides, which present certain problems with regard to storage and projection. Fortunately, many of these lantern slides have been duplicated into a 2-by-2-inch format. Staffing for the slide library is limited: one full-time graphics curator, one half-time temporary research clerk, and two or three part-time student workers. The staff is responsible for all the normal cataloging, reference, circulation, and general housekeeping duties and also for the in-house production of new slides. During the conversion project, the staff also performed all research, worksheet completion, and data entry associated with the process. The staff is also responsible for collections of architectural drawings, maps, plans, models, microfiche, microfilm, records, and tapes, which we anticipate including in the online catalog at a future date.

Although the slide library is housed within the Architecture Library, it is a separate entity that was developed to support the faculty and curriculum of the School of Architecture. The old classification system was based on medium (architecture, painting, etc.) and was filed according to a loose combination of historical, chronological, and geographical determinants. The scheme was changed several times over the years and by 1985 resembled a synthesis of the "Metropolitan Museum of Art" classification listing for periods and styles and the "University of California at Santa Cruz (Tansey)" system for categorizing visual content. Architecture slides were arranged chronologically, and fine arts slides were arranged alphabetically by the artist's name. Subject areas – i.e., architectural design, architectural practice, planning, and building construction – were given new classification numbers in accordance with the Architecture Library's Vertical Filing System. By 1985, there were over thirty separate subject categories, each with its own distinct classification scheme. Some were arranged alphabetically, others numerically, and still others by subject. Despite the fact that an authority file and card index had been developed and maintained to help the user, slide retrieval became an art form in itself; only the most sophisticated patrons could hope to find what they might need in a reasonable amount of time.

IDENTIFICATION OF REQUIREMENTS AND SPECIAL PROBLEMS

Before we could even begin to give serious consideration to a retrospective conversion of the slide collection, we needed to identify the particular problems requiring correction. By monitoring usage and patron commentary, we quickly identified several areas of difficulty:

- The existing system was extremely limited in its capacity to accommodate new or expanded subject areas. If catalogers wanted to integrate new material into the existing system, they had to "force" it into the beginning of an existing subject or style area. For example, a slide of a Viking fishing village would be forced to fit between English Norman and Gothic.

- The system was not designed to accommodate particular non-Western and technological subject areas needed to support the changing curriculum of the School of Architecture.

- The existing catalog suffered from severe fragmentation in some very important architectural subject areas. One particular building (e.g., St. Peter's in Rome) could be found listed and stored in as many as nine different categories ranging from early Christian through 20th century to architectural practice and maps.

- Most important, there had never been a professional curator or librarian in the slide library, which caused inconsistent and sometimes erroneous cataloging. User complaints covered lack of thorough cross-referencing, difficulty in browsing because both sizes of slides were filed in the same drawer, and length of search time required to retrieve the needed slides because of the dispersion and fragmentation of subject areas. These and other less immediately obvious problems demanded attention during the development of a new system.

The identification of specific requirements and considerations was the second area we needed to explore. The main purpose of the project was to develop and implement a system that would serve patrons more effectively and efficiently. If it also made the curator's duties less complicated, all the better. Several distinct areas of consideration were identified:

- A new call number system had to be devised that would allow the entire collection to be integrated into only three distinct headings (architecture, fine arts, and generic subjects/reference examples) and yet that would be flexible enough to accommodate new or different subject areas within that framework.

- Cataloging practices and descriptive terminology had to be standardized to the greatest extent possible to improve consistency. Extensive cross-referencing was needed to improve retrieval time so that a topical lecture on daylighting, for example, or a survey of bridges might be compiled quickly and efficiently without the patron's having to know the names or locations of specific subjects.

- New subject areas needed to be developed to meet the changing demands of not only the faculty of the School of Architecture but also patrons from other curricula and from outside the Institute.

- Labor-saving devices had to be built into the system to whatever extent possible. Particular attention needed to be given to the automatic printing of slide labels and accession cards.

- Future compatibility with videodisc technologies was also a goal.

To accommodate these special considerations, we needed to approach the material in an entirely different way. Conventionally, art and architecture slides have been viewed and cataloged as surrogates of works of art. Compositions have focal points, and those focal points become the primary subjects described by the cataloger. It appeared, however, that for our purposes it would be more appropriate to view a slide as a document, similar to a manuscript that contains more information than just the title page and author. While the title (e.g., Sydney Opera House) is still the primary denotation, the slide document itself contains information on a variety of subjects (RIDGE BEAMS, GLASS CURTAIN WALLS, TILES, SHELL VAULTS, PRECAST CONCRETE RIBS, CONCERT HALLS, etc.). Adding each of these different references now makes that slide available to patrons needing examples of different types of materials, structures, or designs. It means that a slide of a statue in a 15th-century Gothic cathedral is now available to the student or professor of medieval history who needs examples of armor or dress from the Middle Ages. Viewing a slide as a document instead of as a composition significantly increases its usefulness as a visual resource. A single slide can now be approached from many subject paths, so there is no longer a need to duplicate slides for filing into various subject categories. Ultimately, this will mean a savings in terms of storage space and collection development.

DEVELOPMENT

Once our needs were identified and the various options reviewed, it was decided that we should utilize the computer technologies available at Rensselaer. In 1984, the library had instituted an online information system called InfoTrax™ to replace the card catalog. The system uses the Stanford Public Information Retrieval System (SPIRES) database management system operating under the Michigan Terminal System (MTS). The Architecture Library's holdings were included in this system, so our patrons were already familiar with it. It was important that the slide database be compatible with this existing system to allow for future integration.

It was also our intention to test the usefulness of the *AAT* terminology in a working slide library. The ways in which we decided to use the *AAT* hierarchies will become clear once the composition of the data entry worksheet is understood. The structure of the *AAT* Styles and Periods hierarchy was used as the basis for devising a new classification system, and the entire *AAT* was used as our authority file.

The first cataloging worksheet design had twenty-one fields that could be easily manipulated to meet data entry, display, and printing requirements and to create indexes. After the original worksheet had been completed and tested we became aware of the new OCLC Audiovisual Media format, which was consistent with *USMARC Format for Bibliographic Data*, and decided to convert to it to make the slide database more compatible with Rensselaer's online information system. This decision required an expanded definition of the fields and subfields.

This redefinition stage was the most difficult and time-consuming step in the entire process. With the generous help of Rensselaer's cataloging department's staff, we attempted to match and merge the fields we had devised in our first worksheet with the fields and subfields defined by MARC. Difficulties arose during this step because the majority of slides in our collection were either purchased before 1935 (lanterns) or locally produced, thereby lacking the bibliographic documentation needed to develop a standardized MARC record. Our slides did not fit neatly into the criteria used by MARC to define its fields and subfields. This situation inevitably led us to reinterpret and expand the MARC field definitions in a very open ended manner. Instead of trying to adhere strictly to the criteria set down in MARC, we reinterpreted and expanded several of the field definitions to meet our particular needs. (For example, architectural slides, which don't usually have a uniform title, as paintings do, were put into the 245 field: the Title Statement Field, and generic/reference titles into field 242, Translation of Title by Cataloging Agency. See Figure 1.)

During the reinterpretation process, we attempted to predict the direction of the collection's future development. Fields that were not useful immediately were included in anticipation of future need. In deciding to use MARC field codes and definitions, we gained consistency and compatibility; however, we gave up some flexibility and a measure of control over our own work process. It also multiplied the number of necessary fields, nearly doubling the size of the worksheet.

Figure 1 Current Worksheet Design

CURRENT WORKSHEET DESIGN

°= blank space

DATA ENTRY WORKSHEET FOR SLIDE COLLECTION

TYPE " G " (SLIDE)	;GMT " SLIDES "	;007 PHYSICAL DESC.	RECORD (IRN) NUMBER
" O " (KIT)		"°°+HJ (2x2") +db (b&w)	
" K " (2-0)		"°°+HZ (3½x4") +dc (color)	
" R " (3-0)		+dz (other) "	

CALL NUMBERS ARCHITECTURE
;059 "

"°°+d _____ (AAT List 2)   +p _____ (Country)
+far   +r _____ (State)
+g _____ (AAT List 1)   +t ____._ (Title)
+L _____ (Site)   +v _____ (AAT List 3)
+n ___._ (City)   +z _____ (Detail #) "

FINE ARTS
;059

"°°+ffa
+n _____-__ (Artist Name)
+t _____-__ (Title)
+v _____ (AAT List 4)
+z _____ (Detail #) "

GENERIC
:059

"°°+frf
+v _____ (AAT List 5)
                "

PERSONAL NAMES
;100 ARTIST-ARCHITECT-DESIGNER ETC.
"0°+a _____ (SINGLE NAME)
"1°+a _____, _____ (LAST, FIRST)
"2°+a _____ - _____ (HYPHENATED)
    +c _____ (TITLE) +d _____ "(DATES)

;110 CORPORATION-PARTNERSHIP-FIRM-ORGANIZATION
"0°+a _____ (SURNAME, INVERTED)
"1°+a _____ (PLACE NAME)
    +b _____ (DEPT, AGENCY)
"2°+a _____ "(CORPORATION NAME)

;111 EVENT-EXHIBITION-COMPETITION-PROJECT
"0°+a _____ (PERSONAL NAME)
"1°+a _____, _____ (PLACE NAME)
"2°+a _____ (TYPE NAME)
    +n _____ (NUMBER IN SERIES) +d _____ (DATES)
    +c _____, "(SITE OF EVENT)

TITLES
;240 FINE ARTS TITLES
"01+a _____ (NO ARTICLE) +
"02+a _____ (1 LETTER ARTICLE)
"03+a _____ (2 LETTER ARTICLE)
"04+a _____ (3 LETTER ARTICLE)
    +p _____ "(VIEW OR PART)

;242 GENERIC-REFERENCE TITLES
"00+a _____ (SUBJECT-TITLE)
    +p _____ "(VIEW OR PART)

;245 ARCHITECTURE TITLES
"00+a _____ (SLIDE TITLE)
    +p _____ " (VIEW OR PART)

GENERAL NOTES FIELD
;500 NOTES
"°°+a _____
     _____ "

;583 LIBRARY ACTION INFORMATION
"°°+a _____ (ACTION NEEDED) +c _____ (DATE ACCESSIONED)
    +h _____ (REQUESTED BY) +J _____ (SOURCE)
    +k _____ " (LIBRARY NOTES)

LOCAL USE NUMBERS
;590 CATALOG AND ACCESSION NUMBERS
`‡a` _____ / _____ (ACCESSION/CATALOG #)
`‡a` _____ (ACCESSION NUMBERS
`‡a` _____ " IN THE SET)

SUBJECT ENTRIES
;600 SUBJECT OF THE WORK OF ART OR PHOTO
`"0"‡a` _____ (SINGLE NAME)
`"1"‡a` _____ , _____ (LAST, FIRST)
`"2"‡a` _____ - _____ (HYPHENATED)
`‡c` _____ "(TITLE)

;650 LIBRARY OF CONGRESS HEADINGS FOR GENERIC SLIDES
`""0‡a` _____ "

;650 ART AND ARCHITECTURE THESAURUS TERMINOLOGY
`""7‡a` _____ (PRIMARY AAT TERMS)
`‡a` _____
`‡a` _____
`‡a` _____
`‡a` _____
`‡a` _____
`‡a` _____
`‡a` _____
`‡a` _____ "(STYLE AND PERIOD)

;651 GEOGRAPHIC TERMS
`""0‡a` _____ (SITE) `‡a` _____ (CITY) `‡a` _____ (STATE OR PROV.)
`‡a` _____ (COUNTRY) `‡a` _____ "(ALTERNATE SPELLINGS)

;653 NON-AAT TERMS, FREE-FORM TERMS AND DESCRIPTORS
`""‡a` _____
`‡a` _____
`‡a` _____
`‡a` _____ (MEDIUM) `‡a` _____ (DIMENSIONS OF WORK)
`‡a` _____ (DATES OF PRODUCTION, CONSTRUCTION OR MANUFACTURE) „

ASSOCIATED NAMES
;700 ASSOCIATED ARCHITECTS, ARTISTS, PERSONS NAMES
`"0"‡a` _____ (SINGLE NAME)
`"1"‡a` _____ , _____ (LAST, FIRST)
`"2"‡a` _____ - _____ (HYPHENATED)
`‡c` _____ (TITLE) `‡d` _____ "(DATES)

;710 ASSOCIATED CORPORATION-PARTNERSHIP-FIRM-ORGANIZATION
`"0"‡a` _____ (PERSONAL NAMES)
`"1"‡a` _____ (PLACE NAME) `‡b` _____ (DEPT, AGENCY)
`"2"‡a` _____ "(CORPORATION NAME)

;711 ASSOCIATED EVENT-EXHIBITION-COMPETITION-PROJECT
`"0"‡A` _____ (PERSONAL NAME)
`"1"‡a` _____ (PLACE NAME)
`"2"‡a` _____ (TYPE NAME) `‡d` _____ (DATES)
`‡n` _____ (# IN A SERIES) `‡c` _____ "(SITE OF EVENT)

;740 HOLDINGS - SETS OF SLIDES
`"01‡a` ____ (Plans) `‡a` ____ (SECTIONS) `‡a` ____ (DRAWINGS) `‡a` ____ (AERIAL VIEWS) `‡a` ____ (EXTERIOR VIEWS)
`‡a` ____ (INTERIOR VIEWS) `‡a` ____ (DETAILS) `‡a` ____ (GARDENS) `‡a` ____ (PAINTING) `‡a` ____ "(FURNISHINGS)

In retrospect it appears that we may have attempted too many tasks at once. It simply wasn't possible for us to second-guess the future and provide for every alternative. In order to keep the worksheets logical and useful to both cataloging personnel and data entry personnel, our plans for including printing formats for slide labels and accession cards had to be postponed. Although our first worksheet was straightforward enough, it was quite collection-specific and eventually would have proven to be just another stopgap. The worksheet we ended up using was so complicated, it hardly seemed worth the effort.

It was at this point that we decided to abandon the attempt to incorporate a printing format into the layout of the worksheet because it limited each field to a single line of text with space for only thirty-five characters per line. This limitation seemed counterproductive to our goal of trying to include as much information as possible on the worksheets to achieve greater access. We also tried to streamline the worksheet to its most basic components, purposely leaving out exact field numbers and subfield codes. These second- and third-generation worksheets required the cataloger to provide the basic bibliographic information (title, subject, location, descriptors, etc.) and essentially to ignore the delimiters of MARC fields and subfields. The correct field delimiters were then determined by the curator and added to the worksheet just before data entry. Therefore, someone with less training could fill in the worksheets by copying the information gathered from books, labels, and accession records. Then the curator could check this information for errors and determine and fill in the appropriate field numbers and subfield codes. Using this third version of the worksheet, we began to convert the slide collection in March of 1986.

IMPLEMENTATION

We had been using that third worksheet for about three months before we actually began data entry. The worksheet, as implemented online, was a list of all necessary fields in numeric sequence. We discovered that it took approximately twenty minutes to enter the record for one slide! It soon became evident that our third worksheet was not very efficient in terms of data entry, and we found it necessary to devise yet another. This latest worksheet, seen in Figure 1, includes all the necessary fields and subfields, thereby making it easier for untrained staff to move between the paper worksheet and the online data entry worksheet. This worksheet may appear to be very complicated and overworked, but it has cut down on errors in both cataloging and data entry, and it approaches the process in a very straightforward and logical manner.

Because the slide library had been designated as a test site for the *AAT*, we needed a device by which we could monitor its usefulness. We decided to place all of the *AAT* terms in the 650 field and all non-*AAT* terms in field 653. This distinction allows us to monitor user terminology by means of transaction logs, a nonintrusive way to observe user activity.

Once we became familiar with the various field definitions, filling in the worksheets required less and less time. The initial research required for each separate building or site varied according to available resources. We started our conversion process with the Prehistoric section for two reasons: First, we felt the subject would be a good test area as far as research procedures were concerned; and second, it was one of the smallest sections in the collection and would serve as a good gauge of time requirements. By the time we had reached Stonehenge, we knew that many of our worksheets pertaining to the same site or building contained almost the same information with only minor variations concerning details. At that point we began simply to photocopy the first complete worksheet and add the variable information such as accession number and view to the copied sheets.

This decreased our conversion time, especially when a particular subject, such as the caves at Lascaux, France, contained as many as forty slides. The basic information was constant; the particulars had to be appended. A backlog of data entry resulted from this increase in worksheet production. In addition, the data entry became repetitive and boring because the same information was being entered over and over again. We needed a way to create copies of the same entry record, which could then be modified to contain the particular information pertinent to each individual slide. The systems analyst created a "clone" command, which duplicated a single entry record as many times as needed. The data entry person would then access each of these cloned records and change or add the pertinent information that distinguished that particular slide from others with the same title.

The next logical step was to stop photocopying the worksheets and just to make out the primary worksheet and fill in on the subsequent sheets only the information that was distinctive from the primary sheet (different size, color, source, view, etc.). With each of these learning steps, we cut more and more time off the conversion process.

THE BREAKTHROUGH

Once all these implementation problems were successfully identified and solved, the conversion project proceeded at a slow yet steady pace. By the end of 1986, we had converted two entire architecture sections, Prehistoric and Egyptian, and had just begun converting the 20th-Century Architecture collection. It had taken two half-time employees almost eight months to convert and enter approximately thirteen hundred slides. At that rate it would take us fifteen years to convert the entire collection! The National Endowment for the Arts grant was due to end in February 1987, at which point we would lose our temporary staff. It was impossible to imagine ever being able to continue, let alone finish, this conversion to an online database. We needed a new strategy.

As we mulled over this problem, we found that we had ignored one very important factor: A computer display or printout would never replace the visual image itself. Since our patrons were actually looking for visual images, they would never choose to use a slide based on a written record alone. The online record was simply a step in the process. Users would always go to the drawers and pull out the slides to see if they were the images needed. If they were looking for a plan or a cross-section of the Crystal Cathedral by Philip Johnson, all they really wanted to know was whether we had one and, if we did, where it was located. Because all the slides of the Crystal Cathedral are stored together in the same place, under the same call number, and in view sequence, all that was necessary was to treat all slides with the same title as a *set*. This idea proved to be our breakthrough.

Our solution was to have only one entry record per set, or group of slides relating to a building or a work of art. That record contains all the appropriate information pertaining to the building, the accession numbers of the slides in the set, and a holdings listing of the different views contained in that set (see sample catalog entries in Figure 2). As new slides are added to the set, or damaged ones removed, all that is necessary is to update one record by adding the new information to those two fields.

As a result of this change in approach, instead of having to store seventy · thousand-plus records, we have to store about twenty-five thousand records. Searching is greatly simplified because the patron must find only one record for, say, the Sydney Opera House instead of fifty, and that one record contains all the necessary information needed to decide if it is worth looking in the cabinets at all. If the record indicates that the holdings on that particular subject are limited to one exterior view and two details and the patron needs a plan, he or she then knows not to bother going to the slide drawers.

The sections we cataloged first (Prehistoric and Egyptian) using the clone method have now been collapsed into sets to maintain record-format consistency throughout the entire database.

Figure 2   Catalog Entry Samples

```
IRN = 13102;
DATE-ADDED = 02/10/87;
DATE-UPDATED = 05/31/89;
TYPE = G;
GMT = SLIDES;
007 = "  ¬hz¬hj¬db¬dc";
059 = "  ¬d4¬far¬gf¬np232¬pfr¬tp232¬vg";
100 = 1 ¬aGarnier, Jean-Louis-Charles¬d1825 - 1898;
245 = 00¬aParis Opera House¬pcutaway perspective job;
500 = "  ¬aCeiling painted by Marc Chagall in 1964. Sculptural groups
by J. B. Carpeaux ";
583 = "  ¬anone¬c1986¬hlibrary";
590 = "  ¬ac21841/19:FR:P:OH:2";
590 = "

¬a1660/19:FR:P:OH:6¬a6136¬a6147¬a1741¬a1662¬a1814¬a11304¬aC15631¬a10942
650 = " 7¬aOpera houses perspective drawings¬aBeaux art¬amodern
European¬aBaroque revival¬amosaics¬aloggias¬aarcades¬acaryatids¬abird's
eye perspectives¬aaxial building¬avaulted ceilings¬aauditoriums¬aconcert
halls¬aperforming arts buildings";
650 = " 7¬astages¬astaircases¬astairways¬astairs¬amarble¬aRococo
revival¬aorchestras¬arotundas¬adomes¬ametal
domes¬acopper¬acolonnades¬avestibules¬agabled towers¬afoyers¬adressing
rooms";
651 = " 0¬aParis, France";
653 = "  ¬a1862 - 1875¬acandelabras¬achandeliers¬aescalier d'
honneur¬agilt¬agabled flytowers¬alateral domes¬alateral pavilions";
740 = 01¬a2in by 2in slides: 2 perspectives (1 color), 4 exteriors (1
col), 2 interiors (1 col), and 6 3in by 4in. slides ( 1 plan, 1 section,
2 interiors, 2 exteriors);
```

```
IRN = 13285;
DATE-ADDED = 02/25/87;
DATE-UPDATED = 06/05/89;
TYPE = G;
GMT = slides;
007 = "  ¬hj¬db";
059 = "  ¬d4¬far¬gf¬nv662.1¬pau¬ts822.6¬vg";
100 = 1 ¬aLoos, Adolf¬d1870 - 1933;
245 = 00¬aSteiner House¬pview from the garden, an early photograph;
500 = "  ¬aThe facade on St. Veitgasse has been  radically tampered
with, that the original curved & plated roof having been replaced by a
pitched roof. The interior has also been subjected to substantial
alterations";
583 = "  ¬anone¬cNovember 1979¬jRowland: A History of the Modern
Movement";
590 = "

¬a21302/20:AU:VI:STH:6¬a14985¬a14986¬a14987¬a14988¬a14989¬a14990";
650 = "  7¬aArchitect-designed houses¬ahouses¬adwellings¬adomestic
architecture¬aresidences¬aresidential¬adetached
houses¬aroofs¬ametal¬alaminated¬aflat
roofs¬abalconies¬awindows¬aplaster¬alime mortar";
651 = " 0¬aVienna¬aAustria¬aWien";
653 = "  ¬a1910¬acurved roof¬awood cement¬abays";
740 = 01¬a1 plan, 1 section, 1 elevation, 3 exteriors, 1 interior;
```

Figure 3 Detail Display Samples

```
    TITLE :  Sydney Opera House: post 1945 aerial view
       BY :  Utzon, Jorn
  SUBJECT :  Opera Houses, Auditoria, auditoriums, ceramic tiles,
                performing arts buildings, concrete halls, music
                halls, music auditoria, symphony halls, movie
                theaters, theatres, cinemas, restaurants, ribbed
                vaults, ribbed arches
             concrete beams, concrete paint, podium, roof trusses,
                roofing, roofing tile, ribs, vaulted roofs, shell
                roofs, reinforced concrete, lattice roofs, shell
                structures, shell vaults, towers, steel trusses,
                ceremonial ways
             workspaces, workshops, wood walls, wood ceiling,
                wooden ceilings, concrete vaults, concrete
                structures, concrete pilings, concrete joints,
                glass, glass walls, laminated materials, cables,
                cable roofs, cable-stayed structures, ridge boards
             precast concrete, granite, granite powder cement,
                bronze window mullions
             ridge beams
     SITE :  Australia, Sydney, New South Wales, Benelong Point
    DATES :  1957 - 1973
     SIZE :  2x2 in. color
 HOLDINGS :  3 plans, 11 sections/drawings, 2 aerial views, 29
                exteriors, 3 interiors, 3 details
  CALL NO :  20:AUS:SY:SOH:5
```

```
    TITLE :  The Crystal Cathedral, Garden Grove Community Church
                exterior, general view
       BY :  Johnson, Philip
             Johnson/Burgee
  SUBJECT :  glass buildings, glass doors, glass roofs, glass
                windows, glass walls, curtain walls, non-bearing
                walls, enclosure walls, window walls,
                heat-resisting glass, heat-strengthened glass,
                space frames, gussets, web mwmbers
             plates, structural frames, steel trusses, chords,
                pipe, concrete, concrete columns, concrete pilings,
                mechanically operated doors, horizontal sliding
                doors, girders, marble pools, fountains,
                clerestories, porticoes
             space trusses, hangar doors, neo-fundamentalist church
                architecture
     SITE :  Garden Grove, California, USA
    DATES :  1983
     SIZE :  2x2 in. b&w color
 HOLDINGS :  1 plan, 1 section, 1 aerial view, 6 exteriors ( 4
                col.), 3 interiors (2 col.).
    NOTES :  designed for Rev. Dr. Robert Schuller
  CALL NO :  20:US:CA:GA:CC:6
```

THE PUBLIC DISPLAY

Rensselaer's InfoTrax information system is an integrated set of databases that provides information about the different types of resources available at both the Folsom Library and the Architecture Library. The catalog database contains a general listing of books, Rensselaer theses, art prints, cassettes, phonograph records, and audiovisual items. The journal database lists journal titles and information on the volumes and years held by the library. The orders database lists materials on order and materials received but not as yet cataloged. The homework database contains uncataloged material such as homework answers, lecture notes, and practice exams for many classes. The IEEE database lists abstracts as well as journal articles and conference papers from the Institute of Electrical and Electronic Engineers. This database also lists some materials not owned by the library. InfoTrax also has message and news databases.

InfoTrax was designed so that all fields and subfields are searchable in data entry mode, the mode used to input the worksheets. By using the simple FIND command, the staff can search fields not available to the patron. Some of these are medium, action needed (the condition of the slide), IRN number (record number), requester (name of person who requested that the slide be purchased or produced), and source (the source from which the slide was purchased or produced).

The public can search the database in several ways. Slides may be searched and identified by title, subject, name, geographic location, accession number, call number, date of completion, source, and/or descriptors, both *AAT* and non-*AAT*. SPIRES allows the user to search by single words or strings of words. The user begins a search with the command FIND. The search can be expanded with the word OR and narrowed with the word AND. By combining several search terms (i.e., FIND *about* HOUSES AND Pennsylvania AND *by* Frank Lloyd Wright) the patron can very quickly zero in on exactly what he or she needs. The visual display format for the public mirrors that used in the general information system.

- The BRIEF command displays title, architect/artist and site on one line.

- The CALL and PRINT commands display and print the information above given in the BRIEF format plus the accession number, original call number (necessary until new call numbers are included), and the size of the slide.

- The DETAIL command gives all of the above CALL command information plus a truncated listing of the subject/descriptor fields, dates, notes, and a list of current holdings in the set (see Figure 3).

Changes to the public display format can be made as we receive feedback from our patrons as to what other information they would like to see displayed.

FUTURE CONSIDERATIONS

Rensselaer's Slide System is still not complete. A series of fine-tuning changes will continue to be made as new problems surface and more refined technologies come into use. As soon as it is economically feasible, the database will be linked to a videodisc of the slide images. This link will allow patrons to scan the videodisc for needed images instead of searching through slide drawers. This will also cut down on slide handling, refiling, breakage, and general wear and tear on the collection.

The use of videodiscs will eliminate the need for a call number altogether and will allow the slides to be filed in accession number order. This also solves storage problems because new slides would be added to the end of the collection and not interfiled as they are now, resulting in the constant shifting and reordering of drawers.

The idea of cataloging a series of same-subject slides as sets has proved to be a significant time-saving device. It does not hamper the patron's ability to retrieve relevant material, and at the same time it saves considerable time inputting and updating records. It serves as an optimal compromise. The set method of cataloging has precedent in both the cataloging of monographs under a series entry and the cataloging of sets of records by archivists. By extension, one can even look on the cataloging of a monograph as a single record representing a collection of chapters and sections on a single topic. Museums have long used this approach when cataloging items such as sets of dishes, jewelry, silverware, and dresser sets. Using the set method of cataloging puts online conversion within reach of slide libraries with staff or budgetary restrictions.

CONCLUSION

As a response to the questions posed at the beginning of this account, the following is a summary of the conclusions arrived at during the process of developing the Rensselaer Online Cataloging System for Slides.

Is AAT *terminology useful for catalogers and patrons?* The catalogers found the terminology to be very useful, especially the Styles and Periods hierarchy. Any attempt at standardization of terminology in that area is bound to be helpful. The breakdown by culture and reign is especially helpful in categorizing historical periods during which several distinctive styles were in evidence. It also serves as our authority file and as a comprehensive guide for cross-referencing terminology. The *AAT* leads both the cataloger and the patron to terms they would have never thought of using previously. It details particular components in such a way that there can be little room for confusion. Since the database has been available to the public, there has been a positive response from our patrons, especially from those interested in less specific subjects such as LIGHTING TECHNIQUES, CONSTRUCTION METHODS, and STYLISTIC REVIVALS. The use of *AAT* descriptors now allows users to pull together materials on these subjects quickly; it also gives them access to the most recent additions to the collection. Slides produced for a lecture on PRECAST CONCRETE, for example, are now easily retrievable by a patron looking for slides that illustrate different methods of construction. These options are invaluable to patrons using a collection that is classified according to historical periods or artistic styles.

What problems are encountered when AAT *terminology is applied to an established collection?* We did not encounter any problems applying the terminology itself. The problems were in learning to deal effectively with the draft printouts of the *AAT* because each of the twenty-two completed hierarchies had to be searched individually. With the newly published merged alphabetical listing, we are less likely to miss the appropriate terminology.

What level of expertise is necessary for an indexer or cataloger to use the AAT *to its fullest extent?* A basic knowledge of art and architectural history and good clerical and research skills are necessary. Undergraduate-level course work in classical, European, and American history are also very helpful. An initial training period of at least three months was needed before the acceptable level of competence and efficiency was reached. This training period might be shortened if the indexer were to have previous cataloging experience, a broad knowledge of art and architectural history, basic familiarity with Latin and other romance languages, and training in basic logic and critical thinking.

How much time would be involved in converting a small part of a collection to the online catalog format? How much time would it take to convert an entire collection of approximately fifty thousand slides? After the training period was completed and while we were still making out one worksheet per slide, it took two half-time employees (or one full-time employee) approximately one month to complete two hundred and fifty worksheets and enter them into the database. That means that we researched, recataloged, and entered 1.5 slides every hour. The breakdown was an average of twenty-seven minutes per worksheet and about ten minutes for data entry. To convert a small collection (ten thousand slides) would take one full-time employee approximately three and one-half years. It would take nearly seventeen years to convert fifty thousand slides. After our decision to recatalog sets of slides, it took two half-time employees (or one full time) one month to research and recatalog approximately five hundred and twenty slides and to enter the same number into the database. At this present rate, it will take less than two years to complete ten thousand slides or eight years to convert fifty thousand. (Divide that time by two for every added full-time employee.) The major advantage is that once a subject area has been converted, no extra worksheets are needed for additional slides. The existing record is updated by adding the new accession numbers and any different descriptive terminology that might apply. Worksheets and data entry are necessary only for new titles or subject areas.

The larger the slide collection, the greater the need for an online database. In the three years of the project, we have come to appreciate how much less busywork we have to do to keep our records up to date. Now when a slide is added to the collection, we first check to see if a record for that title already exists in the database. If it does, all we do is add the accession number and particular view to the existing record. The majority of our new accessions are different or better views of existing sets. Once the entire conversion is completed, the time it takes to process a slide and add it to the collection will be cut by 75 percent. Of course, worksheets still have to be completed for new titles, but we anticipate that these additions will be limited to selected contemporary buildings and works of art. When we eventually devise a format for printing our slide labels and accession cards from our online records, we will then be able to reduce significantly that processing time.

SUMMARY

The use of the *MARC Audiovisual Materials Format* has its supporters and its detractors. I have found out firsthand its application problems, especially the limitations of its field definitions for cataloging unpublished audiovisual materials. Nonetheless, I agree with its supporters that consistency and standardization of terminology in these types of collections must be encouraged and pursued. As long as MARC can be reinterpreted and extended beyond its existing perimeters to meet the distinct needs of specialized collections, it will continue to be a useful tool.

Consistency and standardization, which both MARC and the *AAT* promote, should be a primary concern of those of us responsible for the original cataloging of nonbook materials. This concern, though, should not put unnecessary restrictions on our ability to catalog comprehensively unpublished nonbook materials, thereby limiting the user's access to that material. Nonpublished materials such as slides generated in-house are very subject-specific (e.g., the Empire State Building) and are very difficult to catalog using MARC without some open interpretation of the field definitions. In designing the Rensselaer Online Catalog System for Slides, we decided to give up some standardization to ensure greater access. We consider this a fair trade-off.

REFERENCES

Art and Architecture Thesaurus. New York: Oxford University Press, 1990.

The Metropolitan Museum of Art. "Photograph and Slide Library." *The Metropolitan Museum of Art Slide Library*, May 1968.

Michigan Terminal Systems Ver. 6.0 (MTS 6.0). Ann Arbor, Mich.: Regents of the University of Michigan, 1988.

Simons, Wendell W., and Luraine C. Tansey. "A Slide Classification System for the Organization and Automatic Indexing of Interdisciplinary Collections of Slides and Pictures." Santa Cruz, Calif.: University of California, 1970.

Stanford Public Information Retrieval System Ver. 87.04 (SPIRES 87.04). Palo Alto, Calif.: Stanford University, 1987.

■ The Object as "Subject": Providing Access to Genres, Forms of Material, and Physical Characteristics

JACKIE M. DOOLEY
HELENA ZINKHAM

Many features of special materials other than creator, title, and subject play important roles in research. Among these are genre, form of material, and physical characteristics, referred to collectively in this paper as *object characteristics*. For example, the physical properties of the books are critical when comparing vellum bindings by place and date of production; authorship and subject content may well be irrelevant. With genres and forms of material, such as lyric poems and voting registers, the form of the intellectual content is a shorthand expression for its probable subject content. A researcher may also rely on object characteristics to limit an author or subject search, such as when an art historian requires etchings by Rembrandt, but not his paintings or works in other media, or when a historic preservation firm needs architectural drawings and photographs of the Statue of Liberty, but not cartoons or posters.

Researchers who want special format materials are accustomed to seeking out a rare book room, archives, graphic collection, slide library, art museum, or film repository to locate a catalog of materials in nonbook formats. During the 1980s, however, changes to the *USMARC Format for Bibliographic Data*[1] have made it possible for special materials in such repositories to be integrated into the same automated catalogs that previously described primarily books and periodicals.

Researchers may welcome the opportunity to discover in a single catalog a variety of media related to a topic, but the catalog must include mechanisms to replace the distinctions in medium formerly made through the context imposed by physically separate catalogs. Consider, for example, the need both to locate and differentiate:

- Actual daguerreotypes.

- 35-mm slide reproductions of daguerreotypes.

- Books about daguerreotypes.

These examples demonstrate the objects themselves (their genre, form of material, or physical characteristics), representations of objects (some of which are reproductions), and works about the objects.[2] Bibliographic records have long described materials in ways that make these distinctions fairly clear, but the differences between object, represented work, and subject have been less clear in indexing.

Because identical terms are often used to express both object and subject, it is important to make object/subject distinctions through separate USMARC field designations. The implementation of fields for genre and form of material (Field 655, Index Term – Genre/Form) and physical characteristics (Field 755, Added Entry – Physical Characteristics) has made it possible to index object characteristics and to differentiate them from subjects in USMARC bibliographic records. Conflicting approaches to indexing object characteristics are emerging, however, in different special format communities. These practices are also frequently in conflict with rules of application for the *Library of Congress Subject Headings*, which are used for much special format cataloging.[3] The goal of distinguishing objects from subjects may be lost unless current variations in indexing practices settle into more widely agreed upon patterns.

The four basic approaches to indexing object characteristics are:

- Assign object terminology (i.e., the indexing vocabularies used to describe object characteristics) to fields separate from subjects.

- Assign object terminology in the same USMARC fields as subjects.

- Use object terminology as subdivisions of subject headings.

- Code a limited number of characteristics in the 007 Physical Description Fixed Field and other data such as book illustration features in the 008 Fixed-Length Data Elements Field.[4]

Further variation results from a choice of several USMARC fields when coding headings for object characteristics (fields 650, 654, 655, 755, and subdivisions of 600, 610, 611, 630, 650, and 651), from disagreement concerning the scope of fields 655 and 755, and from numerous sources of indexing vocabulary with sometimes conflicting terminology. Confusion is escalating at a time when access to object characteristics is becoming more important, now that growing numbers of special collections librarians, archivists, and museum curators are adding descriptions of their materials to integrated bibliographic catalogs. Even if a special collections library isolates its automated catalog records from other materials, it must think about distinguishing objects from subjects without relying on old techniques of separate card catalog drawers, different colors of card stock, and different typeface styles for subject headings.

This paper assumes the importance of access to object characteristics and focuses on ways to distinguish object from subject. Occasional references are made to "represented work" issues, which require separate study. The main concern addressed is that of the researcher interested in identifying, for example, *actual* newsreels, without also sorting through bibliographic records for books and posters *about* newsreels.

The paper concentrates on the specialized USMARC fields 655 and 755 as means of distinguishing objects from subjects. Because use of these specialized fields to index the objects themselves is a new venture, many issues are only now becoming apparent; consequently, the paper touches upon numerous points that are not explored in depth. Necessary background information is introduced by reviewing the development of fields 655 and 755, comparing the thesauri developed by various special format cataloging communities, and describing the roles of the *Art and Architecture Thesaurus*[5] and *Library of Congress Subject Headings* vis-à-vis this terminology. The paper also outlines issues related to effective retrieval of object terminology in bibliographic records and suggests questions for future research. It is hoped that this initial work will be followed by more analytical discussions that can lead to shared solutions to common problems.

DEVELOPMENT OF USMARC FIELDS 655 AND 755

Fields 655 and 755 were added to the *UFBD* based on proposals submitted in 1979 by the Ad Hoc Committee on Standards for Rare Book Cataloguing in Machine-Readable Form of the Independent Research Libraries Association (IRLA).[6] The interests of IRLA focused on rare books, and the field 655 and 755 proposals were developed in response to this particular community's need to draw distinctions among subjects, intellectual genres relevant to printed texts, and physical attributes of rare books that result from printing, publication, distribution, and ownership. Recognition of the relevance of the fields to other special formats was not far behind; Shatford, for example, stated in her analysis of descriptive cataloging of pictorial materials that "isolation of genre/form as different from other types of subject access is a crucial advance."[7]

No thesaurus had been prepared for either field before it was added to the *UFBD*, and consistent indexing of object characteristics was in its infancy. Consequently, the fields were not developed based on systematic analysis, and the data element definitions have evolved in response to the needs of various special format communities. As will be seen, this situation has led to significant problems and confusion.

In one sense, 655 terms are related to the content of materials, while 755 terms pertain to physical features of tangible objects. Therefore, 655 terms remain appropriate to all manifestations of a work regardless of physical medium – a daguerreotype portrait duplicated on microfilm remains a portrait. On the other hand, 755 terms usually change when a work is expressed in a different medium. In the case of a roll of microfilm containing images of daguerreotypes, the tangible object is a microfilm, not a collection of daguerreotypes. In some cases, 755 terms apply to features of a specific *copy* of an object, such as a hand-colored copy of an engraving, an armorial binding, or a book containing a presentation inscription.

The distinctions between fields 655 and 755, however, often remain ambiguous. As Mayo points out, "Many of the terms . . . have physical and intellectual aspects that cannot be easily separated";[8] she cites chapbooks, diaries, and registers as examples of genres that suggest aspects of their physical medium. Other forms of material implying a physical format are broadsides and posters; their assignment to field 655 in some thesauri opens the way for other physically oriented object characteristics such as photographs and sculpture.

When form of material is understood as "format" or "type of object," the intellectual-physical boundary between fields 655 and 755 disappears. Terms such as PHOTOGRAPHS, for example, seem equally appropriate for both fields. Faced with two fields, thesaurus compilers have sketched out several ways to distinguish between them: subject content versus bibliographic description; intellectual category versus physical medium; physical format type versus specific physical characteristics; universal attributes versus copy-specific attributes.

It merits notice that in June 1983 the American Library Association's RTSD/LITA/RASD Committee on Representation in Machine-Readable Form of Bibliographic Information (MARBI) questioned the need for the proposed field 755 and recommended that it be subsumed within field 655. The LC USMARC Review Group objected, however, on the grounds that the two types of data were different and belonged in separate field blocks (6xx and 7xx).[9] Arguments pertaining to the value of one field or two are presented more fully below in the context of retrieval issues.

One essential attribute that the fields share is the use of subdivision facets for general topics, dates, and places (designated in the *UFBD* by subfields $x, $y, and $z, respectively). These facets make it possible to bring out features of objects in more detail than can be done when object terminology is used in subdivisions of subject headings. For example, DAGUERREOTYPES – COLORED – GERMAN – 1855,   or   HYMNALS – RHODE ISLAND – PROVIDENCE – 18TH CENTURY.

Now that we have seen some of the attributes of fields 655 and 755, let us examine the field definitions found in the *UFBD*. The scope of field 655 (Index Term – Genre/Form) is as follows:

> This field contains terms indicating the genre and/or form of the materials being described. Genre terms for textual materials designate specific kinds of materials distinguished by the style or technique of their intellectual contents, for example, biographies, catechisms, essays, hymns, or reviews. Form terms designate historically and functionally specific kinds of materials as distinguished by an examination of their physical character, subject of their intellectual content, or the order of information within them, for example, daybooks, diaries, directories, journals, memoranda, questionnaires, syllabi, or time sheets.
>
> In the context of graphic materials, genre headings denote categories of material distinguished by vantage point, intended purpose, characteristics of the creator, publication status, or method of representation.

The definition of *form terms* was added when the specifications for Archival and Manuscripts Control (AMC) were published in USMARC Update no. 10 in 1984; the graphic materials context was added on the initiative of the Library of Congress Network Development and MARC Standards Office after *Descriptive Terms for Graphic Materials*[10] was published in 1986. Thus, the original field scope was substantially expanded to accommodate the needs of two additional communities. Inclusion of the phrase "physical character" appears to have opened the door for future differences of interpretation as to field 655's scope and its relation to field 755.

In contrast to the detailed definition of field 655, that of field 755 (Added Entry – Physical Characteristics) assumes the field name to be self-defining: "This field contains terms indicating the physical characteristics of the material described."

The original IRLA proposal called for this field to be entitled Publishing/Physical Aspects and included seven indicators to trigger display labels to categorize the types of information that field 755 was initially intended to cover: publishing and bookselling; printing; paper and papermaking; typography; illustration and graphics; and provenance.[11] The proposal was rejected in part because no vocabulary list had been developed and in part because a new mechanism was requested to link a particular 755 field with another 7xx field – for example, to link the 755 term AUTOGRAPHS with a 700 field containing the name of the person whose autograph appears in a book.

The present field definition was approved for all forms of material in 1984.[12] The definition has not been updated to reflect the scope of vocabularies published by ALA's Rare Books and Manuscripts Section, discussed below, which follows the broader concept originally set forth by IRLA.

THESAURI AND LISTS FOR SPECIAL FORMATS

A flurry of thesaurus-building activity began with the approval of the 655 and 755 fields, and this activity is likely to continue as additional thesauri are developed to fill the major gaps in terminology that still exist.[13] Each community and thesaurus define their own domain; yet there is considerable overlap. Many headings appear in more than one thesaurus, but their syntax may differ. In some cases, the same term is assigned to field 655 by one thesaurus and to field 755 by another. Despite efforts on the part of thesaurus compilers to avoid establishing conflicting terminology, simultaneous development of thesauri and differing points of view have made total consistency difficult to achieve.

Each thesaurus has been assigned a source code for use in USMARC records; these codes are listed in the *USMARC Code List for Relators, Sources, Descriptive Conventions*.[14] The codes are entered in subfield $2 of bibliographic access point fields and allow the source thesaurus to be identified by users of a system; they can also facilitate control of multiple thesauri in systems that incorporate such features. Throughout this paper, thesaurus source codes are used as shorthand for the titles of thesauri, and all of the codes are listed in the appendix at the end of this essay.

There is no provision in the *UFBD* for using vocabulary from unspecified sources in fields 655 and 755.

Rare Books

The rare book community has a long tradition of using discrete manual card files to provide access to object characteristics of printed books. As described by the IRLA proposals, a rare book room typically keeps separate files for genres, printing and publishing characteristics, illustration techniques, bindings, paper, typographic evidence, and provenance information. Mayo outlines the history of special files in rare book rooms, the IRLA proposals, and the ensuing work of the Standards Committee of ALA's Rare Books and Manuscripts Section (RBMS) to develop a family of thesauri to cover rare book needs.[15] RBMS elected to publish the thesauri separately in order to make each one available as quickly as possible but hopes eventually to combine them into a single publication having a single alphabetical listing and separate hierarchical listings corresponding to the existing thesauri.

The first thesaurus to appear following approval of field 655 was *Genre Terms: A Thesaurus for Use in Rare Book and Special Collections Cataloguing*, issued in 1983. Three additional thesauri have followed:[16]

> Title: *Genre Terms* (1983)
> Field: 655
> $2 code: rbgenr
> Size: 332 terms
>
> Title: *Printing and Publishing Evidence* (1986)
> Field: 755
> $2 code: rbpri, rbpub
> Size: 158 terms
>
> Title: *Binding Terms* (1988)
> Field: 755
> $2 code: rbbin
> Size: 268 terms
>
> Title: *Provenance Evidence* (1988)
> Field: 755
> $2 code: rbprov
> Size: 76 terms

Genre Terms includes "intellectual genres of textual materials in general rare book libraries . . . [and] has a literary-historical bias . . . genre may be defined as a recognized category of works (not their physical manifestations) characterized by a particular form, purpose or content."[17] It is strongest in its coverage of literary genres but also includes terminology for religious, record-keeping, instructional, illustrated, and other works. Terminology for maps, legal works, and music are only marginally represented, but the RBMS Standards Committee has expressed its eagerness to receive submissions from experts in these areas.[18] Examples include:

> Alphabet books
> Artists' books
> Cartoons
> Expurgated works
> Hornbooks
> Lyric poems
> Miracle plays
> Missals
> Parodies

> Romances
> Voting registers
> Yellowbacks

A second edition of the thesaurus, which will include additional terms, scope notes, and a hierarchical display, is in progress.[19]

Each RBMS thesaurus for field 755 contains the same statement of purpose and scope: to "assist researchers interested in studying the physical characteristics of books as evidence for their production, distribution, or further history." *Printing and Publishing Evidence* also states that it provides terminology for "physical evidence of printing and publishing practices."[20] Terms include:

> Cancelled gatherings
> Composition errors
> Errata slips
> Forgeries
> Galley proofs
> Half-sheet imposition
> Miniature books
> Photographic facsimiles
> Shaped books
> Vellum printings

Binding Terms includes "descriptors relating to techniques for binding construction, and to the style, materials, and decoration of bindings."[21] Some sample terms are:

> Accordion fold format
> Binding errors
> Dos-a-dos bindings
> Folding errors
> Islamic bindings
> Marbled calf bindings
> Rebacking
> Silver clasps

Provenance Evidence contains terms referring "not only to former owners in the legal sense, but also to any who may have had temporary custody of the material (such as auction houses or library borrowers) and have left their mark in some way on it."[22] Examples are:

> Armorial stamps
> Association copies
> Auction copies
> Autographs

Bookplates
Extra-illustrated copies
Marginalia
Presentation inscriptions

Most of this terminology describes "physical" evidence, but the thesauri also contain terms that could be applied based on information obtained from sources independent of the book being described; examples include FORGERIES and PIRACIES from *Printing and Publishing Evidence*, as well as AUCTION COPIES and AUTHORS' COPIES from *Provenance Evidence*. Much of the RBMS terminology for field 755 is copy-specific. This is universally true for *Provenance Evidence* and sometimes true for *Printing and Publishing Evidence* and *Binding Terms*, especially for books printed before the mid-18th century.[23]

Additional RBMS thesauri are forthcoming for characteristics of paper and typographic evidence, which also will be designated for the 755 field.[24] Although rare book collections include illustrated materials and limited illustration terminology appears in existing RBMS thesauri, RBMS will not develop a thesaurus of illustration types and techniques. Instead, RBMS recommends use of *Descriptive Terms for Graphic Materials*, described below.

The RBMS thesauri usually are used in catalog records that describe single items, and they tend to be applied selectively to provide access to particularly interesting or important examples of genres or physical attributes. Because rare book catalogers assign terms based on their knowledge of the importance of a book's content and artifactual value, this practice allows retrieval of the most significant and interesting examples rather than what might be an unmanageable file of every broadside, sermon, morocco binding, presentation inscription, printer's error, and so on. An alternative approach would be to index every example thus providing as broad a sample pool as possible to support study of genres, printing practices, and other characteristics of books.

Graphic Materials

Although several thesauri contain some terminology for prints, photographs, drawings, ephemera, and other two-dimensional pictorial materials, *Descriptive Terms for Graphic Materials* covers the broadest range of relevant terminology in a single alphabetical list. Staff of the Prints and Photographs Division of the Library of Congress, under the sponsorship of the RBMS Standards Committee, began compiling the list in 1983, and it was published in 1986. *GMGPC* is a companion list to a topical subject thesaurus, *LC Thesaurus for Graphic Materials (LCTGM)*.[25]

Title: *Descriptive Terms for Graphic Materials*

Fields: 655, 755
$2 code: gmgpc
Size: 513 terms

Terms meeting the following criteria are coded for the 655 field: "Genre headings denote distinctive categories of material: an established class of pictorial types (CARTOONS), a vantage point or method of projection (BIRD'S-EYE VIEWS) . . . intended purpose (ADVERTISEMENTS; COMPETITION DRAWINGS) . . . characteristics of an image's creator (STUDENT WORKS) or a publication status or occasion (CENSORED WORKS; NEW YEAR CARDS). Others imply a subject but also designate a method of representation (ABSTRACT WORKS; LANDSCAPES). Terms denoting artistic movements and styles are not included in this definition of genre.[26]

In field 755, "Physical characteristic headings designate graphic materials distinguished by production processes or techniques (ALBUMEN PHOTO-PRINTS), production stages or versions (PROOFS; REPRODUCTIONS), instrument employed (PINHOLE CAMERA PHOTOGRAPHS; AIRBRUSH WORKS), markings (WATERMARKS), shape and size (SCROLLS; MINIATURE WORKS), and other physical aspects of graphic materials."[27]

Detailed though these statements may be, some terms are difficult to assign to one field rather than the other. Compound terms sometimes contain aspects appropriate to both fields, such as STILL LIFE PHOTOGRAPHS and PORTRAIT DRAWINGS; these terms are assigned to field 655. POSTCARDS (field 655) are often thought of as a physical format in the same way that STEREOGRAPHS (field 755) express a particular size and shape. POSTCARDS, however, are described in *Descriptive Terms for Graphic Materials* with an emphasis on their purpose as stationery for sending a message. They are therefore designated for field 655, as they can be issued in varied physical media such as photographs, prints, or tree bark. In another example, the term DRAWINGS is designated for field 755 as a broad category of physical media, while SKETCHES is assigned to field 655 as a type of representation associated with a variety of physical media. Both terms are likely to be thought of as object characteristics; coding them in separate fields spells retrieval confusion unless fields 655 and 755 are indexed jointly.

In other instances, the goal to be consistent with rare book thesauri led *GMGPC* compilers to assign physical format terms such as ALBUMS, BROADSIDES, and POSTERS to field 655, and nonphysical terms such as FORGERIES to field 755. Ironically, some borrowing from drafts of the *Art and Architecture Thesaurus* Drawings hierarchy introduced compound terms such as SILVERPOINT DRAWINGS, which *AAT* later dropped in favor of separate terms (SILVERPOINT and DRAWINGS), which may be combined into complex headings by indexers. What was once common terminology may now conflict, depending upon the headings that are constructed.

As mentioned earlier, the difficulty of distinguishing genres and forms of material from physical characteristics calls into question the need for separate fields. In the absence of universal agreement on field scopes, *GMGPC* puts all 655 and 755 vocabulary in a single alphabetical listing so that catalogers and researchers may more easily locate terms in the thesaurus. Also, *GMGPC* assigns a specific field tag to each term to promote consistency in indexing and retrieval.

As with the RBMS thesauri, each repository using *GMGPC* may set its own policy about assigning object terminology on a selective basis to identify examples of special interest or assigning certain terms (such as POSTERS or DAGUERREOTYPES) in every applicable case in order to enable total recall when searching by object characteristics.

False drops from assigning subject and object terminology to separate fields are sometimes a problem. A poster *about* Susan B. Anthony, for example, may feature portraits of the people she inspired, but not Anthony herself. A search for ANTHONY, SUSAN B. and PORTRAITS would retrieve this record unless a technique for linking, subdividing, or faceting is used to maintain clarity among term relationships. This Boolean retrieval problem, described in more detail below, is of particular concern because catalogers of graphic materials frequently describe groups of materials with different features in a single catalog record, in a fashion similar to that of archivists.

Archives and Manuscripts

The archives and manuscripts community has long incorporated form of material terminology in its collection descriptions. In a collection's physical arrangement, for example, each series often corresponds to a form of material (correspondence, diaries, photographs, translations, periodical articles, personnel records, legal files, ephemera, etc.).[28] Widespread provision of access points for direct retrieval by form of material, however, is quite new, as is machine-readable cataloging for these materials.

The list of terms most widely used by archivists is *Form Terms for Archival and Manuscript Control*, issued in 1985:[29]

> Title: *Form Terms for Archival and Manuscripts Control*
> Field: 655
> $2 code: ftamc
> Size: 368 terms

FTAMC is a list of "basic document types . . . not intended to be comprehensive."[30] It defines form of material and genre as in the *UFBD*, which is not surprising because the definition of *form terms* was added to field 655 at the request of the developers of the AMC format. Much *FTAMC* terminology is relevant to printed as well as manuscript formats, and 25 percent of the terms also appear in *Genre Terms*. Sample terms include:

Account books
Albums
Baptismal records
Case histories
Diaries
Field notes
Insurance policies
Motion pictures
Racing forms
Scrapbooks

FTAMC explicitly excludes terminology for audiovisual and machine-readable archival materials and includes few literary genres, so archivists needing such terminology must find another source. The list contains about thirty terms for visual formats, including AMBROTYPES, ARCHITECTURAL DRAWINGS, ETCHINGS, and LANTERN SLIDES. *Descriptive Terms for Graphic Materials* designates most of these terms for coding in the 755 field; hence, the same terms are found sometimes in field 655 and sometimes in field 755, depending upon which thesaurus is used.

The *National Union Catalog of Manuscript Collections* is one of the archival community's major users of subject and form of material access points.[31] For its records entered into the RLIN database since 1988, *NUCMC* staff select terms from *FTAMC* for the 655 field. *NUCMC* does *not* use all the terminology found in *FTAMC* in field 655, as it prefers to maintain consistency with RBMS and *GMGPC* practice and so uses field 755 for terms designated in those lists for field 755. The fact that Columbia University's Avery Library architectural drawings collection, which draws vocabulary from the *Art and Architecture Thesaurus*, also uses field 755 for physical media terms, may have further influenced *NUCMC*'s decision to identify physical media and assign them to a field specifically designed for physical characteristics access.

Since *FTAMC* is authorized for use only in the 655 field and lacks terminology for a variety of object characteristics, *NUCMC* currently uses thirty-eight terms from *AAT* in the 755 field, including AUDIO TAPES, AUTOGRAPHS, DRAWINGS, GLOBES, MACHINE-READABLE RECORDS, and VIDEO RECORDINGS. (As described below, *AAT* includes considerable terminology outside the fields of art and architecture.) The desire for a single source of terminology that would encompass the wide variety of forms of material reported to *NUCMC* and provide guidance on application issues such as topical subdivision has led *NUCMC* staff to begin developing a thesaurus that will be based on *FTAMC*, *GMGPC*, RBMS lists, *AAT*, *LCSH*, and the form terms used in published *NUCMC* index volumes beginning with the volume covering collections reported in 1985. Terms will be submitted for inclusion in *AAT*.[32] Depending upon the outcome of current discussions about fields 655 and 755, all terms may be designed for field 655 or for both fields.

On another archival front, the RLIN Government Records Project, a continuation of the RLIN Seven States Project, has as one of its goals the establishment of uniform terminology for forms of material.[33] Project coordinators began working with *AAT* staff in 1989 to develop guidelines for usage of form of material terminology, to add vocabulary relevant to government archives to the *AAT* Document Types hierarchy, to write scope notes for existing terms in order to standardize usage, and to understand the relationship between *form* and *function* as it pertains to archival materials.[34] If successful, this cooperative effort will benefit government archivists by providing them with extensive form and function terminology from a single source and with ongoing maintenance by *AAT* staff.

Archivists have expressed little interest in developing a thesaurus for field 755, although some terms in *FTAMC* are identical or similar to vocabulary designated in RBMS thesauri and *GMGPC* for field 755. Their predominant need for access to forms of material rather than to detailed physical characteristics of archival materials may lead archivists to advocate the point of view that all object characteristics fall within the scope of field 655, enabling them to avoid using field 755 at all.

Archivists have identified false drops as a particularly acute problem because most archival catalog records describe collections of materials, not single items. A single archival collection often encompasses many subjects and many forms of material; for retrieval purposes, it may be crucial to maintain the relationships of particular subjects to particular forms. For example, in a collection of family papers containing women's diaries, photographs of clergymen, and legislative bills relating to bank robbers, Boolean searching of terminology split between subject and object fields could result in retrieval of this collection by a researcher looking for photographs of bank robbers or diaries of clergymen. Such potential for false drops has led some archivists (including *NUCMC* staff) to advocate subdivision of subject by form and, conversely, of form by subject. The 1986-1987 *NUCMC* form and genre index, for example, includes terms subdivided by topic, as in CASE FILES – REFORMATORIES – NEW JERSEY – 20TH CENTURY. The indexing practices used for rare book cataloging, in which subjects and object characteristics are described in separate headings and coded in separate fields, need investigation as to their effectiveness for collection-level cataloging. An alternative would be to propose an enhancement to the *UFBD* to make it possible to link related access points for retrieval purposes, such as that proposed (unsuccessfully) by IRLA.

It is important to note that object terminology for medieval manuscripts and other nonarchival manuscripts has not been addressed as part of the activities described above, nor has such terminology been developed by rare book librarians.

Moving Image Materials

A recent addition to the growing list of genre and form thesauri is *Moving Image Materials: Genre Terms*, published by the Library of Congress for the archival film community in 1988:[35]

> Title: *Moving Image Materials*
> Field: 655
> $2 code: mim
> Size: 189 terms

MIM emphasizes that forms and genres characterize *works*, regardless of the physical format in which a particular title appears. "*Form* is used rather broadly to encompass any recognized category of works characterized by a particular format or purpose . . . *Genre* is used rather narrowly to encompass any recognized category of fictional works which is characterized by recognizable conventions, i.e., a group of works all of which tend to explore the same themes and use the same plot formulae, character-types and icons . . ." Examples of *MIM* genres are:

> Gangster drama
> Horror drama
> Mysteries
> Westerns

Examples of *MIM* form terms are:

> Animation
> Commercials
> Documentaries and factual works
> Game shows

MIM further states that "since subject matter can easily influence form or genre, it can be difficult to distinguish subject from form or genre."[36] Examples include WAR DOCUMENTARIES, NATURE WORKS, and WAR DRAMA.[37]

In comparison with the concepts found in other special format thesauri, moving image genres have much in common with the literary genres used by the rare books community. Many *MIM* terms do not refer explicitly to motion pictures, reminding one of the need for mechanisms beyond 655 and 755 headings to draw distinctions among types of objects. The terms PLAYS and

CARTOONS in *MIM* refer to motion images; in other thesauri, they refer to texts or two-dimensional graphics. The thesaurus source or fixed-field coding may become critical components in leading researchers to the appropriate materials, such as to moving image cartoons rather than to newspaper editorials in the form of political cartoons.

A distinctive feature of *MIM* is its explicit concordance with *LCSH*. Whenever *LCSH* and *MIM* include the same concept, but with different term syntax, the *LCSH* term is identified and included as a cross-reference. This reflects the reliance of many moving image catalogers on *LCSH* for subject terminology and the desire to correlate a community's subject indexing thesaurus to its object terminology. An example:

> Industrial works
> UF Moving-pictures in industry (*LCSH*)

The moving image cataloging community has yet to develop a thesaurus for the 755 field, and there appears to be no pressing need. An elaborate coding scheme in the 007 Physical Description Fixed Field provides adequate access for identifying features such as color, size, dimensions, and sound track characteristics. A few unusual physical characteristics, such as IB Technicolor, might prove to be useful access points.

THESAURI USED FOR BOTH SUBJECT AND OBJECT INDEXING

The Art and Architecture Thesaurus

The *Art and Architecture Thesaurus* is a project of the Getty Art History Information Program, and has been under development since 1980. The *AAT* is relevant to the context of this paper for two reasons: (1) Its object terminology overlaps considerably with several special format thesauri, and (2) some members of the archives and manuscripts and graphic materials communities use selected the *AAT* hierarchies for indexing object characteristics. The *AAT* is a faceted, hierarchically structured vocabulary meant for indexing and retrieval of art and architecture information in any format, including texts, visual images, and three-dimensional objects. To the extent that the study of art and architecture relies on a wide variety of documents, the vocabulary is also applicable to other disciplines. The *AAT* is issued in printed and electronic form.

> Title: *Art and Architecture Thesaurus*
> Fields: 650, 654, 655, 656, 657, 755
> $2 code: aat
> Size: ca. 35,000 terms

Unlike the thesauri previously described, the *AAT* consists largely of single-indexing terms that may either be used alone or combined into complex headings by indexers. For example, while *GMGPC* has established the term ABSTRACT DRAWINGS, the *AAT* has the separate terms ABSTRACT and DRAWINGS. In a more elaborate example, terms are chosen from four separate hierarchies to form a complex heading: ROCOCO GILDED PAINTED WOOD CHAIRS includes terms from Styles and Periods, Processes and Techniques, Materials, and Image and Object Genres hierarchies.

Within its seven facets and thirty-eight separate hierarchies, the *AAT* includes terms for many of the same concepts that appear in other special format thesauri. The Document Types hierarchy has considerable overlap with *RBGENR*, *FTAMC*, and *GMGPC*, although numerous terms in these lists are not yet represented in *AAT*, and vice versa. As described earlier, a group of archivists is working with *AAT* staff to incorporate governmental forms of material into the Document Types hierarchy. The Processes and Techniques, Drawings, and Image and Object Genres hierarchies cover much of the same ground as *GMGPC* terminology but with greater specificity. The Photographs[38] and Prints hierarchies will do the same. A Book Arts and Calligraphy hierarchy is planned and is likely to overlap with RBMS thesauri. Extensive music, legal, literary, religious, and oriental art vocabularies remain out of scope, as do iconographic subjects and personal, corporate, and geographic names.

One of the great virtues of a thesaurus like the *AAT* is that every conceivable compound concept need not be enumerated; therefore, it will be possible to build far more complex headings using *AAT* than currently are authorized in any other thesaurus. The *AAT*'s use of simple terms that may be combined into headings by indexers also means that the final syntax of indexing strings exists only when the thesaurus is actually applied. The burden that this may place on catalogers and users is only beginning to be evaluated.

In order for the *UFBD* to accommodate the *AAT*'s complex faceted structure, *AAT* staff proposed a new field 654 (Subject Added Entry–Faceted Topical Subject Heading), which was approved by MARBI in 1988.[39] Complex term expressions from the *AAT* and other faceted thesauri now can be coded in the *UFBD*, the hierarchy from which each element of the string was taken can be identified, and systems designers can utilize the facet coding for indexing and display purposes. The field is too new for evaluation of application practices or retrieval implications.

AAT users are free to devise their own rules for applying *AAT* vocabulary, but to assist those wanting guidance, sample applications protocols will be available.[40] Toward this end, *AAT* staff have begun to analyze how the vocabulary might be used in fields 655 and 755.[41] The *AAT* will not establish separate terminology for subjects and objects. Rather, this distinction will be made by use of the plural for subjects and the singular for object terminology such as processes and materials. For example, DAGUERREOTYPES (plural form) would be used when indexing a book about daguerreotypes, and DAGUERREOTYPE (singular form) for indexing an example of this type of photography.

The *AAT* will not specify particular terms for use in particular fields. Rather, *AAT* staff hopes that *UFBD* definitions for genre, form of material, and physical characteristics will be rendered unambiguous so that catalogers will be able to determine easily the correct field tag in each case. An applications protocol might recommend, however, that the 755 field be used only for terms from the Processes and Techniques and the Materials hierarchies and that all other object terminology be coded in the 655 field. This could mean, for example, that an abstract drawing would be indexed partially in the 655 field (ABSTRACT) and partially in the 755 field (DRAWING). Compare this with *GMGPC*, which would enter ABSTRACT DRAWINGS in the 655 field.

The *AAT* considers reproductions of works of art to be surrogates for original works and will recommend that they be indexed in similar fashion. For example, PAINTING (655) would be used to describe both Leonardo's *Mona Lisa* and a slide reproduction; SLIDE (655) would also be used in the latter case. This holds serious implications for effective retrieval, as Shatford has warned.[42] In an integrated database containing both of these media, searchers interested only in examples of actual paintings might have to learn to exclude slides, microfilm, and other reproduction media in their search queries to retrieve only records for original paintings. It does not seem appropriate to expect catalog users to construct such intricate requests. One solution might be the addition of a "reproduction" facet to indexing strings for object surrogates so that they would be differentiated from "originals" in a browse display.

AAT users must resolve a variety of other applications issues as well. When indexing texts, will subject and form terms be split between fields 654 (e.g., BAROQUE CHURCHES) and 655 (BIBLIOGRAPHY)? When indexing photographs, will the data be split among three fields, such as for a DAGUERREOTYPE (755) PORTRAIT (655) of ABRAHAM LINCOLN (600)? Much of the power of the *AAT*'s vocabulary would be lost if indexers were to code each term in a separate field rather than to construct complex headings because, as noted earlier, this can cause false drops in Boolean retrieval. In order to remedy this, *AAT* staff may propose that a linking mechanism be added to the *UFBD* to indicate relationships among headings coded in separate fields within a record. *AAT* staff also are contemplating proposals to add to the 655 and 755 fields the same faceted structure that exists in the 654 field. This would make it possible to code faceted terms in the 654 field and repeat them in 655 or 755, as appropriate, utilizing an object characteristic as the focus term in subfield $a. This would enable separate indexing of object characteristics but could result in a considerable amount of redundant data storage.

LIBRARY OF CONGRESS SUBJECT HEADINGS

As the most widely used source of subject heading terminology for general research libraries in the United States, the role of *Library of Congress Subject Headings* must be considered in almost any discussion of indexing vocabulary. *LCSH* is particularly relevant in the present context, as it is used for assigning *subject* headings by many of the special format communities discussed in this paper. Also, *LCSH* contains extensive object terminology and is authorized for use in field 655 but not in field 755.[43]

> Title: *Library of Congress Subject Headings*
> Fields: 600-651, 655, 656, 657
> $2 code: lcsh
> Size: 162,000+ terms

Although *LCSH* *may* be used in the 655 field, the Library of Congress currently has no plans to use field 655 in catalog records for books, in part because the field has not been implemented in LC's in-house online catalog and in part because of the enormous effort that would be required to retrain catalogers and develop rules for application. Consequently, fields 655 and 755 have been implemented in LC's local automated system only for graphic materials and moving image materials. Only one library is known to have coded *LCSH* form terms in 655;[44] nevertheless, potential for widespread use exists. Because *LCSH* does not indicate which of its terms are genre or form of material terms, libraries wanting to code *LCSH* terms in field 655 would have to identify the terms on their own.[45]

LCSH has been developed principally for use in assigning subject headings to books. Its use is not inherently limited to any particular medium, but *LCSH* rules of application are heavily biased toward published texts. *LCSH* includes many form and genre terms but tends to use them for materials about the form or genre and for published collections of examples, not for individual works. For instance, *LCSH* uses the heading LEGENDS for books about the history of legends and for compilations of legends but not for single legends. The same holds true for *LCSH*'s numerous form subdivisions. In some cases, the *presence* of a form subdivision indicates that the heading describes a work's form, not its subject (e.g., CALIFORNIA – PHOTOGRAPHS or MISSALS – TEXTS); in other cases, *absence* of a form subdivision may indicate that the work's form is being described (ALMANACS or SLAVE RECORDS).

Where there are no specific instructions in a term's scope note or in LC's *Subject Cataloging Manual*,[46] catalogers should assume that the term is to be used only to indicate an item's subject, not its form. Catalogers also should assume that, without explicit instructions to the contrary, exactly the same heading is used regardless of the physical format. As Chan states, ". . . the same types and forms of headings are assigned to works on the same subject whether they are in book form or not . . . the medium of publication of a work is not brought out in the subject headings."[47] There are, however, exceptions to this pattern.

In the context of fields 655 and 755, *LCSH* presents four major problems: Use of object terminology is highly inconsistent; the same headings are usually constructed for works about and examples of an object characteristic, without any consistent technique for differentiating subjects from objects in retrieval; *LCSH* rules of application normally do not allow form headings or subdivisions to be applied to individual examples of an object characteristic; and it is not possible for users to propose extensive form subdivisions for addition to *LCSH*. The following discussion of selected terms relevant to special format materials will help illustrate why use of *LCSH* does not suffice for indexing *examples* of these materials and how current *LCSH* practice contributes to retrieval confusion. The examples cited can be substantiated by reference to the *Subject Cataloging Manual* or to *LCSH* itself.

It should be noted that *LCSH* contains some (but not all) of the vocabulary found in special format thesauri and can be used for individual examples of genres and forms of material by any library willing to identify the relevant terminology and compose rules of application. Those tasks, unfortunately, are daunting to most *LCSH* users, including the Library of Congress.

Rare Books

Although the basic rule in applying *LCSH* is that it not be used for individual examples of a genre or form, exceptions to this rule abound. Examples include CATALOGS, PUBLISHERS'; CATALOGS, BOOKSELLERS'; ARTISTS' BOOKS; and ALMANACS. *RBGENR* uses these terms in natural language order: PUBLISHERS' CATALOGUES, BOOKSELLERS' CATALOGUES, and so on. For religious works, *LCSH* applies form terms to actual liturgical books, followed by the subdivision TEXTS (e.g., PSALTERS–TEXTS) to distinguish them from books about liturgical forms. *RBGENR* uses the liturgical forms without such a subdivision. *LCSH* employs the subdivision SPECIMENS under "types of publications, printed matter, etc., as a form subdivision for actual specimens of the material," seemingly opening the door wide to coding actual examples of objects in field 650, but *LCSH* editorial practice does not allow use of this subdivision under headings such as ALMANACS and ARTISTS' BOOKS.[48]

LCSH applies genre headings to individual literary works in a variety of very specific circumstances, including collections of two or more independent works by different authors; collected works by an individual author, but only if they combine form and topic (WESTERN STORIES, LOVE POETRY) or if the form is highly specific (AMATEUR THEATRICALS, DIDACTIC DRAMA, CONCRETE POETRY); individual works of drama or poetry, but not fiction, which combine form and topic or represent a highly specific form; individual works of biographical fiction, historical fiction, and animal stories; and children's poetry and plays.[49] Needless to say, these categories omit many individual works and spell confusion for the catalog user who may thereby expect to find form headings for many more individual literary works.

LCSH employs free-floating subdivisions that match some of the terms in *RBGENR*. These subdivisions include BIBLIOGRAPHY, CATALOGS, GUIDE-BOOKS, INDEXES, and JUVENILE LITERATURE. To further complicate matters, the form of the terms sometimes differs. For example, *RBGENR* uses BIBLIOGRAPHIES, CATALOGUES, and GUIDEBOOKS; *LCSH* uses these subdivisions when assigning headings to individual works, so in such cases, the same term may be coded as a subfield of a topical subject field (such as 650) and as the main term in field 655.

Rare book librarians are not alone in their interest in genre access to individual literary works. In response to the needs of public libraries and other constituencies, a subcommittee of the American Library Association's Subject Analysis Committee has drafted a *Genre List for Individual Works of Fiction, Drama, Etc.*[50] Many of the terms in the *Genre List* are also found in *RBGENR* (CONFESSIONS, EPISTOLARY NOVELS, EROTICA, MIRACLE PLAYS, ROMANS A CLEF), but others are not (EDWARDIAN NOVELS, LIGHT VERSE, MELODRAMA, OCCULT FICTION, TALL TALES). The Subcommittee on Subject Access to Individual Works of Drama, Fiction, Etc., which developed the list, has recommended that terms in the *Genre List*, as well as all *LCSH* terms for genres and forms, be used for individual works and coded in field 655.[51] Whether or not its parent committee, or the Library of Congress, will support this recommendation remains to be seen.

Graphic Materials

LCSH terminology includes many of the artistic media enumerated in *GMGPC*, although the vocabulary varies somewhat. CHROMOLITHOGRAPHY, DRY-POINT, MEZZOTINT ENGRAVING, PAINTING, and SERIGRAPHY in *LCSH* become CHROMOLITHOGRAPHS, DRYPOINTS, MEZZOTINTS, PAINTINGS, and SILKSCREENS in *GMGPC*. Until 1977, *LCSH* established such terms in the singular and the plural. The singular was applied to treatises about the medium, and the plural to collections of reproductions published separately from treatises. This practice was abandoned and all of the plural forms were deleted because changing book publication practices blurred the distinction between the two circumstances.[52] *LCSH* does not address use of these terms in the context of original works or reproductions of single items. As described earlier, *GMGPC* is used to index individual works of art, codes them in field 655 or 755 as appropriate, and uses the plural noun form. The *AAT* does not designate a field choice and establishes many terms in both the singular form (for indexing object characteristics) and the plural form (for indexing subjects).

LCSH includes the subdivisions AERIAL PHOTOGRAPHS, ART, ILLUSTRATIONS, PHOTOGRAPHS, PICTORIAL WORKS, PORTRAITS, POSTERS, and VIEWS, which are added to topical, geographic, personal, and corporate name headings to indicate their pictorial nature. In those cases where instructions are given, the *Subject Cataloging Manual* specifies that these subdivisions are to be used for collections of *reproductions* of visual images; single images and original materials are not addressed. Also, application guidelines can lead the indexer down some tortuous paths that searchers may have difficulty retracing. PORTRAITS, for example, is used as a subdivision under names of persons who lived after 1400 A.D., while ART is used for those who lived in the previous centuries.

Archives and Manuscripts

One of the most detailed sections of the *Subject Cataloging Manual* addresses headings for manuscripts (section H1855).[53] The focus is on facsimiles of and works about manuscripts, but some instructions are included for collections of original materials. An unusually lengthy (for *LCSH*) list of headings is assigned, including headings for the form of a single manuscript (e.g., PSALTERS; HOURS, BOOKS OF). For collections, however, H1855 suggests that the probable multiplicity of forms precludes describing them all. Original manuscripts also receive headings in the form MANUSCRIPTS – [language] – [place where currently located], as this "provides retrieval in the subject catalog by form." H1855 states that "because of [their] unique characteristics," manuscripts need many subject headings. This suggests that the need to provide extensive subject and form access to original source materials is recognized and implies that the policies enumerated elsewhere in the *Subject Cataloging Manual* do not sufficiently meet this need.

LCSH assigns form headings, such as ARCHIVES, BUSINESS RECORDS, MARRIAGE LICENSES, PUBLIC RECORDS, SLAVE RECORDS, and WILLS, to compilations of materials considered of value to genealogists. In these cases, therefore, book catalogers would enter object terminology for published versions of these forms of material in field 650, while catalogers of original archival materials would enter the same terminology in field 655. In systems that index fields 650 and 655 in separate indexes, searchers may locate only some of the relevant materials.

LCSH also uses a variety of form subdivisions for published versions of historical source materials, including the subdivision SOURCES. If archivists were to employ this subdivision, it would apply to literally everything in their collections. In any event, precise retrieval on SOURCES would be muddied by additional usage of this subdivision under names of persons for discussions of their sources of ideas or inspiration. The subdivision GENEALOGY is used for "works of value in the study of the origin, descent, and relationship of named families, especially . . . family papers, deeds, wills, public records, parish registers, [etc.]"[54] As in the case of SOURCES, the usefulness of this subdivision is lost in the context of archives, where a majority of materials are of value for such purposes. Use of the form subdivisions ARCHIVAL RESOURCES and ARCHIVES is slanted toward published compilations of archival materials; these subdivisions do not appear to be intended for the sources themselves. *LCSH* subdivides names of persons by CORRESPONDENCE, but for no more than three writers and two recipients per collection; this is clearly a book-oriented rule that would not suffice when indexing original materials.

Even if these various subdivisions were useful for original source materials, archivists might be hard-pressed to choose among them; their distinct meanings, designed for published collections of archival materials, become obscured in the context of the originals.

Moving Image Materials

The *Subject Cataloging Manual* has recently added instructions for assigning subject headings to films (3d ed., section H2230), and *LCSH* contains a variety of relevant scope notes. Moving image catalogers at the Library of Congress have added form terms to *LCSH* for certain film genres, such as ANIMAL FILMS, COMEDY FILMS, EXPERIMENTAL FILMS, HORROR FILMS, SHORT FILMS, TELEVISION ADVERTISING, WAR FILMS, and WESTERN FILMS. *LCSH* includes specific instructions to assign these headings to individual films as well as to books about these genres.[55] The subdivision HISTORY AND CRITICISM is added to headings for books about film genres.[56] Compare the *LCSH* terms listed above with the equivalent *MIM* headings for examples of moving image genres and forms: ANIMAL DRAMA, COMEDIES,

PERSONAL/INDEPENDENT   WORKS,   HORROR   DRAMA,   COMMERCIALS,
SHORTS, WAR DRAMA, and WESTERNS.

Catalog records for original archival films at the Library of Congress
contain a genre term from *LCSH* in the 650 field and the corresponding *MIM*
term in 655, but this use of 650 may be abandoned when LC implements
indexing of the 655 field for its visual materials application. Catalog records
for commercial audiovisual material may continue to carry only a 650 field
for film genre terminology.

LCSH also uses terms with the syntax "[topic] in motion pictures,"
including DEATH IN MOTION PICTURES and YOUTH IN MOTION PICTURES, for
books about such subjects in films. These terms designate "subjects of
individual works of fiction," not genres, and are appropriate for tagging in the
650 field, as are similar headings for "[topic] in television" and "[topic] in art."
These present an interesting contrast to LC practice for other media, for
which no such "[topic] in [medium]" headings have been established.

RETRIEVAL ISSUES

Two Fields or One?

As we have seen, uses of fields 655 and 755 vary widely. The rare book
community takes a broad view of the scope of field 755 but might consider
placing all of its vocabulary in a single field when faced, for example, with the
type of retrieval conflict that occurs when BOOKPLATES is considered both a
form of material (field 655) and physical evidence related to provenance
(field 755).

The graphic materials community is struggling with two approaches:
designating terms for both fields in what often seems an arbitrary fashion
(the *GMGPC* approach) or narrowing the scope of field 755 to include only
materials and processes such as CHARCOAL and PAINTING (the *AAT*
approach). The first approach has made one field seem desirable, while the
second could place all RBMS and *GMGPC* vocabulary into field 655, as they
do not use simple material or process terms.

The archives and manuscripts and moving image film communities see
little use for field 755, although for different reasons. Library of Congress
book, map, and music catalogers use neither field, although *LCSH* contains
extensive relevant terminology. Uniform indexing among communities is not
feasible if the conflicting field distinctions drawn by RBMS, *GMGPC*, and
AAT are maintained. All of these communities overlap in the materials they
collect, the terminology they use, and the catalogs they build, so these
differences promise to have a negative effect on retrieval success.

If, as we have found, much of the relevant terminology contains strong elements of both description and content, is the field separation in fact conceptually possible for these data? The situation is different from that of authors and topical subjects, where there is a real need to use the distinction between descriptive USMARC tag groups (1xx and 7xx) and subject content tags (6xx). For example, the catalog must distinguish books *by* Shakespeare from those written *about* him. In contrast, a broadside, a charcoal drawing, a videorecording, a fountain, a daguerreotype, and a heraldic binding are what they are. Each need never appear in both the 655 and 755 fields *if* the field definitions can be made unambiguous. The fact that the Research Libraries Group has opted to construct an RLIN index that combines field 655 and 755 terms, while separating them from traditional subjects, suggests that the fields are perceived to contain common information.

Why *not* collapse fields 655 and 755 into a single field? One argument against doing so, suggested above, is that cataloging practice and the *UFBD* distinguish between access points based on a work's intellectual form or content and those based on a work's physical or descriptive characteristics and that fields 655 and 755 must be retained to honor this split. A second argument can be found in the *AAT* recommendation that the type of object (DAGUERREOTYPE or PAINTING) be coded in field 655 but that the process or material (DAGUERREOTYPE or CHARCOAL) be coded in field 755. It may be that compound terms such as CHARCOAL   DRAWING, which is part medium and part type of object, should be coded in field 655 despite whether the term is drawn from a thesaurus that enumerates all authorized headings (such as *GMGPC*) or one that lists primarily single concepts (such as *AAT*).

The field definition problem could be likened to that of many proper-named entities such as ships, airports, bridges, zoos, and fictional characters, for which the Library of Congress serves as the de facto arbiter of the correct USMARC field in which they should be coded. If separate fields 655 and 755 are to be maintained, perhaps such an arbiter is necessary. When the data are so difficult to pin down, an arbitrary decision is preferable to erratic retrieval. Coding the same terminology in both fields is unacceptable.

Variations in Indexing Practice

The one-field-or-two dilemma notwithstanding, variations in indexing practice contribute to haphazard retrieval of genre, form of material, and physical characteristics data.

As we have seen, *LCSH* and *AAT* blur the differences between subjects and objects by using the same terminology, coded in the same 6xx fields, without application guidelines to distinguish terminology for works *about* from *examples of* an object characteristic. *LCSH* describes object characteristics only under very specific circumstances, possibly leading searchers to believe erroneously that no examples of a particular characteristic exist. The *AAT* does not limit the circumstances under which object characteristics may be indexed but does not yet provide guidelines for promoting consistent practice.

The various special format thesauri, on the other hand, are designed to draw a clear line between subjects and objects. They exist for the explicit purpose of indexing individual examples of object characteristics, and they tag object terminology separately from subjects by assigning it to field 655 or 755. Because these thesauri are frequently applied in the same bibliographic records as *LCSH* subject headings, however, one is faced with extensive duplicate storage of data, variant forms of headings, and variant *meanings* of headings or with the prospect of violating nationally accepted *LCSH* practice in order to avoid such duplication.

The special format thesauri themselves vary in ways that affect retrieval. They use various degrees of precoordination, recommend different subdivision practices, sometimes express the same concept using different terminology, and differ in their treatment of originals and reproductions. In many cases, the terminology is applied very selectively, although it is probably safe to assume that catalogers index the most significant examples. In collection-level cataloging records, and to a lesser degree in item-level records, tagging of related subjects and forms in separate fields can result in false drops, leading some libraries to subdivide subject by form *and* form by subject or to contemplate proposals to enhance the *UFBD* to link related data coded in separate fields.

If all online systems provided optimal retrieval mechanisms, including similar indexes, Boolean and keyword search capabilities, and permutation of subdivisions, these differences would be less critical. In the absence of such a scenario in the foreseeable future, however, variations in indexing practices spell confusion for the searcher.

Construction of Online Indexes

There is no standard model for online indexing of fields 655 and 755. Their unique field tags make it possible to index them separately from each other as well as from subjects and other related data. The expense of each index in an online system, however, is so high that a powerful rationale must exist for each one.

Expense notwithstanding, what would be the best model for indexing 655 and 755 data? Given that object characteristics are frequently difficult to distinguish from subjects, is it wise to try to force searchers to understand the differences between separate indexes? Even more difficult, perhaps, would be the task of differentiating to the public the theoretical difference between form/genre and physical characteristics. If the experts cannot adequately define the differences for their own purposes, how can they explain them to their users?

These problems are overstated for environments in which a single medium, such as rare books or two-dimensional artworks, comprise the entire catalog. Many institutions, however, collect a wide variety of media and describe them in integrated catalogs. One cannot, in such cases, describe a 755 index as being strictly printing and publishing evidence, or as artistic materials and processes. The vague scope of field 755 presents a particular dilemma.

Each of the possible scenarios for index construction spells confusion for catalog users if online catalog *displays* are not designed effectively. If, for example, subjects and object characteristics are combined in a single index, search results that retrieve both types of information could be labeled so as to differentiate them. The searcher could be told, "Your search has retrieved twenty works *about* DIARIES and sixty-two *examples of* DIARIES. Please select . . . etc."[57]

Many systems do not yet index the 655 and 755 fields at all, so the available models are limited. Examples include the RLIN system, which has a combined form and genre index containing both 655 and 755 terms and a separate subject index, and the University of California's MELVYL online union catalog, which indexes field 655 in the subject index but does not index 755. The *National Union Catalog for Audio-Visual Materials* (*NUC-AV*) indexes 655 and 755 terms in its subject index but prints and displays them separately from subjects in full-record displays. LC's in-house MUMS system,[58] UCLA's ORION system, and the INNOPAC implementation at the University of California, San Diego, all follow the *NUC-AV* model, primarily because of the cost of mounting separate indexes. The OCLC system does not yet index either field.

Originals versus Reproductions

As mentioned above, various thesauri have taken different approaches to indexing reproductions of objects, such as facsimile printings, 35-mm slides of paintings, or daguerreotypes reproduced on microfilm. *RBPRI/RBPUB*, *GMGPC*, and the *AAT* contain terms such as FACSIMILES and REPRODUCTIONS but do not provide a way to link them with terms for characteristics of the originals. For example, a 35-mm slide of an oil painting such as the *Mona Lisa* is indexed in *GMGPC* under REPRODUCTIONS and SLIDES, both in field 755, but the indexing does not reflect that it is a reproduction of a *painting*. The *AAT* would recommend that both PAINTING and SLIDE be coded in field 655 for the 35-mm slide.

It will be ironic if the distinction between original special format materials and reproductions becomes muddied in online indexes after such an investment of effort has been put into special thesauri. Perhaps free-floating subdivisions such as FACSIMILES and REPRODUCTIONS should be considered by way of solution.

Multiple Thesauri

The scopes of the various special format thesauri overlap considerably. There can be merit in this if a particular community need not use a multiplicity of thesauri because relevant terminology from another area has been included in that community's thesaurus. For example, if rare book libraries did not need *FTAMC* or *GMGPC* because the RBMS thesauri included all the archival and visual terminology relevant to rare books, there would be no multiple thesauri problem for that community.

This is not the case. No community's vocabulary is comprehensive or self-contained. It is important, therefore, that the special format thesaurus compilers communicate and cooperate as much as possible to avoid vocabulary conflicts. Exact term matches will not always be possible, but by including cross references between each others' terms (as *MIM* does with *LCSH* terms, and as *GMGPC* does with RBMS terms) and by composing explicit scope notes, many problems can be avoided.

Cataloging agencies that use several thesauri would be well advised to establish a hierarchy of thesauri for term selection. For example, a rare book library would probably prefer *RBGENR* over *GMGPC*; therefore, BROADSIDES and other terms found in both thesauri would always be tagged with the source code *RBGENR*. The importance of such a practice will become more evident when the special format thesauri, with their syndetic structure and scope notes, become available online and searchers are able to move back and forth between linked thesaurus terms and bibliographic access points.[59]

As for *LCSH*, its widespread usage for subject indexing by special format communities makes it highly relevant in the context of multiple thesauri. *LCSH* includes extensive object terminology, but the headings frequently are in a different form from that found in other thesauri. As many *LCSH* headings are gradually being changed to bring the list into accordance with the ANSI standard for thesaurus construction, variant syntax and spellings will gradually diminish.

The pitfalls of multiple thesauri are numerous and most easily avoided when a community can agree to use a single family of lists or when several communities can share a single list. Efforts such as those of RLIN's Government Records Project to develop vocabulary for inclusion in the *AAT*, as well as RBMS' acceptance of *GMGPC* for indexing graphic materials, are important steps in the right direction.

Nonusers of 655 and 755

The inconsistent and incomplete use of form terminology in *LCSH* has been described in some depth. *LCSH* intermingles form and subject headings in the 650 field and does not label form terms as such so that interested libraries can code them in 655; this greatly hampers reliable retrieval of object terminology in catalogs containing *LCSH* headings.[60] Internally, LC has no immediate plans to use field 655 except in the visual materials application.[61] It would be a great advance if LC were to adopt the use of field 655 for cataloging book materials; the recommendations of ALA's Subcommittee on Subject Access to Individual Works of Drama, Fiction, Etc. are an important step toward encouraging such a change.

Some special format communities, notably maps and music, have not yet chosen to employ the 655 or 755 fields.[62] Both of these communities have long traditions of using form terminology in *LCSH* subject headings in the 650 field and apparently have identified no compelling reason to change. This can be attributed, at least in part, to the fact that *LCSH* accommodates these media by including the form terminology they need and by authorizing it for indexing individual works in those forms. On the other hand, music and maps appear in archival collections, rare book rooms, and collections of art and graphics. The implication for retrieval is that music and map forms of material will be coded in different fields depending upon the cataloging agency.

QUESTIONS FOR FURTHER RESEARCH

The preceding discussion raises numerous questions that must be resolved if retrieval of object characteristics is to be effective in integrated online catalogs.

We still know too little about the users of genre, form of material, and physical characteristics data. How do they search for such information? How often do their needs encompass materials in multiple formats? Would combined or separate online indexes best serve their retrieval needs? Do they, or could they, understand the distinctions that technical experts draw among subjects and objects? Do differing subdivision practices make union databases difficult to use? Does selective indexing of object terminology render sharing of these data minimally useful to scholars?

How are the special format thesauri being used by indexers? How many institutions are using the special thesauri? How many use several thesauri in a single database? Are indexing practices uniform among institutions? Is it desirable to incorporate this terminology into subject heading lists in order to reduce the number of cataloging tools?

Are new indexing techniques needed for collection-level cataloging records, for which postcoordinated Boolean searching poses dangers more severe than for item-level records? Or would techniques for linking related fields in USMARC bibliographic records be sufficient?

We are also still learning about the data. Can definitions be devised for fields 655 and 755 that will eliminate the present ambiguities? Or can the structure of online indexes and displays be made to compensate for the different points of view of the special format communities? What is the value of separate 655 and 755 fields if the same terminology is found coded in both? How can the special format communities cooperate and resolve as many discrepancies as possible?

How does object terminology fit into the context of traditional indexes, particularly subject indexes? To what extent is use of fields 655 and 755 an asset when the same terminology, applied to the same materials, is also found in *LCSH* terminology in field 650? How can indexing strings, index structure, and online catalog displays best distinguish subjects from objects and reproductions from originals? Should subject, genre, form of material, and physical media terminology all be combined in complex indexing strings, using a specific subfield tag to identify the object characteristic terms, or is object terminology best separated from subjects at the field level and postcoordinated during retrieval?

Finally, fields 655 and 755 clearly are of little use if few systems index them at all. Are systems developers and administrators unwilling, or are they waiting for a unified message from the user communities that a consistent approach has been agreed upon?

CONCLUSIONS

The special format communities have confirmed that access to genre, form of material, and physical characteristics data is essential in order to make special format materials fully accessible, and they are gaining experience in compiling thesauri and indexing object characteristics. The right moment has arrived to take stock of the evolving situation and to work together to solve the problems that have developed.

There is considerable overlap in the materials held by various communities. Rare book libraries often encompass manuscript and archive collections; archival repositories frequently hold materials in every conceivable physical format; graphics collections are likely to include materials extracted from books or manuscript collections as well as printed ephemera; motion picture archives also collect still images; art collections encompass materials in all formats; and concepts such as provenance are relevant to all communities.

Widely varying scopes, structures, and application methodologies of the thesauri provide clear evidence, however, that needs and interpretations vary significantly from one community to the next. Overlapping needs result in the communities' sharing thesauri, so conflicts in interpretation of 655 and 755 field definitions, term syntax, and hierarchical structure have immediate implications for effective retrieval. Differing views of the scope of the two fields, coupled with *LCSH*'s highly restrictive rules of application and the *AAT*'s current lack of guidance for users, appear to pose the most serious problems. An increasing number of online catalogs integrate descriptions of materials in many formats, intermingling the terminology from a variety of lists; this lends additional urgency to the need for control of multiple thesauri. Catalogers need guidelines that allow them to index object characteristics and that are in widespread use, so they can accurately interpret and utilize each other's catalog records.

It is not difficult to identify the unresolved issues in an area where so many questions exist and where so little work has been done. The difficulty is in determining where to begin in the search for answers and solutions. Nevertheless, it is important to continue to describe and index object characteristics so that databases will contain the data necessary for future research. Despite the conflicts that may result temporarily, members of the special format communities should work together to identify workable solutions to their common problems. Consensus must be reached while vocabularies and indexing practices are still fluid enough to change.

APPENDIX: ACRONYMS

AAT: *Art and Architecture Thesaurus*
AMC: Archival and Manuscripts Control
ANSI: American National Standards Institute
FTAMC: *Form Terms for Archival and Manuscript Material*
GMGPC: *Descriptive Terms for Graphic Materials*
IRLA: Independent Research Libraries Association
LC: Library of Congress
LCSH: *Library of Congress Subject Headings*
MARBI: American Library Association. RTSD/LITA/RASD Committee on Representation in Machine-Readable Form of Bibliographic Information
MIM: *Moving Image Materials*
NUC-AV: *National Union Catalog for Audio-Visual Materials*
NUCMC: *National Union Catalog of Manuscript Collections*
RBBIN: *Binding Terms*
RBGENR: *Genre Terms*

RBMS: Rare Books and Manuscripts Section, Association of
College and Research Libraries, American Library Association
RBPRI/RBPUB: *Printing and Publishing Evidence*
RBPROV: *Provenance Evidence*
UFBD: *USMARC Format for Bibliographic Description*

NOTES

1. Library of Congress, Network Development and MARC Standards Office, *USMARC Format for Bibliographic Data* (Washington, D.C.: Library of Congress, 1988). Hereinafter cited as *UFBD*.

2. Representations of works are discussed more fully in Sara Shatford, "Describing a Picture: A Thousand Words Are Seldom Cost Effective," *Cataloging & Classification Quarterly* 4, no. 4 (Summer 1984): 13-30.

3. Library of Congress, Subject Cataloging Division, *Library of Congress Subject Headings*, 12th ed. (Washington, D.C.: Library of Congress, 1989). Hereinafter cited as *LCSH*.

4. Although these fixed-field codes cover numerous basic object characteristics, they cannot accommodate the hundreds of specific genres and forms of material, such as Thanksgiving Day proclamations, that appear in specialized object characteristic thesauri. This paper focuses, therefore, on issues relating to headings for object characteristics.

5. *Art and Architecture Thesaurus* (New York: Oxford University Press, 1990). Hereinafter cited as *AAT*.

6. Independent Research Libraries Association, "Proposals for Establishing Standards for the Cataloguing of Rare Books and Specialized Research Materials in Machine-Readable Form" (Worcester, Mass.: December 1979). For a summary of the IRLA proposals, see John B. Thomas, "The Necessity of Standards in an Automated Environment," *Library Trends* (Summer 1987), 125-39.

7. Shatford, "Describing a Picture," 17.

8. Hope Mayo, "Form and Genre Terms for Rare Books and Manuscripts: Some Reflections on the Work of the RBMS Standards Committee" (Unpublished paper presented to the Society of American Archivists, Atlanta, Georgia, 1 October 1988), 5.

9. American Library Association, RTSD/LITA/RASD Committee on Representation in Machine-Readable Form of Bibliographic Information

(Unpublished minutes, 27 June 1983). Library of Congress, MARC Review Group (Unpublished minutes, 29 July 1983).

10. Helena Zinkham and Elisabeth Betz Parker, comps., *Descriptive Terms for Graphic Materials: Genre and Physical Characteristics Headings* (Washington, D.C.: Library of Congress, 1986). Hereinafter cited as *GMGPC*.

11. *UFBD*, Proposal LC-220, March 1980.

12. *UFBD*, Proposal 82-21 (Additions/Changes to the Films Format so as to Accommodate Two-Dimensional Material).

13. The thesauri conform to the national standard: American National Standards Institute, *American National Standard Guidelines for Thesaurus Structure, Construction, and Use*, 2d ed. (New York: ANSI, 1980) (ANSI Z39.19-1980).

14. Library of Congress, Network Development and MARC Standards Office, *USMARC Code List for Realtors, Sources, Description Conventions* (Washington, D.C.: Library of Congress, 1988).

15. These developments are detailed in Mayo, "Form and Genre Terms."

16. The RBMS thesauri are: (1) *Genre Terms: A Thesaurus for Use in Rare Book and Special Collections Cataloguing* (Chicago: Association of College and Research Libraries, 1983). Hereinafter cited as *RBGENR*; "Genre Terms: Additions and Changes," *College & Research Libraries News* 48, no. 9 (October 1987): 558-60. (2) *Printing and Publishing Evidence: Thesauri for Use in Rare Book and Special Collections Cataloguing* (Chicago: ACRL, 1986). Hereinafter cited as *RBPRI/RBPUB*. (3) *Binding Terms: A Thesaurus for Use in Rare Book and Special Collections Cataloguing* (Chicago: ACRL, 1988. Hereinafter cited as *REBBIN*. (4) *Provenance Evidence: A Thesaurus for Use in Rare Book and Special Collections Cataloguing* (Chicago: ACRL, 1988. Hereinafter cited as *RBPROV*.

17. *RBGENR*, i.

18. *RBGENR*, iv.

19. It is sometimes thought that a second thesaurus of rare book genres exists, because the *USMARC Code List for Relators* includes the subfield $2 code ESTC for the *Eighteenth-Century Short-Title Catalogue*. The code is not used by the ESTC, however, as ESTC uses only five genre codes in an indexed fixed-field byte. The codes stand for the terms Advertisements, Almanacs, Directories, Publishing Proposals and Prospectuses, and Songs and Single-Sheet Verse.

20. *RBPRI/RBPUB*, i. This thesaurus has two subfield $2 codes because it is considered by RBMS to be two separate thesauri. The publication contains a single alphabetical list in which each term is coded for printing, publishing, or both.

21. *REBBIN*, [v].

22. *RBPROV*, [1].

23. Since so much terminology for field 755 is copy-specific, a future proposal to amend the *UFBD* to authorize use of subfield $5 in this field may be in order.

24. Tentatively entitled *Paper Evidence* and *Type Evidence*, both thesauri are forthcoming from ACRL.

25. Elisabeth Betz Parker, *LC Thesaurus for Graphic Materials: Topical Terms for Subject Access*, introduction by Jackie M. Dooley (Washington, D.C.: Library of Congress, 1987). Separate subject and object thesauri were compiled to reinforce the object-subject distinction, but each *GMGPC* term also resides in *LCTGM* in recognition of the fact that objects may also sometimes be the subjects of images. For example, a cartoon (object) may depict postcards or stereographs (subjects).

26. *GMGPC*, vi.

27. *GMGPC*, vii.

28. For a detailed description of the use of object terminology for describing and indexing archives and manuscripts, see Helena Zinkham, Patty Cloud, and Hope Mayo, "Providing Access by Form of Material, Genre, and Physical Characteristics: Benefits and Techniques" (Manuscript submitted to the *American Archivist*, Spring 1989).

29. Thomas Hickerson and Elaine Engst, comps., *Form Terms for Archival and Manuscripts Control* (Stanford, Calif.: Research Libraries Group, 1985). Hereinafter cited as *FTAMC*. *FTAMC* has no syndetic structure and does not follow the ANSI standard for thesaurus construction.

30. *FTAMC*, 1.

31. *National Union Catalog for Manuscript Collections* (Washington, D.C.: Library of Congress, 1959). Hereinafter cited as *NUCMC*.

32. Conversations with Harriet Ostroff, *NUCMC* editor, and with Toni Petersen, *AAT* director, in February 1989.

33. Telephone conversation with Kathleen Roe and Alden Monroe, March 1989. The Project will expand RLIN database holdings of descriptions of governmental records from thirteen states and the District of Columbia.

34. Functions terminology is coded in field 657 of the *UFBD*. The project coordinators plan to combine terminology developed for the RLIN Seven States Project with the *AAT* Functions hierarchy.

35. Martha Yee, comp., *Moving Image Materials: Genre Terms*. Compiled for the National Moving Image Database Standards Committee (Library of Congress: Cataloging Distribution Service, 1988). Hereinafter cited as *MIM*.

36. *MIM*, 11.

37. An update to *MIM* is scheduled to appear in the *Cataloging Service Bulletin* and to announce numerous changes, including substitution of "films and programs" or "films and video" for "drama" and "works" in all relevant terms. Telephone conversation with Martha Yee, May 1989.

38. The Photography hierarchy will be based on an extensive glossary compiled by Diane Vogt-O'Connor and Richard Pearce-Moses.

39. Proposal 88-10 was approved by MARBI in July 1988 and implemented with *UFBD* Update no. 1 in 1989. Proposal 88-7, for a new field 677 (Subject Synthesis Information), in the *USMARC Authority Format*, was also approved.

40. A preliminary set of application guidelines has been issued: "AAT Application Protocol" (Unpublished draft, May 1987).

41. Information throughout this section is taken from telephone conversations with Toni Petersen, *AAT* director, in May and June 1989.

42. Shatford, "Describing a Picture," 18-19.

43. *LCSH* was authorized for use in field 655 because it was obvious that it contains numerous genre and form terms. Its inclusion of terms appropriate to field 755 was less obvious, so the Library of Congress opted to wait until users might request that *LCSH* be authorized for use in 755. No such request had been received as of Spring 1990.

44. The Hoover Institution at Stanford University reported using *LCSH* as a source for field 655 in Max Evans and Lisa B. Weber, *MARC for Archives and Manuscripts: A Compendium of Practice* (Madison: State Historical Society of Wisconsin, 1985).

45. Northwestern University has expressed interest in coding *LCSH* terminology for music in field 655 but has been stymied by the need to

identify which terms refer to forms, which to subjects, and which to both. In a telephone conversation in March 1989, Velma Veneziano noted the importance of making these determinations and suggested adding a byte to the 008 field of the *USMARC Authority Format* to indicate that a term can be used as form, subject, or both.

46. Library of Congress, Subject Cataloging Division, *Subject Cataloging Manual: Subject Headings*, 3d ed. (Washington, D.C.: Library of Congress, 1989).

47. Lois Mai Chan, *Library of Congress Subject Headings: Principles and Application*, 2d ed. (Littleton, Colo.: Libraries Unlimited, 1986), 221.

48. *Subject Cataloging Manual*, H1095, 37.

49. Chan, *Library of Congress Subject Headings*, 257-64.

50. *Genre List for Individual Works of Fiction, Drama, Etc.* (Compiled by Barbara L. Berman et al. for the Subcommittee on Subject Access to Individual Works of Drama, Fiction, Etc. Unpublished draft, 1988).

51. American Library Association, Cataloging and Classification Section, Subject Analysis Committee, Subcommittee on Subject Access to Individual Works of Drama, Fiction, Etc., "Draft of Recommendations to Be Sent Directly to the Library of Congress" (Unpublished draft, January 1989).

52. "Art Headings," *Cataloging Service Bulletin*, no. 121 (Spring 1977): 13-14.

53. *NUCMC* has developed its own rules of application for *LCSH*, so does not follow H1855 or many other sections of the *Subject Cataloging Manual*.

54. Chan, *Library of Congress Subject Headings*, 318.

55. The scope note under Motion pictures–Plots, themes, etc., states: "Films on specific topics are entered under specific headings, e.g., Horror films; War films; Children in motion pictures; Death in motion pictures." The ". . . in motion pictures" syntax is used for topics not well established as film genres.

56. *LCSH* adds the form subdivision Juvenile Films to headings for films intended for children, thus breaking its usual prohibition against indicating an item's format in the subject heading.

57. The authors are indebted to Sara Shatford Layne for her ideas on displays. Related ideas are found in Mia Massicotte, "Improved Browsable Displays for Online Subject Access," *Information Technology and Libraries* (December 1988): 373-80.

58. Fields 655 and 755 are indexed in the LC MUMS subject index, but are retrievable separately from subject terminology only when the field tag is specified in the search query.

59. For a thorough discussion of the problems posed when multiple thesauri are used in a single database, see Carol A. Mandel, *Multiple Thesauri in Online Library Bibliographic Systems: A Report Prepared for Library of Congress Processing Services* (Washington, D.C.: Library of Congress, 1987).

60. The confusing results generated by *LCSH* practice are described in Barbara L. Berman, "Form Headings in Subject Cataloging," *Library Resources & Technical Services* 33, no. 2 (April 1989): 134-39.

61. LC's Rare Book and Special Collections Division has expressed interest in indexing and retrieval of object terminology since 1980.

62. The Bibliographic Control Committee of the Music Library Association has plans to develop a limited thesaurus of rare and manuscript musical genres. (Telephone conversation with Helen Bartlett, March 1989.) Map librarians appear to be satisfied with the *LCSH* form headings and subdivisions currently in use. (Telephone conversation with Elizabeth Mangan, March 1989.)

BIBLIOGRAPHY

"AAT Application Protocol." Unpublished draft, May 1987.

American Library Association, Cataloging and Classification Section, Subject Analysis Committee, Subcommittee on Subject Access to Individual Works of Drama, Fiction, Etc. "Draft of Recommendations to Be Sent Directly to the Library of Congress." Unpublished draft, January 1989.

American Library Association, RTSD/LITA/RASD Committee on Representation in Machine-Readable Form of Bibliographic Information. Unpublished minutes, 27 June 1983.

American National Standards Institute. *American National Standard Guidelines for Thesaurus Structure, Construction, and Use*. 2d ed. New York: ANSI, 1980 (ANSI Z39.19-1980).

Art and Architecture Thesaurus. New York: Oxford University Press, 1990.

"Art Headings." *Cataloging Service Bulletin*, no. 121 (Spring 1977): 13-14.

Berman, Barbara L. "Form Headings in Subject Cataloging." *Library Resources & Technical Services* 33, no. 2 (April 1989): 134-39.

Berman, Barbara L. et al., comps. *Genre List for Individual Works of Fiction, Drama, Etc.* Compiled for the Subcommittee on Subject Access to Individual Works of Drama, Fiction, Etc. Unpublished draft, 1988.

Binding Terms: A Thesaurus for Use in Rare Book and Special Collections Cataloguing. Chicago: Association of College and Research Libraries, 1988.

Chan, Lois Mai. *Library of Congress Subject Headings: Principles and Application.* 2d ed. Littleton, Colo.: Libraries Unlimited, 1986.

Genre Terms: A Thesaurus for Use in Rare Book and Special Collections Cataloguing. Chicago: Association of College and Research Libraries, 1983.

"Genre Terms: Additions and Changes." *College & Research Libraries News* 48, no. 9 (October 1987): 558-60.

Hennessey, Christine. "The Smithsonian Institution Art Research Databases and Their Use of the MARC Format." In *Beyond the Book: Extending MARC for Subject Access.* Boston: G.K. Hall, 1990.

Hickerson, Thomas, and Elaine Engst, comps. *Form Terms for Archival and Manuscripts Control.* Stanford, Calif.: Research Libraries Group, 1985.

Independent Research Libraries Association. "Proposals for Establishing Standards for the Cataloguing of Rare Books and Specialized Research Materials in Machine-Readable Form." Worcester, Mass.: December 1979.

Library of Congress, MARC Review Group. Unpublished minutes, 29 July 1983.

Library of Congress, Network Development and MARC Standards Office. *USMARC Code List for Relators, Sources, Description Conventions.* Washington, D.C., Library of Congress, 1988.

Library of Congress, Network Development and MARC Standards Office. *USMARC Format for Bibliographic Data.* Washington, D.C.: Library of Congress, 1988.

Library of Congress, Subject Cataloging Division. *Library of Congress Subject Headings.* 12th ed. Washington, D.C.: Library of Congress, 1989.

_____. *Subject Cataloging Manual: Subject Headings.* 3d ed. Washington, D.C.: Library of Congress, 1989.

Massicotte, Mia. "Improved Browsable Displays for Online Subject Access." *Information Technology and Libraries*, December 1988, 373-80.

Mayo, Hope. "Form and Genre Terms for Rare Books and Manuscripts: Some Reflections on the Work of the RBMS Standards Committee." Unpublished paper presented to the Society of American Archivists, 1 October 1988, Atlanta, Georgia.

National Union Catalog for Manuscript Collections. Washington, D.C.: Library of Congress, 1959-.

Parker, Elisabeth Betz. *LC Thesaurus for Graphic Materials: Topical Terms for Subject Access*. Introduction by Jackie M. Dooley. Washington, D.C.: Library of Congress, 1987.

Printing and Publishing Evidence: Thesauri for Use in Rare Book and Special Collections Cataloguing. Chicago: Association of College and Research Libraries, 1986.

Provenance Evidence: A Thesaurus for Use in Rare Book and Special Collections Cataloguing. Chicago: Association of College and Research Libraries, 1988.

Shatford, Sara. "Describing a Picture: A Thousand Words Are Seldom Cost Effective." *Cataloging & Classification Quarterly* 4, no. 4 (Summer 1984): 13-30.

Thomas, John B. "The Necessity of Standards in an Automated Environment." *Library Trends*, Summer 1987, 125-39.

Yee, Martha, comp. *Moving Image Materials: Genre Terms*. Compiled for the National Moving Image Database Standards Committee. Library of Congress: Cataloging Distribution Service, 1988.

Zinkham, Helena, and Elisabeth Betz Parker, comps. *Descriptive Terms for Graphic Materials: Genre and Physical Characteristics Headings*. Washington, D.C.: Library of Congress, 1986.

Zinkham, Helena, Patricia Cloud, and Hope Mayo. "Providing Access by Form of Material, Genre, and Physical Characteristics: Benefits and Techniques." Manuscript submitted to the *American Archivist*, Spring 1989.

■ Mapping LCSH into Thesauri: The AAT Model

CATHLEEN WHITEHEAD

In building its vocabulary, the *Art and Architecture Thesaurus* (*AAT*) records the form of the concepts that it covers as they are found in what it calls *major sources*. These sources are the *Library of Congress Subject Headings* (*LCSH*), the Royal Institute of British Architects *Architectural Keywords*, *Revised Nomenclature for Museum Cataloging*, and authority lists for nonproper name headings maintained by the *International Repertory of the Literature of Art* (*RILA*) indexing service and the *Avery Index to Architectural Periodicals*.[1] The process of tracing the form of headings and their status (whether the heading is permitted for use or is a nonpreferred "see" reference) in these sources to the appropriate term in the *AAT* is called *mapping*. This essay will focus on the process of mapping into *AAT* terminology from *LCSH*, including why and how it is done and what the implications of this procedure are. The differences and similarities between *LCSH* and the *AAT* in vocabulary construction principles, term form, and vocabulary structure will also be explored.

WHY MAP *LCSH*?

The limits of *LCSH* have been set forth in the past decade. Cochrane and Kirkland noted the problem of lack of specificity for particular subjects.[2] Petersen later noted the weaknesses in *LCSH*'s syndetic structure when LC headings relating to art and architecture were arranged conceptually (hierarchically) rather than alphabetically.[3] This finding was substantiated recently in a study of the *LCSH* machine-readable file by Markey and Vizine-Goetz. They reported that nearly 40 percent of LC topical subject headings have no Broader Terms and that a substantial number of them do not have Narrower Term references (75.5 percent of all headings).[4]

Recent criticism of *LCSH* has centered on the dangers in the move to adopt standard thesaurus coding in the eleventh edition.[5] According to Dykstra, this move gives the incorrect impression that thesauri and subject headings are the same thing. Dykstra notes that the major distinction between subject headings lists like *LCSH* and thesauri is that the thesauri consist of *terms*. Thesaurus construction standards developed by the British Standards Institute (BSI)[6] and American National Standards Institute (ANSI),[7] state that terms are discrete semantic units designed to be used in rule-based ways. In contrast, *LCSH* consists not only of terms but also of many complex subject statements comprised of terms plus punctuation and/or prepositions. Hence, the use of thesaurus conventions is not appropriate. As Dykstra notes, the standard thesaurus codes BT (Broader Term), NT (Narrower Term), and RT (Related Term) are appropriate only to elicit relationships between terms as defined by the standards. While LC's use of these codes does violate the standards and gives the false impression that LC headings are terms in all cases, the references do point the user to broader and narrower headings. Perhaps this criticism might have been avoided if LC had used conventions such as BH (Broader Heading), NH (Narrower Heading), and RH (Related Heading).

Despite the weaknesses and the critical assessments that have plagued *LCSH* over the years, the fact remains that *LCSH* is the standard vocabulary used by the majority of information resources, especially libraries, in the United States. Efforts to improve or replace it in particular disciplines must take into account not only that its use is widespread but also that it will be maintained for a long time to come.

When the *AAT* began, its compilers were aware of the hegemonic role *LCSH* had played in shaping the nature of information access in the art library community. Libraries and other collections in the field either used *LCSH* or derived their subject access terminology from *LCSH* even though many were unhappy with it. Although it was unfair to expect that *LCSH* could meet all the information access needs of the art historical community, it was also unfair to *AAT*'s LC-based constituencies to ignore the existence of *LCSH* in building the thesaurus. By keeping track of relevant headings from *LCSH* and by aiming for compatibility with *LCSH* wherever possible, the *AAT* could gain legitimacy among groups using *LCSH* and ease the transition from one vocabulary to another.

To remain as compatible as possible with *LCSH*, it was decided that relevant LC headings would be used as *AAT* terms whenever possible. As work on the *AAT* proceeded, however, it became more and more difficult to achieve total compatibility with *LCSH* because many subject headings violated the rules on term form and term relationships as outlined in the standards. This forced the *AAT* to look not only at the content of *LCSH* but also at the form of LC headings and to devise a scheme that would help map those relevant headings that did not meet thesaurus standards to related *AAT* terms.

In planning its vocabulary, the *AAT* also had to deal with the fact that information resources, such as art and architecture libraries that might be potential users of a discipline-specific vocabulary like the *AAT*, were rooted in the USMARC communications formats and were dependent on *LCSH*. The *AAT* had already made a commitment to mapping LC terminology, but there had to be a connection to both the *USMARC Bibliographic Format*[8] and the *Authority Format*.[9] The first step was to seek approval for use of *AAT* in MARC. In 1986, the *AAT* was issued a source code allowing *AAT* terms to be entered in USMARC records. The use of *AAT* varies but in general *AAT* terms have been used in the 650 (Subject Added Entry–Topical Subject), 655 (Genre/Form Heading), 755 (Physical Characteristics), 656 (Index Term–Occupation), and 657 (Index Term–Function) fields. Obtaining a code for use in MARC was an important step, but it was not entirely satisfactory because the types of content designation provided in the subject portion of the *Formats* was geared toward *LCSH* constructs and could not be used to implement the rule-based indexing/cataloging system being recommended by the *AAT*.[10]

Just as many specialized fields such as archives have affected change in the MARC structure to accommodate their specialized description needs, the *AAT* sought changes. With the aid of the Library of Congress Network Development and MARC Standards Office, the *AAT* proposed a new field that accommodates either individual thesaurus terms or complex subject statements created by the combination of single *AAT* terms.[11]

The development of the mapping process and the addition of new content designations to the MARC format are steps toward the peaceful coexistence of a discipline-specific vocabulary like the *AAT* and the foremost subject access standard, *LCSH*.

DIFFERENCES IN EDITORIAL POLICIES

The *AAT* and *LCSH* share the common function of alleviating problems of language that interfere with information management and retrieval by, for instance, controlling synonyms, distinguishing between homographs, and aiding in the selection of words or headings through establishing relationships between them. Because of the different methods by which these ends are achieved, however, *LCSH* and the *AAT* must be viewed as very different entities having different philosophies of what controlled vocabularies are, how they are constructed, and what purposes they serve.

LCSH is a subject heading system that grew in a relatively ad hoc fashion. *LCSH* reflects the subject content of LC's collection and was not intended, as one might assume, to be the principle tool by which to organize collective knowledge. The brief introduction to the eleventh edition and auxiliary aids such as the *Subject Cataloging Manual*[12] discuss the structure of LC headings a posteriori. Although historical reasons exist for the formation of headings, the form of headings generally lack consistently applied linguistic and syntactical logic. Foskett cites Haykin's *Subject Headings: A Practical Guide*[13] and Chan's *Library of Congress Subject Headings: Principles and Application*[14] as two attempts to offer guidance on the content of *LCSH* but adds that "it is difficult to find any rationale for the development of (*LCSH*) headings."[15]

New headings were and continue to be added to *LCSH* on an as-needed basis, and the form of headings follows policy in place at a particular time. As stated in the introduction to the eleventh edition, "Inconsistencies in formulation of headings can usually be explained by the policies in force at the varying dates of their creation."[16] The introduction also notes that little attempt was made to convert older headings to new approaches. Even though LC recognizes the inconsistencies, the rules for the creation of headings are not self-evident, making it difficult for the uninitiated to predict what a given form of a heading may be.

In contrast, the *AAT* grew out of a tradition that began with the post-World War II information explosion. This period saw revolutionary changes in information retrieval techniques. The first was the use of *uniterms* – keywords taken directly from indexed documents – as access points to information and the application of Boolean search techniques in retrieval. Shortly after this, thesauri (such as the *Thesaurofacet*[17]) and rule-based indexing systems (such as PRECIS[18]) emerged as improvements over the uniterm approach. These methods better served the management and retrieval of information in an automated environment than did traditional precoordinate library subject headings. In twenty years, no major advancements over these methods have occurred in libraries, although the techniques of machine-aided indexing and the development of natural-language processing systems may prove as revolutionary as postcoordinate systems. Despite the perceived benefits of the postcoordinate method, the promise of machine-aided indexing and artificial intelligence, and the advent of online public access catalogs, little attempt has been made by library systems to adopt these basic approaches to controlled vocabulary and subject access.

In keeping with current approaches to vocabulary development and information management and retrieval, the *AAT* decided to build a discipline-based vocabulary that would exist independent of any particular application or medium – that is, it would not serve as any one institution's authority file. Rather than adding terms when needed as in authority file creation, the *AAT* began by developing, a priori, a conceptual structure for the field. This approach allowed a logical, rule-based system to be set in place that could be used in flexible, yet predictable ways.

The conceptual structure of the *AAT* is based on the theory of facet analysis, which organizes terminology into generic, fundamental classes of knowledge relevant to a particular field.[19] The faceted approach to thesaurus construction states that compound terms consisting of words from two or more facets are not to be included as thesaurus terms. Instead, *keywords* from each facet should be combined syntactically by the indexer at the time of indexing or assigned separately by the indexer and combined at the time of searching. This approach allows greater precision in its application because new combinations can be made as needed rather than chosen from a fixed universe of precoordinated headings.

MAPPING *LCSH* IN *AAT* TERM RECORDS

In general, only topical subject headings are mapped in the *AAT*. All proper name headings that are found in *LCSH*, such as names of families or persons, corporate headings, names of meetings, uniform titles, and geographic names, are outside the scope of the *AAT* and therefore not mapped.

LCSH terms are mapped at both the *concept* level and the *status* level. Tracking at the concept level means that any match between an *AAT* concept and an *LCSH* concept is recorded, regardless of differences in their forms. When there is no exact match between *AAT* and *LCSH*, the closest possible LC heading is recorded in the *AAT* term record. For example, the LC heading DOCUMENTS IN MACHINE-READABLE FORM is mapped to the *AAT* term MACHINE-READABLE RECORDS because they denote synonymous concepts. Tracking at the status level means recording whether the *AAT* term is an established heading or a "see" or "USE" reference in *LCSH*.

Mapping information resides in an in-house thesaurus maintenance database system (TMS). Along with editing functions such as adding and deleting terms, TMS allows information such as sources, definitions, and illustration citations to be recorded for each *AAT* term. (TMS was used to generate statistics and other information reported in this chapter.) With regard to *LCSH*, information that may be extracted from TMS includes:

1. The *AAT* term that an LC heading maps to, regardless of form.

2. The LC heading that an *AAT* term maps to, regardless of form.

3. The *AAT* term that an *LCSH* USE reference maps to.

4. The status (i.e., preferred, nonpreferred, precoordinated) of an *LCSH* heading in the *AAT*.

5. The status of an *AAT* term in *LCSH*.

The TMS term record display provides a synopsis of *AAT* term information and illustrates the mapping process. Figure 1 shows the term record display for the *AAT* Main Term ROYAL CHAPELS. As shown in the UF portion of the display, the terms COURT CHAPELS, PALACE CHAPELS, and CHAPELS ROYAL are treated as nonpreferred terms in the *AAT*.

Figure 1 Typical term Detail Display from *AAT* Maintenance System

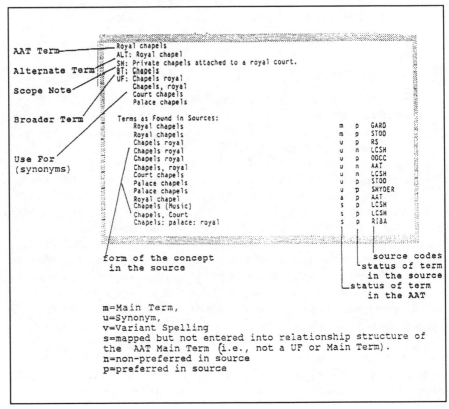

By looking at the Term as Found in Sources portion, we see that the term ROYAL CHAPELS was not found in *LCSH*. However, *LCSH* lists both CHAPELS ROYAL and COURT CHAPELS as USE references. In the *AAT* term record, the status of these terms in *LCSH* is indicated by code "n" (nonpreferred), as shown in the third column of the Term as Found in Sources portion of this example. When an *AAT* Main Term is listed as a USE reference in *LCSH*, the established heading to which it refers is noted in the record of the *AAT* term. The example in Figure 1 shows that CHAPELS (MUSIC) and CHAPELS, COURT are the preferred LC headings and are indicated in the *AAT* record by the code "p."

Other elements of *LCSH* syndetic structure (Broader Term, Narrower Term, And Related Term) are not directly mapped in the *AAT*. This is because the *AAT* provides exhaustive displays of genus/species classification for the fields it covers and does not add terms selectively as in an authority file. The *LCSH* syndetic structure often omits hierarchical levels in, for example, a BT/NT relationship (e.g., DOORS BT ARCHITECTURE – DETAILS). In the *AAT*, the sections on DOORWAYS and OPENINGS are the next broader levels to *doors*. In addition, *LCSH* NT references are often not hierarchical but indicate some other relationship (e.g. WOMEN IN ART NT MODELS, ARTISTS').

The BT/NT/RT relationships provided in *LCSH* are sometimes used to determine the probable meaning of an ambiguous heading to ensure that the *LCSH* heading represents the same concept as the *AAT* term. This is used especially for terms that are morphologically identical. If an LC heading clearly is used differently than its exact match in the *AAT*, it is not mapped at that occurrence. For example, the *AAT* term DETAILS is a homograph in the *AAT* because it has several meanings that are each within the scope of the thesaurus. It appears once as a Main Term and three other times as a Lead-in Term. As shown below, the Lead-in Terms occur with qualifiers that point to their different meanings. A Scope Note at the Main Term occurrence guides the user on the form of term to be used in specific cases (Figure 2).

In *LCSH*, the word DETAILS appears in the USE reference, DETAILS, ARCHITECTURAL, and in the established heading to which it refers, ARCHITECTURE – DETAILS. By looking at this heading's NT relationships, such as BALCONIES, CORBELS, FIREPLACES, and DOORS, one can discern that LC's usage of the term maps most closely to the *AAT* Main Term occurrence.

As of July 1990, TMS contained approximately 42,000 terms. Of these, 23,000 are Main Terms and 19,000 are nonpreferred synonyms and spelling variants. Thus far, over 7,000 LC headings, both established headings and USE references, are relevant to the scope of the *AAT* and have been mapped in some way to the appropriate *AAT* terms. This figure represents about 5 percent of the total number of existing LC topical subject headings and approximately 16.9 percent of the total number of terms in the *AAT*.

Figure 2 Sample *AAT* page

Det–Dev

ALT detachable key
 SN Keys so constructed that the bit or portion that actuates the tumblers may be detached from the shank or handle of the key for convenience in carrying. (STEIN)
 UF keys, detachable
 CN V.TF.AFU.ALO.ARI.AFU.ARI

detachable legs
   TG.955
ALT detachable leg
 UF legs, detachable
 CN V.TG.ALO.FIM.AFU.ALO.AFU

detached
   DC.30   (B)
 UF separate
 CN D.DC.AFU.ALO.ARI.BCW

detached houses
   RK.259   (A)
ALT detached house
 UF houses, detached
 CN V.RK.AFU.ALO.ALO.AXC.ALO.AFU.CRG.ALO

detail assemblies
USE subassembly drawings

detail drawings
   VD.150   (L)
ALT detail drawing
 SN Use for drawings of construction or design details. For minute parts of a larger structure, object, or image, use details. For preparatory studies of pictorial or design details, use detail studies.
 UF details (drawings)
     drawings, detail
 CN V.VD.AFU.BIQ.ARI

detail drawings (studies)
USE detail studies

detail drawings, standard
USE standard detail drawings

detail sketches
USE detail studies

detail studies
   VB.64
ALT detail study
 SN Use for preparatory studies of pictorial or design details. For minute parts of a larger structure, object, or image, use details. For drawings of architectural construction or design details, use detail drawings.
 UF detail drawings (studies)
     detail sketches
     drawings, detail (studies)
     sketches, detail
     studies, detail
 CN V.VB.AFU.ALO.BOK.AXC.ALO

detailing, architectural
USE architectural drawing

details
   VB.92   (A,L,B)
ALT detail
 SN Use for minute parts of a larger structure, object, or image. For architectural drawings of design or construction details, use detail drawings. For preparatory studies of pictorial or design details, use detail studies.
 CN V.VB.ALO.BOK.ARI

details (drawings)
USE detail drawings

detection systems, fire
USE fire detectors

detectives
   HG.716   (L)
ALT detective
 CN H.HG.AFU.BCW.BUE

detectors, fire
USE fire detectors

detectors, flame
USE flame detectors

detectors, ionization
USE ionization detectors

detectors, photoelectric
USE photoelectric detectors

detectors, smoke
USE smoke detectors

detectors, temperature
USE temperature detectors

detention camps
USE concentration camps

detention centers
   RK.731   (A,L,B)
ALT detention center
 SN Use for places of relatively short confinement for youthful offenders pending transfer or trial.
 UF centers, detention
     centers, juvenile detention
     detention centers, juvenile
     detention facilities
     detention homes
     detention homes, juvenile
     facilities, detention
     homes, detention
     homes, juvenile detention
     juvenile detention centers
     juvenile detention homes
 CN V.RK.AFU.ALO.ALO.CXA.AFU.BCW.AFU

detention centers, juvenile
USE detention centers

detention facilities
USE detention centers

detention homes
USE detention centers

detention homes, juvenile
USE detention centers

detergents
   MT.2422   (L)
 SN Materials which have a cleansing action like soap, usually applies to synthetic chemicals, or soapless soaps. (MH)
 UF detergents, synthetic
     synthetic detergents
 CN M.MT.AFU.ARI.CLM.AFU

detergents, synthetic
USE detergents

deterioration
   KT.893   (L)
ALT deteriorated
 SN Use broadly for the action or process of growing worse or becoming impaired in quality, state, or condition. (W)
 UF degeneration
 CN K.KT.ALO.BCW

deterioration, oxidative-reductive
USE oxidative-reductive deterioration

determinate structures
USE statically determinate structures

determinations
USE decisions

determinism
   BM.508   (L)
 SN Doctrine that all acts of will result from causes which determine them either in such a manner that people have no alternative course of action, or that the will is still free in the sense of being uncompelled. (W)
 CN B.BM.BIQ.AXC.BCW

detoxification
   KT.70
ALT detoxified
 SN The act of removing the poison or effect of poison from something. (W)
 CN K.KT.AFU.ALO.BIQ.AFU

Devagiri
USE Daulatabad

Developed Orientalizing
   FL.2571
 UF Orientalizing, Developed
 CN F.FL.ALO.AXC.ALO.AFU.AFU.ARI.ARI.ALO

developed sketches
USE design development drawings

developers
   HG.620
ALT developer
 SN Individuals, companies, or corporations engaged in the development and improvement of land for construction purposes. (STEIN)
 CN H.HG.AFU.AXC.BZY.ARI

Approximately 16.5 percent of *AAT* Main Terms (over half of the total number of tracked LC headings and 9 percent of all *AAT* terms) match exactly in form and status to *LCSH* (e.g., *LCSH*: ABBEYS; *AAT*: ABBEYS). These are usually single nouns. About 3.8 percent of *AAT* Main Terms map exactly to LC USE references (e.g., *LCSH*: WORKING DRAWINGS USE ARCHITECTURE – DESIGNS AND PLANS – WORKING DRAWINGS; *AAT*: WORKING DRAWINGS). Interestingly, almost an equal number of *AAT* nonpreferred synonyms derive from LC established headings (e.g., *LCSH*: SUGAR FACTORIES; *AAT*: SUGAR FACTORIES USE SUGAR REFINERIES). Sometimes this results from the fact that the form of the LC established heading is in violation of the direct or natural language order as set forth by thesaurus construction standards and followed by the *AAT* (e.g., *LCSH*: LIBRARIES, SPECIAL; *AAT*: SPECIAL LIBRARIES). In other cases, the LC heading is simply a variant spelling (e.g., *LCSH*: METAL-WORK; *AAT*: METALWORK). The remainder do not meet *AAT* Main Term selection criteria, such as currency, literary warrant, and expert opinion (e.g., *LCSH*: MOVING-PICTURE THEATERS; *AAT*: MOVIE THEATERS).

Each *AAT* term is checked in *LCSH* including synonyms and variant spellings. About 6 percent of *AAT* nonpreferred terms (or 2.8 percent of all *AAT* terms) are also found as USE references in *LCSH*, although they usually do not point the user to the same Main Term/established heading. In an example used above, CHAPELS ROYAL is nonpreferred by both *AAT* and LC, but in the *AAT* the Main Term is ROYAL CHAPELS and in *LCSH*, the established heading is CHAPELS, COURT.

Of the total number of LC headings that are related to *AAT*'s scope, 4 percent have not been incorporated into *AAT*'s syndetic structure and so are not Main Terms or Lead-in Terms. These are subdivided headings (e.g., ARCHITECTURE – DESIGNS AND PLANS) and complex, precoordinated headings (e.g., *LCSH*: ART, BYZANTINE). Before explaining how these are accommodated, *AATs*'s policies on term form need to be explained.

In selecting the form of its terms, the *AAT* seeks to increase the probability that its vocabulary will match that brought by the researcher to an information resource. With the rise of individual workstations, the possibility of unmediated searches and the use of thesauri in natural language processing systems, the criterion of literary warrant practiced by the *AAT* becomes crucial.

For the *AAT*, the chosen form of its thesaurus terms must exist in primarily written sources within the field. Terms that have literary warrant are usually in natural word order and occur without punctuation. Headings such as CATALOGING OF SPECIAL COLLECTIONS IN LIBRARIES have no literary warrant other than their occurrence in *LCSH*. Although *LCSH* was supposedly developed according to the principle of literary warrant because LC headings reflect actual works written on those subjects, the *form* of the concept is often based on editorial policy that dictates how the concept is to be expressed. It is unfortunate that an artificial construct is used (e.g., Architecture – Designs and Plans – Presentation Drawings).

In addition to following a strict literary warrant policy, *AAT* follows term form guidelines outlined by BSI. BSI states that "complex subjects should be represented by combinations of terms, these separate terms be used as search keys in a post-coordinate retrieval system, or as components or pre-coordinated index entries." The BSI standard makes general recommendations as to when a compound term should be allowed but states that they "should not be applied rigidly in all indexing situations."[20]

Following this recommendation, individual *AAT* terms may be used as the building blocks of complex headings to catalog or index the subject of a text, to name and describe objects, or to formulate research questions. The *AAT* factors, or separates, many compound terms that might be acceptable as thesaurus terms according to BSI standards, including phrases that occur frequently in the field, such as PAINTED GREEK VASES. This is done because so much of *AAT* terminology relates to objects and could yield an almost infinite number of possible term combinations.[21] Phrases like PAINTED GREEK VASES may be constructed using two or more *AAT* terms.

As a rule, compound phrases that contain terms from two or more *AAT* facets – BYZANTINE CHURCHES (Style plus Object) or HALF-TIMBER CRAFTSMAN BUNGALOWS (Activity plus Style plus Object), are not explicitly enumerated in the *AAT*. They contain one or more *modifying* terms plus a *focus* term, each term found in the *AAT*. The focus term is the word that is modified by other words in a phrase. (CHURCHES is the focus term of the phrase BYZANTINE CHURCHES, which contains two *AAT* terms.)

The mapping process has shown that some headings in *LCSH*, such as CHURCHES and PIGMENTS, do meet the definition for being a *term*. As shown above, many *LCSH* "terms" are easily mapped into the *AAT*. In order to map LC headings not considered terms in the *AAT*, the *AAT* determines what the focus of the heading is and maps the heading in the record for the focus term. Examples of LC headings mapped to *AAT* focus terms are shown below, with the focus term in boldface:

> Bronze **doors**, Byzantine
> Half-timbered **buildings**
> **Buildings**, Octagonal
> **Buildings**, Plastic
> Spherical **buildings**
> **Accreditation** (Education)
> **Decoration** and **ornament**, Ainu
> Bridges – **Abutments**
> **Symmetry** (Art)
> **Cultural property**, Protection of

Forgery of inscriptions
Comic books, strips, etc.

As shown by these examples, many precoordinated LC headings map to the same focus term in the *AAT*. For example, the term BUILDINGS appears in several precoordinated headings. One can also see that several LC headings contain more than one focus, in which case the heading maps to more than one *AAT* term. (DECORATION AND ORNAMENT maps to the separate *AAT* terms DECORATION and ORNAMENT.) One can also see from these examples that precoordinated LC headings take several forms, including:

- "and" headings (Caricatures and Cartoons)

- "in" headings (Ruins in art)

- "of" headings (Forgery of manuscripts; Promotion of special events)

- "for" headings (Access for the Physically Handicapped)

- subdivided headings (Pavements – Live loads)

- Parenthetical phrases (Symmetry (Art))

- Modified Terms in natural language order (Brick houses)

- Modified Terms in inverted order (Roads, Brick)

- Combinations of the above (Decoration and Ornament, Renaissance; Bridges, Iron and Steel; Courts and courtiers in art)

In each case, a focus term in each heading can be identified, which makes it possible to map successfully the various mix of natural (single terms in natural word order) and artificial (adjectival and syntactical phrases, inverted headings, and subdivided headings) combinations found in *LCSH* to the appropriate *AAT* term(s). In addition to mapping LC headings to the focus term, it is the policy of the *AAT* to make sure that other relevant terms in these complex headings are listed as *AAT* terms.

The mapping process has pointed to inconsistencies in the form of similar headings. Some are constructed through the use of subdivisions, others, through an adjectival or prepositional phrase, and others, through the use of a qualifier. For example, in the headings MONUMENTS – PRESERVATION and FORGERY OF MANUSCRIPTS, the same syntactic relationship exists. In each heading, an action is being performed on an object: preservation *of* monuments and forgery *of* manuscripts. Yet two different methods of conveying this relationship are used. This example points to the unpredictability of LC headings.

The use of subdivisions is also confusing. Sometimes a whole/part relationship is expressed (e.g., BRIDGES – ABUTMENTS); at other times, a kind of hierarchical relationship exists between the words in a heading (e.g., ARCHITECTURE – DESIGNS AND PLANS – WORKING DRAWINGS). LC acknowledges these problems, but it will be difficult to implement changes given the thousands of *LCSH* users and millions of records containing LC headings. It is hoped that mapping processes, such as those undertaken by the *AAT*, will help form a link between *AAT* and *LCSH* and provide insights into improving LC heading structure.

STRICT SYNONYM POLICY

Terms labeled as nonpreferred in the *AAT* are, as far as possible, true synonyms of the *AAT* Main Term to which they are referenced. Near synonyms, such as MOTELS and MOTOR COURTS, have a Broader Term/Narrower Term relationship in the thesaurus, as shown below.

> Motels
>> Motor courts

Such terms are also given Scope Notes, which convey the fine distinctions between them. This practice results in sometimes exhaustive hierarchies that allow indexers and catalogers to choose the most appropriate terms and allow researchers to achieve a greater level of specificity without loss of information. In an application that uses the hierarchies for retrieval, one might search only for those records that deal specifically with MOTOR COURTS, but a broader search for MOTELS would retrieve records dealing with MOTELS plus those indexed using the term MOTOR COURTS because these terms are linked hierarchically in the thesaurus.

In contrast, many nonpreferred headings in *LCSH* are in fact Narrower Terms to the established heading (e.g., COMMUNITY ART CENTERS USE ART CENTERS). This practice contributes significantly to the problem of specificity that *LCSH* poses for users. If a researcher is interested in a topic represented by the USE reference, those topics are cataloged under more general headings. The researcher must then dig more deeply into the information retrieved by the broader heading to find what he or she is actually interested in. This practice also compels catalogers to assign topical headings that may be imprecise, instead of to assign an exact and appropriate heading.

The use of Narrower Terms as USE references contributes to the use of nonpreferred LC headings as *AAT* Main Terms. Although USE references in the *AAT* are often given a Broader Term corresponding to the established heading in *LCSH*, it would not be wise to assume that one could increase the specificity of *LCSH* simply by converting USE references to Narrower Terms because not all LC USE references are related hierarchically to the established heading. They are often only topically related (e.g., DOCUMENTS USE ARCHIVES). Any attempt to apply a rule of strict synonymy to LC USE references would require intellectual analysis of the reference structure of each heading.

Another characteristic of the *LCSH* USE reference structure is that the reference itself may be from one part of speech, usually a plural noun, and the USE reference from another, usually the gerund, (e.g., ARCHITECTURAL RENDERINGS USE ARCHITECTURAL RENDERING). Even this practice is not applied consistently. For instance the noun, *Architectural drawings* does not appear as a UF at the established heading, ARCHITECTURAL DRAWING, although the reference DRAWING, ARCHITECTURAL PLANS does.

The inconsistency of this practice makes it difficult for *LCSH* to be used as a source of vocabulary for constituencies such as museums and archives, which need controlled terminology for object names and form of material – that is, terms for what a cataloged item *is*, in addition to what it is *about*. Following the strict synonym policy, terms such as DRAWING and DRAWINGS are each listed in the *AAT* and appear in different facets (the Activities and Objects facets respectively). This allows thesaurus users to be as precise as possible when determining subject statements and object descriptions.

Some LC subject headings containing qualifiers are viewed as precoordinated because they indicate the specific context in which a term is used, rather than simply distinguish between homographs (e.g., IRRATIONALISM (PHILOSOPHY)). This is a form of precoordination that in the *AAT* is be handled by the formation of an indexing string. Apparently LC is moving away from this type of heading, but they exist nevertheless.

AVAILABILITY OF MAPPING INFORMATION

Data on the mapping of *LCSH* and other sources can be generated from TMS. In addition, *AAT* source/mapping data are also distributed in field 670 of the *USMARC Format for Authorities*. Subfield $a contains the source used to establish the term or heading in field 150 and subfield $b contains the information found in that source. The *AAT* transmits the source code (e.g., *LCSH*) in subfield $a and the form of term found in subfield $b. The example below shows that the LC heading ARCHITECTURE – DESIGNS AND PLANS IS mapped to the *AAT* Main Term ARCHITECTURAL DRAWINGS.

    00 150 $a architectural drawings. . . .
    00 670 $a *LCSH* $b architecture – designs and plans

CONCLUSION

The *AAT*'s development has been closely tied to an awareness of existing standards. Mapping is critical to facilitating movement between vocabularies, and we plan to continue the mapping process. As more discipline-specific controlled vocabularies like the *AAT* appear in the effort to improve access to information, it is essential that they accommodate existing standards, such as MARC and *LCSH* if improved access to information is to be a common goal. Even though the mapping process is currently a labor-intensive, manual procedure, it will make it easier for users to live with several systems and perhaps make it easier for *LCSH* to live with other vocabularies.

NOTES

1. The statistics reported here are based on headings in Library of Congress, *Library of Congress Subject Headings*, 11th ed., vols. 1-3 (Washington, D.C.: Library of Congress, 1988).

In addition to *LCSH*, other major sources of terminology that are systematically mapped to the *AAT* are the Royal Institute of British Architects *Architectural Keywords*, *Revised Nomenclature for Museum Cataloging*, and authority lists for nonproper name headings maintained by the *International Repertory of the Literature of Art* (*RILA*) indexing service and the *Avery Index to Architectural Periodicals*. In addition to recording the form of headings from these sources, other characteristics of each vocabulary, such as the preferred or nonpreferred status of headings, are noted.

2. Pauline A. Cochrane and Monica Kirkland, "Critical Views of LCSH – the Library of Congress Subject Headings: A Bibliographic and Bibliometric Essay and an Analysis of Vocabulary Control in the Library of Congress Subject Headings" (Syracuse, N.Y.: ERIC Clearinghouse on Information Resources, 1981). (ED208900).

3. Toni Petersen, "The AAT: A Model for the Restructuring of LCSH," *Journal of Academic Librarianship* 9 (September 1983): 207-10.

4. Karen Markey and Diane Vizine-Goetz, "Characteristics of Subject Authority Records in the Machine-Readable Library of Congress Subject Headings" (Dublin, Ohio: OCLC Online Computer Library Center, Office of Research, 1 August 1988).

5. Dykstra addresses these issues in a series of two articles: Mary Dykstra, "LC Subject Headings Disguised as a Thesaurus," *Library Journal*

113, no. 4 (1 March 1988): 42-46, and Mary Dykstra, "Can Subject Headings Be Saved?" *Library Journal* 113, no. 15 (15 September 1988): 55-58.

6. British Standards Institution, *Guidelines for the Establishment and Development of Monolingual Thesauri* (London: BSI, 1987) (BS 5723).

7. American National Standards Institute, *American National Standard Guidelines for Thesaurus Structure, Construction, and Use*, 2d ed. (N.Y.: ANSI, 1980) (ANSI Z39: 1980). Under revision in 1990.

8. See Library of Congress, Network Development and MARC Standards Office, *USMARC Format for Bibliographic Data* (Washington, D.C.: Library of Congress Cataloging Distribution Service, 1988).

9. See Library of Congress, Network Development and MARC Standards Office, *USMARC Format for Authority Control* (Washington, D.C.: Library of Congress, 1987).

10. This system is outlined in a document on *AAT* application guidelines being prepared by a subcommittee of the Research Libraries Group Art and Architecture Program Committee. These guidelines provide instruction on selecting terms from the thesaurus to make complex subject or item descriptions. These term combinations are created according to the faceted scheme mentioned later in this essay.

11. *USMARC Format for Bibliographic Data*.

12. Library of Congress, Subject Cataloging Division, *Subject Cataloging Manual: Subject Headings*, rev. ed. (Washington, D.C.: Library of Congress, 1989).

13. David Judson Haykin, *Subject Headings: A Practical Guide* (Washington, D.C.: Library of Congress, 1951).

14. Lois Mai Chan, *Library of Congress Subject Headings: Principles and Application*, 2d ed. (Littleton, Colorado: Libraries Unlimited, 1986), 9-10. (Foskett cites the 1978 edition.)

15. A. C. Foskett, *The Subject Approach to Information*, 4th ed. (London: C. Bingley, 1982), 427.

16. *Library of Congress Subject Headings*, 9.

17. Jean Aitchison, ed., *Thesaurofacet: A Thesaurus and Faceted Classification of Engineering and Related Subjects* (Whetstone: English Electric Company, 1969).

18. Derek Austin, *PRECIS: A Manual of Concept Analysis and Subject Indexing*, 2d ed. (London: British Library, 1974).

19. The *AAT* defines a *facet* as a mutually exclusive, fundamental class of terms whose members share characteristics that distinguish them from the members of other classes. Facets play an important role in how *AAT* thesaurus terms are applied. *AAT* facets are predicated on the types of knowledge concerned with the recording of and access to information in art, architecture, and related disciplines. The seven facets that have been identified thus far are listed below, along with sample terms from each facet.

1. Associated Concepts (access, copyright, heat, pose)

2. Physical Attributes (blue, square, monumental, motifs)

3. Styles and Periods (Baroque, Nicaraguan, Ancient)

4. Agents (editors, archivists, associations, youth)

5. Activities (analysis, engraving, psychology, painted)

6. Materials (marble, gold, lapis lazuli, solvents)

7. Objects (drawings, maps, murals, arches, chairs)

Because the *AAT* is organized into facets, multiword terms consisting of two or more facets are generally not enumerated because they can be synthesized, or postcoordinated, from the existing vocabulary. These include, for example, terms consisting of:

- Material term plus an Object term (stone walls).

- Style term plus Object term (Ionic columns).

- Activity term plus Object term (prefabricated houses).

- Physical Attribute term plus Object term (round houses).

20. BS 5273, p. 5.

21. Multiword terms, such as adjectival phrases, are allowed if they are considered to be single concepts (e.g, CABINET PICTURES). Such terms are sometimes called *bound terms,* which means that separating, or factoring, them into their component parts would lead to ambiguity when they were rejoined or combined. A Boolean search on the individual terms CABINETS and PICTURES would yield results quite different than a search on the single term CABINET PICTURES.

■ Subject Access to Moving Image Materials in a MARC-Based Online Environment

Martha Yee

The category of moving image materials is a diverse one, covering fictional or dramatic film and television; news programs and newsreels; documentaries; educational films in all subject areas; moving image materials used as a recording medium in specialized subject areas such as medicine, engineering, science, dance, and anthropology; and, finally, art film and video. Naturally, users' needs for subject access are equally diverse, and it is probably impossible to generalize effectively about all of these materials.

The following discussion will first consider the basic principles to be followed in the design of any system for providing subject access and the ways they apply to moving image materials and will present some of the basic decisions that must be made in the design of such a system. Then I will examine some specific types of subject access useful for moving image materials. Finally, I will discuss some problems with the use of the MARC format to provide subject access to moving image materials in online systems.

PRINCIPLES

In designing any type of subject access system, one must consider the needs of the users and potential users of the system, the nature of the subject matter to which access is to be provided, the concept of *aboutness* as it applies to the materials in question, and the depth of indexing necessary.

Users

The needs of users and potential users of the system should be the primary consideration in the decision as to the nature of the subject access to be provided. For example, the University of California, Los Angeles (UCLA), Film and Television Archive inherited the Hearst newsreel collection several years ago. Originally, Hearst newsreel footage was shot and edited to create newsreels that would draw the public and thus have box office value. Later the newsreels were cut down into stories, and the stories were indexed so that they could be reused as stock footage; the indexing reflects this use, with emphasis on objects, geographic areas, and persons depicted. We inherited the indexing along with the footage. We would like to encourage scholarly use of the collection and anticipate interest in such things as the portrayal of women, the coverage of particular events including how much and what the American people were told, and the kinds of bias exhibited in the commentary. It is very likely that our users will need different index terms than those needed by stock footage users.

Depth of Subject Coverage

In evaluating existing lists of subject headings, including *Library of Congress Subject Headings (LCSH)*,[1] to see how well they would adapt to moving image materials such as newsreels, it quickly became apparent to us that particular media tend to vary in their depth of subject coverage. The subjects covered by monographs, which *LCSH* was designed to handle, tend to be more general than the subjects covered by a newsreel story, for example. Thus, many specific headings needed for newsreel stories are not in *LCSH*. Ferris reports findings that educational moving image materials may require more specific headings than books do. A comparison of PRECIS strings needed for educational nonbook materials with those already created by the British Library revealed that 80 percent of the nonbook materials required new PRECIS strings; however, much of this was because of the existence of inappropriate form terms in the existing strings.[2]

On the other hand, a monograph can go into a very specific subject in much more depth than a newsreel story can, and there are times when a more general subject is probably more useful for a newsreel story than the most specific subject heading available in *LCSH*. For example, one of our newsreel stories concerns a prize bulldog with a record-size litter of puppies. *LCSH* contains headings for a number of different breeds of bulldog. It is doubtful that our users would benefit much from our spending the time necessary to identify the breed of bulldog featured in our newsreel story and indexing it!

There is some evidence that users of some types of moving image materials require both specific and general headings.[3] At UCLA, our policy is to use *LCSH* as a source for subject headings but not necessarily to follow the LC practice that calls for choosing the most specific heading; when we judge that a more general heading would be more useful, we use it. We are not planning to use very broad subject headings for all nonfiction materials because the provision of educational nonfiction films for elementary and high school curriculum support is not one of our goals.

Ofness, Aboutness, Etc.

Sara Shatford has written two excellent articles on the cataloging of still image materials. Much of what she discusses is relevant to moving image materials as well.[4] I am indebted to her for the conceptual framework of much of what follows.

There are a number of different subject-like aspects of moving image materials in which users are interested. We must, therefore, consider trying to bring them out in the course of subject analysis. First of all, as pictorial or image materials, these materials depict subjects; there is actually a visual image of the subject. Shatford refers to this aspect as what the picture is *of*. Second, like textual materials, pictorial or image materials may be used to discuss or refer to, to parody or caricature, or to express meanings, themes, moods, or points of view. Shatford refers to this aspect as what the picture is *about*. Finally, pictorial or image materials, like textual materials, can themselves be instances of a category of materials sought by users. To use moving image examples, they can themselves be westerns (genre), animated cartoons (form) or imbibition dye transfer Technicolor prints (physical characteristics).

It is important to be aware of these aspects for two reasons. First, they can remind us of decisions we must make in the design of any subject access system. How important is it to the users being served to bring out ofness, aboutness, genre, form, and physical characteristics? Should all or just some of these be brought out in a given situation? Second, an issue that will be considered further below is the degree to which it is useful to distinguish among these aspects in our systems in such a way as to enable users to specify that a search should be for a particular subject from just one of these aspects, excluding the others. For example, is it useful to allow users to search for materials that actually depict Martin Luther King, excluding materials in which he is discussed but not depicted? Is it useful to allow users to search for animated cartoons themselves, excluding works about the making of animated cartoons?[5] Related to this is the question of how distinctions should be made, if it is felt that they are useful. The headings themselves can be designed to bring out these different aspects, as when we add form subdivisions to topical subject headings for such things as pictorial works (of) or parodies (about, in a particular way). Alternatively, MARC tags can be used to distinguish these aspects, as when genre or form headings (the thing itself) are put in 655 fields, and topical subject headings (both of and about) in 650 fields. The distinctions among these aspects may appear relatively straightforward at first glance, and often they are. However, there are some gray areas, which might bear some examination.

A special case of ofness occurs when a pictorial work depicts another work. Shatford refers to the latter as the Represented Work. A film of a house designed by Frank Lloyd Wright is an example of a work containing a Represented Work: The film is the representation, and the house is the Represented Work. Shatford's discussion of the question of when the Represented Work rather than the representation should be described is well worth reading.[6] The border line between descriptive cataloging and subject cataloging is not always clear-cut, and as we will see in discussion below of problems with MARC format cataloging, this can sometimes create problems in the choice of MARC tags and in the design of indexes. Depending on what one chooses to describe, the representation or the Represented Work, the heading for the Wright house could end up in either the name/title index or the subject index.

Moving image media can easily be used to record performances of various kinds, for example, musical and dance performances. The border line between a performer involved in the creation of the work, and therefore indexed as an Author, and a performer being depicted in the work, and therefore indexed as a Subject, can sometimes be a hard one to draw; the decision will usually hinge on how the work represents the participation of the performer. Moving image materials can record performances of nonhuman creatures, including performing animals like Lassie, or of animated fictitious characters, like Bugs Bunny. Currently in the MARC format, such nonhuman creatures are deemed incapable of authorship and therefore are indexed as topical subjects, more discussion of which will follow below.

The aspect of aboutness covers a lot of territory. When applied to works of art, it can include expressional meaning. In other words, aboutness may encompass an abstract concept expressed by a work of art. Shatford suggests, for example, that Dorothea Lange's *Migrant Mother* might be considered to be "about strength, or suffering, or determination."[7] This meaning, specific to works of art, is relevant to moving image materials as well. Certainly art film and video contain expressional meaning in the same way that still photographic materials do. Dramatic or fictional moving image materials are also full of expressional meaning. This kind of aboutness can be very difficult to bring out, first, because it is so subjective, and second, because one of the differences between a work of art and a factual work is that the former tends to take as its subject the world entire and life itself while the latter tends to map out a relatively narrow single subject. Thoroughly indexing just one work of art could take the lifetime of a diligent indexer!

Aboutness can have its more conventional meaning when applied to factual materials with a textual or discursive aspect. Unlike still image materials, moving image materials often contain both picture and sound and therefore both pictorial material and textual material. While the pictorial material may be "of" particular objects and events, the textual material may consist of a factual discussion of what is depicted and may therefore be "about" what is depicted in the way that a nonfiction monograph is "about" a subject. Some users may wish to limit a search to things actually depicted while others may be mainly interested in the discussion on the sound track.

The question also arises as to whether users would be interested in distinguishing among different kinds of aboutness. If the decision is made to index expressional meaning in works of art (e.g., themes, or concepts such as courage), should we allow users to specify works that discuss the concept of courage in an explicitly discursive way, excluding those that depict it in an expressional way, or vice versa? Currently, this can be coded in the MARC format only for books, using the fiction code in the 008 field. Form subdivisions such as FICTION or DRAMA added to topical subdivisions also fulfill this function to a certain extent for some materials. At least, the user who is *not* interested in expressional aspects can say AND NOT DRAMA or something similar in a system with Boolean searching capability.

It can be hard sometimes to distinguish between the thing itself and a depiction of the thing (ofness). An example may help. One could argue that "baseball game" is a particular television format and as such belongs in a list of genre and form terms to be applied to television programs. In a televised baseball game, there is almost always an announcer who follows certain conventions of sports announcing that can be parodied or caricatured; certain camera techniques are commonly employed; the program takes up a certain amount of broadcast time, divided into innings; and televised baseball games are a category of materials that users may well wish to study as a category. However, one could also argue that such a program depicts a baseball game–that it is "of" a baseball game. Depending on how one analyzes this situation, one would choose a different tag in the MARC format (655 versus 650). The implications of this will be discussed further in the section on problems with the MARC format.

Depth of Indexing

Purely visual materials tend not to be on a single subject or in a single discipline. For example, film footage of Los Angeles in 1900 may interest historians, engineers, filmmakers, costume designers, if people are present, and even ornithologists, if a particular bird can be identified in the footage. For this reason, one may be tempted to provide great depth of indexing for visual materials. Shatford suggests the useful thresholds of detail and pertinence to temper excessive zeal in this area.[8] The *LC Thesaurus for*

Graphic Materials (*LCTGM*) also suggests some useful guidelines, such as historical significance, novelty, and prominent depiction.[9]

ONLINE SYSTEM DESIGN CONSIDERATIONS

What follows are some of the system design decisions one will have to make in the design of any subject access system. All of these decisions should affect choice of indexing terms or subject headings to be used.

Integration

For a system that integrates records with those for many other types of materials, it might be wise to choose subject headings that are appropriate to various types of materials. The UCLA Film and Television Archive is planning to make its records available through ORION, an online public access catalog that also serves scholars and researchers looking for textual materials in the UCLA libraries. Thus, our decision to use *LCSH* will benefit scholars and researchers who could use our materials because it is used to provide subject access to textual materials at UCLA. Users are required to learn just one system.

In integrated systems, decisions must be made about how to communicate to users that many different formats are available. Techniques that allow one to limit a search to a broad format category may be helpful in extensively integrated collections but useless in a collection of a single kind of material. As our records are searchable as a separate file on ORION that contains only motion pictures, video recordings, and sound recordings, we are less interested in access by format than we might be if our records were intermingled with all UCLA library records.

Co-occurrence Rules and Decisions about Pre- and Postcoordination

Co-occurrence rules is a term this writer has invented to refer to the rules that online public access catalogs follow when searching for two or more terms specified by a user. Some systems look for the two or more terms to occur in the same field; other systems look for the two or more terms to occur in the same record; and other systems allow the user to specify which rules the machine should follow. The rules the system is following can have a profound effect on the success of a user's search. No research has yet been done on this issue, but intuitively one can see that the rule that two terms need only co-occur in the same record undoubtedly produces more false drops than the rule that two terms must co-occur in the same field.

The co-occurrence rules the system follows should affect the decision as to whether to adopt a precoordinated or a postcoordinated subject access system. In a precoordinated system, more than one term can be given in a single field. This approach allows the relationship between the terms to be indicated. For example, the *LCSH* heading CHILDREN AND ART refers to the effect of art on children, while CHILDREN IN ART refers to the depiction of children in art. If a user's search has been done using the rule that two or more terms must occur within a single heading, the results can be arranged on display in order by the headings matched, allowing users to discriminate among the results and choose those that best match their information needs.

In the simplest version of a postcoordinated system, each field contains a single term. The only relationship between terms that is demonstrated is that both occur on the same record. In the simplest system, CHILDREN would occur in one field and ART in another. In such a system, it would be imperative to allow co-occurrence in the same record to be specified. This would mean that results of a search could not be displayed by heading matched because a given search might easily match more than one heading. The best that could be done on display would be to display all matched fields; records still could not be arranged by matched headings.

In a sense, the *AAT*[10] is a hybrid between a precoordinated and a postcoordinated system. In the most sophisticated use envisioned of the *AAT*, the cataloger would encode the relationships between single terms, and in a sense the machine rather than the cataloger would actually precoordinate the terms. It is not yet clear whether implementations of this sophisticated approach would display the terms as coordinated headings or whether searching rules would allow specification of co-occurrence within one heading string, but if both display and searching involved coordinated heading strings, the *AAT* would actually be indistinguishable from a precoordinated system from the user's point of view.

One of the problems we noted with *LCTGM* when we investigated its possible use for providing subject access to our newsreel materials was that it tends more than *LCSH* to be a single-term system, designed for postcoordination in the simplest sense described above.[11] This means that searching would produce more false drops and that the system does not allow as much specification of the relationship between two terms. The more in depth the indexing, the more likely false drops are to occur. In other words, the more index terms provided per record, the more likely it is that a search on two keywords will bring up an irrelevant record, one in which the two keywords do not have the meaning or the relationship to each other desired by the user. This also means that it is not possible to arrange retrieved records by headings matched for searches on more than one term, thus making it much harder for a user to browse through a large retrieval.

We are beginning to notice similar problems with *Moving Image Materials: Genre Terms*, which has also taken the approach of avoiding use of subdivisions (precoordination). For example, one heading is PARODIES and another heading is BASEBALL GAMES.[12] A cartoon parody of a baseball game would be given both headings and would come up on a search for baseball games, under the heading BASEBALL GAMES. There would be no way to distinguish parodies from actual baseball games in the heading displays. (Of course, a knowledgeable user could use Boolean ANDs or AND NOTs to exclude or include parodies as soon as he or she realized what was going on; however, there is no way for a user to look at *only* parodies of baseball games without seeing the games themselves.)

Searchable Fields

The MARC format has fields that contain controlled vocabulary of various sorts (topical subject headings in 650 and 690, genre terms in 655, etc.) and descriptive fields that can contain subject-rich vocabulary (contents notes in the 505 field, summaries in the 520 field, etc.). In any given system, decisions must be made as to which fields to make searchable. Maintenance of a controlled vocabulary can be expensive. The creation and maintenance of authority files require trained staff. A quick and dirty method of providing a kind of subject access would be to write summaries and let users search summary fields. This puts the burden of thinking of all synonyms on the user and forces the user to sift through many more false drops. It also means that displays arranged by matched terms will probably not be possible. If the user's search matched one term in the first sentence of the summary and another term in the last sentence (or another term in the title, if that is indexed as well), it would probably not be possible to instruct the computer to display fifty retrieved records in any other order than that determined by the main entry of each record.

Definition of Indexes

Many online catalogs maintain a subject index that is separate from the name/title index and require users to specify which index is to be searched by any given search.[13] As we will see below, this can cause problems for users if they cannot pick the correct index for their particular search. Probably the best solution would be to give the user at least the option of searching a general index; this might also make searching costs rise, however. Another option would be to index in more than one index the types of headings that cause problems, such as names as subjects that some users would search as names and others search as subjects. This option would require that all problem headings be tagged or coded in some way so that the computer could distinguish them from headings that should be indexed only as names or only as topical subject headings. This option might present problems for systems that link authority records to bibliographic records, unless methods could be devised to link the heading in one bibliographic record to two authority records, one in the subject index and the other in the name index.

Displays of Headings from Multiple Lists

A number of existing lists might be candidates for use in providing subject access to moving image materials, either alone or in combination. The decision to use more than one list should be made with full awareness of the problems such a decision is likely to cause users. Currently, most systems that do this seem to display headings with qualifiers to indicate the source of the terms; see, for example, the systems examined by Carol Mandel.[14] If two lists being used employ the same term and if catalogers make two authority records to record this fact, the display of the same heading twice (identified as belonging to two different lists) may confuse users. Most users probably do not know what *LCSH* means. More serious problems occur when two different lists being employed use two different terms for the same concept. The classic example is the heading CANCER in *LCSH* as opposed to the heading NEOPLASMS in *MeSH*. If cross-references are not edited to reflect the fact that both terms are in use, users may discover only half the material available on the subject. Even if cross-references are edited appropriately, users may still find it very confusing that materials on the same subject are located in two different places in the file, indexed under two synonyms.

TOPICAL SUBJECT ACCESS

Nonfiction

In this section, we will consider several types of nonfiction moving image materials: news and newsreels, documentaries and educational works, and record film and video. Because these materials tend to have different bibliographical "behaviors" and their users have different needs, they will be considered separately.

The first thing to be borne in mind in designing a system for providing subject access to news materials is that subject access is of *primary* importance to users of these materials. Rarely do they have the names of specific news programs with broadcast dates or citations to volume and issue number of a newsreel. They are almost always looking for footage of some particular event, personage, place, and the like. If you are not providing subject access to these materials in some fashion, you are probably not providing access to the collection at all!

If it is possible to provide direct access by means of a controlled vocabulary, a number of possibilities exist. Use of *LCSH*, at least when appropriate headings are available in *LCSH*, does have the advantage of providing access similar to that provided to books and journals about the same events, personages, and so on. LC is currently exploring the possibility of instituting cooperative subject cataloging similar to the cooperative name authority work being done through NACO, so institutions providing subject access to news materials by means of *LCSH* may want to consider using this mechanism (or other cooperative mechanisms) for sharing work on establishing new headings for events and other topics not yet found in *LCSH*. If the *LCTGM* is preferred, ongoing revision of that list might be possible as well if the staff of the Prints and Photographs Division at the Library of Congress can handle the volume of work.

A more expensive alternative would be to design a controlled vocabulary locally, specifically for the purpose of providing access to news materials. Such a vocabulary could be tailored specifically to news materials, but it would have the disadvantage of being yet another system for users to master.

A cheaper and less satisfactory method has been mentioned above: that of providing free-text searching of summaries and contents notes of story titles. If this could be offered in addition to access by means of a controlled vocabulary, however, it might actually improve access by providing more lead-ins to the controlled vocabulary than are already provided by whatever cross-references have been made. As one might imagine, indexing of current news is plagued by the problem of devising terminology for events and activities that are in the process of being named as they occur.

Another shortcut might be to encourage users to use existing indexes, such as the Vanderbilt index, or the New York Times index, to determine a span of time when a particular subject was being covered in the news and then to provide direct access under broadcast date to news materials. An indexable broadcast date has recently been added to the MARC format to provide this type of chronological or historical access. This method of providing subject access would shift the burden to the users' shoulders to a considerable extent, as they would have to view many programs that do not cover the topic of interest in order to find those that do.

At UCLA, we are using *LCSH* to provide subject access to each story in a cataloged Hearst newsreel issue. We have not yet determined how we will be able to provide subject access to a recently acquired collection of news programs taped off the air. We will probably use the Vanderbilt index to provide access to the national news. The local news is another matter. We currently have the report of a consultant under consideration. He has discovered that the rule of thumb in similar collections is that it takes ten hours to describe and index one hour of news!

LCSH may be better suited to provide subject access to documentaries and educational works, as they tend to cover subjects similar to those covered in monographs. There is some evidence (cited above), however, that users of these materials may also require access under broad categories. For example, a teacher may need a film on science for her science class, not caring which more specific scientific topic is being covered.

A collection specializing in a particular kind of record film, such as film recordings of dance performances or film recordings of anthropological data, may need quite specialized subject access and may be more likely to develop special local lists or to use lists special to their subject areas. The use of local lists commits the institution to expensive and ongoing maintenance and makes difficult the integration of the resulting records with records from other institutions in a subject-searchable database, so the decision to create a local list should be made with care.

Fiction

The American Film Institute (AFI) catalogs of feature films released in the United States provide extensive subject access to fiction films. Following their lead, the Motion Picture, Broadcasting and Recorded Sound Division of the Library of Congress is also adding a number of topical subject headings to fully cataloged films being distributed on the MARC tapes. We have discussed above some of the problems with bringing out the aboutness of works of art: the inevitable subjectivity and the large number of concepts that could be brought out. Research on the frequency with which scholars and researchers need subject access to these materials has never been done, but my suspicion is that they need access to the names of creators more frequently than they need subject access. For these reasons, at UCLA we have chosen instead to devote our efforts to bringing out the names of all people involved in the creation of a work, hoping that those who need subject access can use the AFI catalogs.

GENRE AND FORM

The National Moving Image Database (NAMID) Standards Committee has recently completed work on a national standard list of genre and form terms to be used by moving image collections to provide access under genre and form terms in the 655 field in the MARC format.

The term *genre* is used somewhat differently for moving image materials than it is for still image materials; its use for moving image materials is more akin to its use for literary materials. The definition in *Moving Image Materials: Genre Terms* is as follows: "any recognized category of fictional works which is characterized by recognizable conventions, i.e., a group of works all of which tend to explore the same themes and use the same plot formulae, character-types and icons."[15] We attempted to distinguish genre from form (any recognized category of works characterized by a particular format or purpose), physical format (which can change from one copy to another), and subject (pertaining to what a work is about, without regard to form or genre).

The NAMID Standards Committee recognized that moving image collections are diverse, that is, they include highly specialized collections as well as very general ones. It was decided that the list should be designed for use in collections at three levels of generality. Those collections that need only a short list of very broad terms can use the broad term list, a subset of the more detailed list. Those collections that need more specialized terms can use the detailed list. The detailed list contains *see* references from unused Narrower Terms. For example, a whole array of specific types of experimental films is listed in the form of unused Narrower Term references to the Broader Term PERSONAL/INDEPENDENT WORKS. The third level of generality available to very specialized collections would be to convert these unused Narrower Terms to used headings. For example, a collection of nothing but personal/independent works could convert the cross-references mentioned above to used headings. The hope is that records from institutions employing any level of generality could be integrated into one national database.

Terms in the list were derived from scholarly literature and from existing lists. We tried to select the most commonly used terms. Sometimes compromises were necessary in order to create terms that were properly inclusive in a hierarchical structure. Terms were designed to cover both film and television. Rather than use the more commonly used phrase, such as, for example, GANGSTER FILMS, we used the somewhat artificial construction GANGSTER DRAMA so that the term would cover television programs as well.[16]

The list is constructed like a thesaurus, with Broader and Narrower Term relationships clearly laid out. This is particularly useful for genre categories because there frequently are narrower subgenres that have grown out of broader ones.

The plan is to produce revised editions of the list to incorporate new terms as necessary.[17]

Because it is so easy to use moving image formats to record music and dance performances, as well as to reproduce works of art such as sculpture and architecture, there was a temptation to include form and genre terms for all these kinds of works in the list. We were quickly disabused of the notion that this would be possible, however, by the enormity of the undertaking, and our lack of expertise in all of these areas. Instead, it is highly recommended that other lists, such as *LCSH*, be used to provide access to music, dance, and the like.

Some of the problems with the use of more than one list have been alluded to above. It should be noted that currently *LCSH* terms go into the 650 field in MARC, even when they are form and genre terms, while terms from our list go into the 655 field. This means that there is not yet a clear distinction made in MARC among aboutness terms, ofness terms, and terms that identify the thing itself, as genre and form terms do. The situation is confused further by the fact that genre and form headings included in our list may also be present in *LCSH*; in the latter, they are meant to be applied only to collections and critical works, but this distinction may be lost on users.[18]

Form subdivision is not used in the genre list. We have discussed some of the problems this causes above in the section entitled Co-occurrence Rules and Decisions about Pre- and Postcoordination.

The form subdivision DRAMA is used when *LCSH* terms are used to provide subject access to fictional moving image materials. At UCLA, we use the form subdivision CARTOONS AND CARICATURES to provide access under the names of persons caricatured either by means of cartoon caricatures or by actors who do imitations. We use the form subdivision PARODIES AND IMITATIONS under the names of parodied works.

If it is desired to clearly separate form and genre access from topical subject access, one issue that must be addressed is that of the disposition of the hybrid headings created by adding form subdivisions to topical subject headings. I would hope that these would still be considered topical subject headings because the emphasis usually is still on their aboutness or ofness and the form subdivisions serve mainly to subdivide large files into subcategories for the user to choose among.

We have recently run across another problem whose source is our use of different lists for providing topical and genre access. When cataloging a film about westerns, one must either use the topical subject heading in *LCSH*, WESTERN FILMS, or one must use the heading from our list, WESTERNS, as a local subject heading (690 in MARC); we have decided on the latter solution.

PHYSICAL FORMAT

The 755 field has not yet been implemented for moving image materials, although the Standards Committee is currently working on a project to create a list of physical format terms, together with definitions and hints on how to identify them. These are meant to be appropriate for inclusion in the 755 field, if desired. The enterprise promises to be a difficult one as there is very little standardization in the use of terminology in the industry, or in the archival world for that matter.

Direct access online under physical format may not be as useful for moving image materials as it is for still image materials. In still image materials, a greater variety of physical processes have been employed to produce the images—for example, painting, print-making, engraving, photography, and drawing. In moving image materials, the basic process is photography.

Format is important, however. It affects access, in that one must ensure that appropriate equipment is available to view particular formats. We plan to use MARC physical format codes to print out offline lists of categories, such as 16-mm films or 1/2-inch videocassettes, to enable us to encourage use of particular formats or to help us in planning storage space. Some sound and color processes may be quite interesting to those doing research in the history of film technology and, in particular, in the history of sound, color, and wide-screen techniques. We have users who might need to see examples of two-color Technicolor prints, for example. It is possible that users might eventually find it helpful to be able to limit searches to material in a particular format, and terms in the 755 field might be helpful for that purpose. For example, the easiest material to book for a viewing appointment at UCLA is 1/2-inch VHS video. If a user is not interested in materials that are more restricted in access, he or she might find it helpful to be able to limit a search to 1/2-inch VHS video. There is a danger, though, with any of these physical formats, that we will have so many items that our online system will not be able to bring up everything online or will bring up so many things that no user in a hurry would browse through all of them. Those stubborn users who persist despite large retrievals can monopolize a limited number of public terminals and increase searching costs.

The general material designation (GMD) is sometimes mentioned as a possible substitute for direct access under physical format. It is part of the title field and so is often indexed along with words from the title. At UCLA, we do not use GMDs for two reasons: First, we often have both a video and a film copy attached to the same bibliographic record; second, much of our television collection is on 16-mm film, and it would be very misleading to put the heading MOTION PICTURE after the title of a television program. In our world, the term MOTION PICTURE refers to the medium of distribution, not to the physical format.

Medical libraries that use *MeSH* add terms such as VIDEOCASSETTES to subject headings as form subdivisions. *LCSH* has few such form subdivisions based on physical format and Jean Weihs, an expert on the cataloging of non-book materials in libraries and a proponent of integrated collections, warns against using them because it is easy for a patron interested in a particular subject to miss nonbook materials that may be available on that subject when they are segregated in the file because of use of form subdivisions.[19]

PROBLEMS WITH USE OF THE MARC FORMAT TO PROVIDE SUBJECT ACCESS TO MOVING IMAGE MATERIALS

In the course of the discussion so far, we have identified several problems, or potential problems, with the provision of subject access using the MARC format in its current state. They involve cases in which the fact that different kinds of data are tagged differently requires catalogers to make the distinction among the different kinds of data. Requiring such choices is legitimate if it serves user needs, but if users have no need for the distinction, cataloging efficiency might be served by dropping the distinction. In each case, it might be informative to consider the following questions:

1. Is the distinction necessary; does it serve user needs?

2. Is the distinction being made in the best possible way? Are users having trouble predicting what will be found where? Do we in fact make the distinction consistently?

3. Should online systems require users to make the distinction in order to do any search?

4. Is it useful for online systems to allow users the option of specifying the distinction in a search?

5. Is it useful for online systems to make the distinction only at the time of display, to allow users a choice at that time without requiring them to make the choice ahead of time?

The first distinction the MARC format requires us to make is the one between entities a work is about or of (6xx fields) and entities capable of authorship (or of being the primary work cataloged) (1xx/7xx fields). Thus, in the case of Represented Works, we must decide whether to treat the Represented Work as the primary work cataloged (1xx), as a related work or work capable of being the primary work cataloged (7xx), or as the "subject" of the work being cataloged (6xx). In the case of performers, we must decide whether a performer is an "author" (7xx) or is being depicted (6xx). Note that this means that the name of a performer in a 700 field indicates that the person is both an "author" and depicted. The user who is looking for a depiction of a performer would have to search both ways. In most online systems, our decision will cause the entry for the Represented Work or the performer to fall into one index or another, and users will be required to specify the correct index to find the Represented Work or performer.

Related to this is the distinction the MARC format requires us to make between a real person (600 or 700 field) and a fictitious character or performing animal (650 topical subject heading field). Because of the tag given fictitious characters and performing animals, they must be indexed in all systems in the same way that other topical subject headings are. In systems in which users must choose between either a subject index or a name/author/title index, they will surely have difficulty understanding why they must search Humphrey Bogart as FIND NAME Bogart but must search Bugs Bunny or Lassie as FIND SUBJECT Bugs or FIND SUBJECT Lassie. The performing animal issue is complicated by the fact that often an animal is portrayed by a number of different animals over time, as Lassie was. In such cases, perhaps we are talking about both a fictitious character (Lassie) and a performing animal (name of a dog that played Lassie). It should also be remembered that topical subject headings currently include a number of other proper names, such as artists' groups, athletic contests, events, and tribes, that users might expect to find in a Names index.[20] If we had some way of indicating proper names to the computer, by either tag or subfield code, systems that create Name indexes could create a more logical and predictable index.

Another distinction the MARC format requires us to make is the one between a topical heading (of/about: 650/690) and a genre/form heading (the thing itself: 655). Because *LCSH* contains many genre/form headings, all of which are currently tagged 650, our practice is clearly not consistent. The main question becomes whether the distinction is useful and whether users need to be able to limit searches to one type of heading or the other. We have indicated some cases, such as baseball games, in which the distinction between "thing depicted" and "thing itself" cannot be clearly drawn, but experienced catalogers realize that it's the gray areas that make us a profession. If we backed away from making distinctions every time we ran into gray areas, we would not be able to catalog at all.

One distinction we *don't* make consistently now that might be useful is the distinction between of (subjects depicted) and about (subjects discussed or alluded to). Another is the distinction between expressional versus discursive, or factual, treatment of subjects. If we can devise tags and codes in the MARC format to make these distinctions, we can have the option of building separate indexes in online systems. If it is felt that users merely need to be able to limit searches or to be able to choose among these categories, we could probably deal with the problem by means of such things as subdivisions.

CONCLUSION

Moving image materials are too diverse for this essayist to feel sure that all possible issues pertaining to all kinds of moving image materials have been addressed here. It is hoped, however, that the preceding remarks will provide at least a start in thinking through some of the stickier problems to be encountered in designing online systems to provide subject access to these materials that are so rich in source material for the study of twentieth-century history and culture.

NOTES

1. *Library of Congress Subject Headings in Microform* (Washington, D.C.: Library of Congress, Cataloging Distribution Service, 1989).

2. Dave Ferris, "Developments in the Bibliographic Control of Audiovisual Materials: The BL/ILEA Learning Materials Recording Study," *Education Libraries Bulletin* 22, no. 2 (Summer 1979): 33-34.

3. Donald Bidd, Louise de Chevigny, and Margo Marshall, "PRECIS for Subject Access in a National Audiovisual Information System," *Canadian Library Journal* 43 (June 1986): 181; James R. Dwyer, "Getting Down to the Reel Thing: Improved Access to Films and Videos through Subject Headings, Added Entries, and Annotations" in *Cataloging Special Materials: Critiques and Innovations*, ed. Sanford Berman (Phoenix, Ariz.: Oryx Press, 1986), 1-12; Dominique Saintville, "La Gestion Documentaire," *Problemes audiovisuels* 22 (November/December 1984): 45-57.

4. Sara Shatford, "Describing a Picture: A Thousand Words Are Seldom Cost Effective," *Cataloging & Classification Quarterly* 4, no. 4 (Summer 1984): 13-30.; Sara Shatford, "Analyzing the Subject of a Picture: A Theoretical Approach," *Cataloging & Classification Quarterly* 6, no. 3 (Spring 1986): 39-62.

5. For an impassioned plea from a library user for the usefulness of allowing this type of search, see: Alexandra Herz, "Scientific Illustration in Some Boston Area Libraries: An Art historian's View of Library Subject Analysis," *Library Resources & Technical Services* 31, no. 3 (July/September 1987): 239-48.

6. Shatford, "Describing a Picture," 13-30.

7. Shatford, "Analyzing the Subject," 43.

8. Shatford, "Analyzing the Subject," 58-59.

9. Elisabeth Betz Parker, *LC Thesaurus for Graphic Materials* (Washington, D.C.: Library of Congress, Cataloging Distribution Service, 1987), xiv.

10. *Art and Architecture Thesaurus*. [Information regarding this portion of the Getty Art History Information Program is available from the offices, located at 62 Stratton Road, Williamstown, MA 01267; telephone, 413-458-2151.]

11. Interestingly, Betsy Betz Parker, in a phone conversation, has pointed out that *LCTGM*, which is subject to continuous revision, is moving over time in the direction of precoordinated phrases and has even begun to use subdivisions in a limited fashion.

12. Actually, BASEBALL GAMES is an unused Narrower Term that we have chosen to use at UCLA.

13. Joseph R. Matthews, *Public Access to Online Catalogs*, 2d ed. (New York: Neal-Schuman, 1985). Of forty-eight systems described in Matthews's *Public Access to Online Catalogs*, 2d ed., forty require the user to choose between author or subject indexes, four require the user to choose between name or subject indexes, and only four do not require the user to choose an index.

14. Carol A. Mandel, *Multiple Thesauri in Online Library Bibliographic Systems* (Washington, D.C.: Cataloging Distribution Service, Library of Congress, 1987).

15. *Moving Image Materials: Genre Terms* (Washington, D.C.: Cataloging Distribution Service, Library of Congress, 1988), 11.

16. At its October 1988 meeting, the Standards Committee decided to revise the list to match our users' vocabulary better; thus, for example, we will now use the heading GANGSTER FILMS AND PROGRAMS.

17. Revisions decided upon at our October 1988 meeting will be distributed and published by the National Center for Film and Video Preservation. It has not yet been determined when a second edition of the list will be published.

18. I am currently a member of the Subcommittee on Subject Access to Individual Works of Fiction, Drama, Etc., Subject Analysis Committee, Cataloging and Classification Section, Resources and Technical Services Division, American Library Association. The subcommittee is in the process of preparing guidelines for publication, along with recommendations for the Library of Congress that, in the current draft, recommend that all genre and form headings from *LCSH* be placed in the 655 field when applied to either collections or individual works. Much will depend on whether LC decides to implement this recommendation.

19. Jean Riddle Weihs, "Problems of Subject Analysis for Audio/Visual Materials in Canadian Libraries," *Canadian Library Journal* 33, no. 5 (October 1976): 455.

20. "Headings for Certain Entities," *Cataloging Service Bulletin* 38 (Fall 1987): 2-9.

The Quest for a Code, or a Brief History of the Computerized Cataloging of Art Objects*

DEIRDRE C. STAM

Like the legendary pursuit of the Holy Grail, a quest which for most Knights of the Round Table resulted in increased knowledge but no grail, the art community's strivings for a cataloging code for objects has resulted in increased sophistication but still no code. No Galahad, or Percival, or Henriette Avram has so far appeared on the art cataloging scene. In the absence of a colorful hero and a satisfactory ending, why should the tale be told? And more particularly, what interest could it hold for librarians? For pragmatists, admittedly, the story has little to offer. There are no useful tricks to learn and no informational riches to plunder. For the theorist and dreamer, however, there are ideas to explore and lessons to learn.

Unhindered by the reality of traditional manual cataloging, those in pursuit of an automated art cataloging code have looked for a kind of perfection in their creation. The elements making up their concept of perfection can be instructive to catalogers of rare books in particular, whose interest in their material, stressing physicality and context, has much in common with the creators of art object information systems. From the point of view of the reference librarian, this topic is of interest in that it begins to explain what museum collection information is (or is not) publicly available in electronic form.

---

*Reprinted with permission from *Art Documentation 8,* no. 1 (Spring 1989): 7-15. This essay has been reproduced directly from the original; this accounts for variations in style between it and the other essays in this volume.

The following account will describe attempts to create a uniform cataloging code, suitable for computer applications, for art objects, here defined as unique objects made by human beings and considered to have aesthetic qualities. Excluded from this discussion are visual resources designed to document works of art, and other multiples such as prints and photographs, even though individual copies of these kinds of works are sometimes considered, as are rare books, unique entities. These categories of materials have their own cataloging histories. This story will concentrate, as has the activity of computerized art object cataloging, on the museum community. The scope is necessarily international for at least two reasons: art is itself an international topic, and significant advances in its recent cataloging have taken place in countries other than the United States.

To recount a "history" of this activity requires that facts be presented in orderly fashion. For historical accounts of most activities of this sort a standard order emerges, shaped in part by the nature of the facts themselves, and in part by the perceptions and interests of its theorists. Theorists of computer-assisted art object cataloging have so far been very few, and it is partly for that reason a standard version of this history has not yet taken shape. Another explanation for the paucity of syntheses is that this activity has lacked focus. In contrast to developments in book cataloging, one cannot cite here a few significant institutions, identifiable leaders, and major publications. For art object catalogers, in contrast to library catalogers, there was no standard code in the manual environment, and there was no tradition of sharing cataloging information.

The lack of focus may be due as well to the variety of purposes intended to be served by art object cataloging. The purpose of library cataloging is fairly well understood and widely agreed upon: it consists of making available to potential users both the resources of collections, and information about such resources. While the desire to catalog the material for inhouse management of collections is often the immediate objective, the more general goal is the service to the user community through communication concerning holdings. It could be reasonably argued that the pursuit of the larger goal has encouraged even rare book and special collections catalogers – who have much in common with art object catalogers – to accept standards such as AACR2 and network requirements, even though these general practices do not always meet inhouse needs, nor do they represent the economy of time that one finds in the cataloging of in-print, trade material. The goal is communication to a fairly well-defined audience, and the modes of communication and the language of that audience have been used for conveying information about items in rare book collections.

Agreement on intention has not been characteristic of the computerized art object cataloging movement. One finds several purposes represented in various cataloging projects in this field: the management of museum inventory, the documentation of legal title, the sorting of puzzling aggregates of objects, the ordering of a corpus of objects, and even the tallying of objects owned by a country in order to define a national patrimony. Heterogeneity of purpose has led to great variety in the form and content of records. In particular, on a theoretical level, one finds widespread misunderstanding between listing (describing) and cataloging. The communication of information to the scholarly community is, for computerized catalogs of art objects, more often a still undeveloped by-product than it is a major objective of a system.

Partly owing to the lack of motivation to communicate beyond the boundaries of a single institution, the use of standardized codes or rules, technical formats, and vocabulary has been minimal. The other reasons which have been cited for the lack of cohesive approaches include the uniqueness of materials in art collections; the "part-whole" problem, which has its parallel in libraries in the debate over the collection-level versus individual-item cataloging; the vast numbers and extremely wide variety of items to be cataloged; the lack of an authoritative body charged with the setting of standards; the low level of funding available for automation among art historians and museum staff; the lack of theoretical foundation, particularly with respect to "aboutness," a term one finds in contemporary archival cataloging theory; the diversity in output desired by art object catalogers; and the proprietary attitude toward research data held by many museum curators.

An additional, and important, explanation for the lack of coherent systems is just now becoming apparent in the field of art object cataloging: that is, the inadequacy of language as a recording medium for describing a work of art.[1] Whereas books carry some words within them which are significant for their identification and indisputable in form, art objects usually lack inherent verbal "labels." Almost all words used to describe works of art represent attributed characteristics – often the interpretations of the catalogers – rather than inherent properties of the object. Even the categories of information recorded vary from one cataloger to another working with the same type of material. As things stand now in object cataloging, an art cataloger – usually a curator – in one museum might be interested in the *function* of Egyptian funerary vessels; that in another museum in their *decoration*; and a third elsewhere in their *provenance*. Each cataloger could therefore devise a record with rather different fields, utterly unique rules of entry for those fields, and idiosyncratic choice and form of words for those fields. Added to this problem of focus are the difficulties caused by the multilingual character of art scholarship. There is considerable interest in adding visual components to art object databases, but so far this refinement is quite rare, and while it is an aid to description, it has not in any case solved the problem of retrieval. There seems no way around the problem of developing controlled language for description, and that is the aspect of art object cataloging which is now receiving the most attention from theorists. While language – authority work – is being sorted out, practitioners – museum registrars and scholars – continue to build and expand systems that are *sui generis* in every sense: the definition data elements, information "architecture," syntax, and terminology.

It should be noted that the staffing of automated art cataloging operations is as diverse as everything else about this activity. Information is generated by curators and registrars. It is systematized for automation in either the curatorial office or the registrar's department (sometimes through the services of a vendor or service agency); enlarged upon by virtually every department in a typical museum; and maintained variously by the systems office (if there is one), the curatorial offices or the registrar's department. Even though the professional degree in museum studies is becoming more common, few programs offer any preparation for automated cataloging. (In the absence of a body of theory, such preparation is virtually impossible to provide.) Training usually takes place on the job. Work with automated catalogers is considered barely professional, ranking far below curatorial status, and is very poorly paid – to judge from the job advertisements in the museum press. All of these organizational factors contribute to the heterogeneity and amateurishness of many automated museum cataloging efforts.

Although the history of art object cataloging is diffuse, it is not utterly chaotic. There are patterns within it, and these patterns correspond in a very rough way to what has happened in library cataloging generally. The phases of automated art object cataloging, while overlapping in time and somewhat isolated from one another in space, seem determined to a large extent by developments in computer technology – from the dominance of a single mainframe, to the availability of powerful microcomputers, to the improvement of communications devices and networks, and most recently to the development of integrating and flexible software. The phases of computerized art cataloging are divided for purposes of this narrative into decades and characterized thus: the late 1960s, unity; the 1970s, multiplicity; and the 1980s, harmonization.

THE LATE '60s: UNITY

The first phase of computer-assisted art object cataloging, ca. 1967 through the early 1970s, was characterized by a vision of large-scale, multi-institutional systems created through concerted effort. Early statements mentioned even libraries as allies, though such alliances were not to be formed for at least fifteen years. The rhetoric was expansive and optimistic. Typical was a statement from 1968 by Everett Ellin, later the executive director of the Museum Computer Network, delivered at a significant conference in 1968 entitled "Computers and their Potential Applications in Museums," sponsored by the Metropolitan Museum of Art and IBM:

> If we are to discharge our duty to education and scholarship and develop our unrealized potentials, we must reconcile ourselves to the cooperative formation of central repositories of information with facilities for handling inquiries from many classes of users. . . . What is called for is the establishment of comprehensive information systems as an integral aspect of museum service. . . . Such an archive or "information system" should be maintained, ideally, at a headquarters location from which the stored information would be retrieved and distributed on request to a great number of users over a network of terminals strategically placed in museums, libraries, and educational institutions throughout the region which the archive serves.[2]

And from Kenneth Lindsay of the State University of New York at Binghamton at the same conference: "Working parameters should be defined by a hardworking consortium of experts, a group consisting of leading art historians in all of the major fields, personnel from both large and small museums, art librarians, slide and photo librarians, computer systems analysts, copyright lawyers, and business management specialists."[3]

And finally, the comments of Thomas Hoving, then director of the Metropolitan Museum of Art in New York City: "The whole idea of a computer network is generating momentum, and is forcing upon museums the necessity of joining forces, pooling talents, individual resources and strengths. Because, obviously, no one of us can do it alone. It is forcing upon us the realization of our interdependence."[4]

The purpose of computerized record keeping for museums was in debate from the outset. The extreme positions ranged from minimal record keeping derived from registrars' manual records for the purpose of inventory control to maximal recording of information derived by professional art historians for curatorial purposes. The debate was subsequently discussed by Robert G. Chenhall, one of the few theorists of this activity, in his 1975 book, *Museum Cataloging in the Computer Age*.[5] Chenhall's argument for a catalog begins with a quote from Carl Guthe:

"To register an object is to assign to it an individual place in a list or register of the materials in the collection in such a manner that it cannot be confused with any other object listed.

"To catalog an object is to assign it to one or more categories of an organized classification system so that it and its record may be associated with the objects similar or related to it."[6]

Chenhall continues:

> The truth is that *most museums do not have any cataloging system at all.* (Many do not have an adequate registration system either, but that is

another problem.) . . . Some museum administrators would claim that a catalog is not an indispensable part of the object documentation, even though it might be a useful finding aid with some collections. A good case can be made, though, for the fact that *any documentation of the objects in a collection must be cross-indexed as many ways as possible or the information contained in the records will not be usable*. A catalog is such a cross-index. . . .[7]

Unlike the library community, the museum community did not have at the outset a shared concept of cataloging. Registrars had some idea of what elements constituted standard record keeping, thanks in part to the publication in 1958 of *Museum Registration Methods* by the American Association of Museums.[8] But even here, in the official statement of the major professional museum association, the descriptions of cataloging consisted not of a synthesis of methods, but rather discussions of several particular approaches in specific museums.

The creators of the first automated systems, which were usually intended for multi-institution use, had therefore to synthesize a cataloging code, define fields, specify data structure, and create a MARC-like structure for transmitting data, all at one stroke. Authority work, currently considered the key to fully integrated databases, was barely considered. It is hardly surprising that the goal of the union catalog was never achieved.

The assumption in the 1960s of the appropriateness of a unified, multi-institutional database was not due entirely to a philosophical position; it reflects to some degree the state of automation. The mainframe, bulky and expensive, was the only form of computer available just 20 years ago. To put museum development in perspective it is useful to recall that OCLC was established as the Ohio College Library Network in 1967, only a year before the conference on computer applications in museums. The MARC format for data elements had become fully operational in 1966.[9]

Art object catalogers struggled with many of the concerns that trouble rare book catalogers. A simple description of the physical object was not enough. It is not primarily physical elements, by and large, which cause art museums to collect their objects in the first place, as might be the case for natural history museums. It is, rather the *significance* of the piece – a concept representing a perceiver's judgment – based on any one of several criteria. For art objects, like rare books, interest in the object might be in its uniqueness, its history, or its aesthetic qualities. These elements are difficult to codify, a necessary step for computerization especially in its early years, and they are even more difficult to classify. How can one classify the most beautiful? The best preserved? The most charming? (For years, I personally have advocated the inclusion of the "ah!" factor in automated catalogs, but I have yet to find a system with enough wit to adopt this suggestion.)

While many of these issues were explored for the first time publicly at the 1968 Met/IBM conference, the story of computerized art object cataloging had begun some years before. Serious discussion about the feasibility of using computers for cataloging museum collections had taken place as early as 1963 when the Automatic Data Processing Committee was set up at the National Museum of Natural History of the Smithsonian Institution, soon to be followed by the development of the SIIRS (Smithsonian Institution Information Retrieval System), a forerunner of the more widely known SELGEM. In the same year, 1963, the Institute for Computer Research in the Humanities was founded at New York University under the direction of Jack Heller. The computer system developed by Heller, GRIPHOS (General Retrieval and Information Processor for Humanities Oriented Studies), was used a few years later by the Museum Computer Network for museum cataloging by six institutions.[10]

It should be mentioned parenthetically that computer applications for museum cataloging were taking place in the 1960s in ethnology, natural history and paleontology museums, but these projects were significantly different from art applications in that they dealt with large numbers of objects, each needing very little identifying data; they were based upon generally accepted taxonomies with stable terminology; and they recorded relatively objective data. A very early system had been set up at the art museum of the University of Miami, Florida, at what is now the Lowe gallery, but this installation did not significantly affect later developments in this field.[11]

The cataloging of art objects by computer in the United States effectively began with the establishment of the Museum Computer Network in New York City early in 1967, when several New York museum directors came together to discuss Jack Heller's proposal to develop a "Fine Arts 'Data Bank.'" They accepted Heller's proposal and began to plan the network and to raise funds for its support.

Supported by seed money from the New York State Council on the Arts and the Old Dominion Foundation, an office was set up at the Museum of Modern Art. Everett Ellin, then assistant director of the Solomon R. Guggenheim Museum, became the first executive director. Member museums included a core of computer institutions, the National Gallery of Art, and nine others. Ellin established contact with the International Council of Museums in 1968, thus giving the MCN international exposure from the beginning. David Vance, later executive director of the MCN, claims that the MCN served as a quasi-National Committee on Documentation. There is some truth to the claim, although it seems that the respect accorded such a body has come largely from outside the United States, where art and museum scholars and administrators expect an official body of this sort and seem to have accepted the MCN as playing this role. The influence on domestic development of art object cataloging has been rather less far-reaching than such a characterization would suggest.

A few concepts from the MCN data structure are significant, and have found their way into many derivative systems, and they are therefore worth reviewing briefly. Heller proposed two groups of data: objective data consisting of identifying elements such as object type, accession number, title of the work, artist, vendor, date, location, size, reference numbers, and medium of application and of support; and subjective or interpretive data, such as subjects and location of those subjects or images within the work. In discussing these elements, David Scott pointed out in 1976 that each of the so-called objective elements is subject to debate for most works of art.[12] While the second category is useful, it is inadequate in that it does not indicate what art historians and critics find interesting in a work of art. To record what interests the scholar one must include two other levels, each more subjective than the last: style, and then evaluation. These discussions touched only lightly on the context of the object, except through mention of provenance, and on the relationship of an object to others in its related group. Scott's objections to the record do not even begin to address the concerns of modern day art historical scholarship which focus in part upon signs, signification, and social context.

Some cautionary remarks from these early days, delivered at the 1968 Met/IBM conference, but not heeded at the time, seem in retrospect to be particularly cogent. Dr. Squires, from the Smithsonian Institution, for example, during a question period, commented upon difficulties which had become apparent in the experience of the British Museums Association: "The problem . . . is . . . of deciding when an object is of sufficient value to be catalogued for inclusion in a national-scale data bank. Perhaps one could add to this the very interesting question of the validity of the information about the specimen."[13] And Robert G. Chenhall, then of Arizona State University, strongly urged that museums approach their computerization, not from the standpoint of information retrieval alone, but from that of systems analysis which "is *vitally* concerned with what is communicated through information retrieval techniques, as well as with why this communication takes place and what is accomplished by it."[14] And further, "the first logical question to ask is, what are the outputs?" Finally, J.-C. Gardin, of the Centre d'Analyse Documentaire pour l'Archéologie, Marseille, spoke to the issue of control:

> "Control" is here to be understood in two ways: as equivalent to ownership on the one hand, and command on the other. . . . The right to fear collectivization holds rather in the second interpretation of the work, in which "control" refers to the actual command of files that have escaped private owners to fall into the hands of public bodies. Then, possible questions are: (a) Isn't there a danger of substituting a kind of mechanistic, superficial knowledge, drawn from a free access to large-scale uncritical

information material, for the more organic and deeper form of culture gained in the process of personally building and perusing a private file? (b) Isn't there a contradiction between the rigid organization of the data in a master file and the multiplicity of intellectual viewpoints reflected in the heterogeneity of personal archives? (c) Doesn't one take the risk in subordinating individual research to de facto monopolies of information that may eventually have the power to control the whos and whats of scientific inquiry. . . ?[15]

And another observation from Gardin, delivered amidst talk of unified systems: "For essentially scientific reasons, the modern trend is away from standardization – a seemingly desperate and somewhat old-fashioned goal, from a methodological standpoint – and in favor of concerted codes, each of which should be free to reflect idiosyncrasies, while required to exhibit compatibility with others."

Following the 1968 conference, efforts toward a unified databank went forward under the auspices of the Museum Computer Network. It was not until David Vance, then associate registrar of the Museum of Modern Art, took a close look at the files of 12 museums that the dimensions of the problem were understood. It had been the hope that a single "data bank" could accommodate the records of all cooperating museums (forming a union catalog), and further that none would have to recatalog material for this purpose. Vance's examination of data categories revealed that not only were they various, but they were nowhere rigorously defined. Vance found not one written definition of even one field label. The same term, e.g., provenance, was used differently in different museums. Said Vance, "The only way to learn what a label meant was to interrogate the staff, who often disagreed among themselves."[16] The encouraging finding was that there was considerable overlap in the kinds of information recorded from one museum to another.

One of Vance's first steps in developing a record format for the GRIPHOS system was to invent a standard set of defined labels. In order to avoid disputes over terminology, numbers were used as field labels. These numbered fields were then submitted to museum staff who either accepted them, or requested new number-labels to accommodate variations in their particular meaning of the concept under discussion. This approach, while logical in the extreme, and strongly reminiscent of MARC tags, ignores the human need for mnemonic devices when dealing with information structures, a need which is rather more acute in museums than in other informational organizations due to the largely intuitive style characteristic of work in the discipline of art history, a tendency nicely described by David Scott in an essay of 1976 entitled "The Yogi and the Registrar."[17]

The strategy for data entry in the early MCN system called for full cataloging of a few items, rather than selective data entry for large numbers of items. This approach led to severe limitations in retrieval, and made the meaningful use of the database impossible in the short term. An additional problem which slowed data entry was the need to rearrange data from manual files to the computerized format. The Metropolitan Museum of Art, after entering a considerable amount of data for a relatively small proportion of its collection, ended its data entry in 1971, citing financial reasons. Other early users of the MCN's adaptation of the GRIPHOS system were the International Museum of Photography at George Eastman House, and the Yale Center for British Art.

Despite its auspicious debut, by 1970 the MCN lacked money, staff, and offices, and was moved to the Museum of Modern Art for Vance to administer in his spare time. It later moved with Jack Heller to Stony Brook, as did David Vance. The MCN has survived to this day, in various forms, and has recently redefined its mission to serve as a focus for discussion and a source of information on museum automation issues in the broadest sense.

Another pioneer in the cataloging of museum objects, in addition to Heller and Vance, was Robert G. Chenhall who served as first chairman of the Museum Data Bank Coordinating Committee (MDBCC) formed in 1972. Chenhall convened experts and produced a significant document in 1975, *Museum Cataloguing in the Computer Age*, which defined data elements for museum records. When funds ran low in about 1974, the group became an informal body, changed its name to the Museum Data Bank Committee, and concentrated its energies upon producing Museum Data Bank Research Reports distributed by the Strong Museum in Rochester, where Chenhall served then as director of data services. In 1977, the MDBCC disbanded.

The last large-scale effort of these early years was centered at the Smithsonian Institution.[18] In 1968 the SELGEM (SELf GEnerating Master) was developed, and its documentation was made available at no charge to the museum community. The system required a considerable amount of programming to make it useful to other institutions, and its creating institution was besieged by requests for technical advice and support. A user-group known as MESH (Museum Exchange of Systems Help) was planned, but funding was not obtained. The SELGEM system continued to be used at the Smithsonian until very recently; an early database from the system is the well-conceived Inventory of American Paintings Executed before 1914, prepared at what is now the National Museum of American Art. This database represents not a single museum collection, but a kind of union catalog of examples – perhaps more properly a corpus – and in its cooperative aspects it is highly significant for the museum field.

On the international front, UNESCO had been active in documentation issues since 1946 when it founded a small documentation service for what was then the Museums Department of UNESCO's Division of Culture. In 1947 the management was turned over to the International Council of Museums

(ICOM) to become the UNESCO-ICOM Documentation Centre in Paris. The Centre serves as the Secretariat for the ICOM International Committee for Documentation (CIDOC), a group whose activity in art object cataloging has increased in recent years.[19]

One of the most highly centralized national art cataloging efforts has taken place in Canada.[20] Conceptually it belongs with United States developments of the 1960s. Begun in 1972, this ambitious program was charged with "creating a data bank of all the public museum collections in Canada and providing access to it through a computerized national network." This National Inventory Programme later became the Canadian Heritage Information Network/Réseau canadien d'information sur le patrimoine.

The notion of a unified catalog for museum objects in Great Britain can be traced as far back as 1888 with the call for "a compendious index of the contents of all provincial Museums and Collections" as a major purpose of the Museums Association.[21] During the 1960s British museums, primarily those concerned with natural science, experimented with automated indexing systems. At a meeting at the University of Leicester in 1966, participants discussed the need for a national data processing center for "systematics collections." A year later the Sheffield City Museum and the Museums Association convened a colloquium to address information problems connected with museum collections. The result of these meetings was the establishment by the Museums Association of working parties to examine data standards, problems of terminology and classification, and the interdisciplinary nature of museum records. The combined "Leicester Group" and the Museums Association working parties joined forces as the Information Retrieval Group of the Museums Association (IRMGA). The early interest in a national index of collections soon gave way to developing a workable method for collection documentation which could be used by individual museums thus moving the organization to the second stage of computerized object cataloging characterized by multiplicity and limited coordination.

THE '70s: MULTIPLICITY

Many of the characters in this tale – most of which are institutions – have already been introduced as players in the '60s. In this story, as in most legends, the protagonists became preoccupied along the way with diversions from the quest, but – also in the manner of legends – returned older and wiser with each new chapter. In this phase, the protagonists pursued their separate paths, often in small groups which are related – usually administratively – to one another. Various individuals or small groups developed cataloging systems for specific purposes. The single-purpose systems were seldom seen as cataloging methods or codes, and seldom were principles articulated. The rules making up the individual systems were characteristically expressed as part of the software documentation, and were often found only in the data dictionary for the application. These applications were characteristically tightly bound up with system software, reflecting its limitations and possibilities. In the course of the 1970s, institutions were able increasingly to use commercially available generalized database management systems, rather than programming their own applications, and thus their codes assumed some degree of technical similarity as the decade passed.

The United States, says David Vance, "is a land of independent museums."[22] Independent, too, to varying degrees, are university art departments, research institutions, and state agencies. Even within one museum, like the Metropolitan Museum of Art, one finds a degree of independence among departments, reflecting separate sources of funds and separate advisory bodies. Many of these separate units attempted small-scale collection documentation systems in the 1970s.

During that decade, museums in the United States pursued the computerization of their collection records with all of the independence characteristic of their other operations. Although the minicomputer became commercially available in about 1971, this breakthrough was less significant for the American museum community than the availability of the inexpensive microcomputer in the following years, allowing immediate online access to data on-site in several administrative units. Numerous minute cataloging and research projects were undertaken on microcomputers in the latter 1970s but most of these applications were frustrated by limitations of machine memory. It was not until the hard disk was available in about 1979, the end of this period, that significant applications were attempted. Little progress was made in this decade toward the development of a universal, or even national, code for cataloging art objects.

One of the lessons of the 1960s was that terminology is more important to cataloging art objects than had been recognized. During the 1970s Robert Chenhall and numerous experts from the museum field worked on a set of terms useful to the history museum, published in 1978 as *Nomenclature for Museum Cataloging: A System for Classifying Man-Made Objects*.[23] While its focus was on the function of objects, a concept more useful to the history than to the art museum, it served as an important prototype and teaching tool for those engaged in systematic description of objects. Significant among its achievements is the introduction of hierarchy in classification language as a way of introducing hierarchical structures into "flat-file" systems.

In 1979 work began on a thesaurus designed specifically for the art field, the *Art and Architecture Thesaurus*, initiated by art historian Dora Crouch, and librarians Toni Petersen and Pat Molholt. The *AAT*, like Chenhall's *Nomenclature*, was undertaken independent of any particular application.

During the 1970s, the Museum Computer Network abandoned the then obsolete GRIPHOS system, and its users went their own ways. The Metropolitan Museum of Art did very little in the following years by way of automating collection records. The National Gallery of Art worked away on its own collection records, publishing almost nothing on its efforts. The Yale Center for British Art continued its cataloging on university equipment, using an all-purpose database management system. The Museum of Modern Art, by contrast, adopted major elements of the GRIPHOS concept and converted its data into its own collections management system.[24]

In 1978, the Detroit Institute of Arts undertook the development of the system now known as DARIS (Detroit Registration Information System) to record their inventory on the computer already in use by other departments.[25] Under the direction of Susan Kalb Weinberg, and later Judith Schulman, a librarian by training, the system staff began a three-year period of parallel design and data entry, during which time data elements and authority lists were refined. Vocabulary was strictly controlled in several fields of the record. A significant conceptual development was the decision to group objects under standard art historical and archaeological terms, and catalog them as groups, rather than to attempt subject indexing of individual items. Another significant decision made by the museum was that such a system required not only a registrar as professional staff, but professional catalogers as well. By 1980, the Detroit Institute offered the use of DARIS for collections records to museums throughout Michigan.

While Great Britain saw the development of several separate attempts to computerize records, the most significant work has turned out to be that of the Museum Documentation Association, an organization "formed by museums themselves to assist with the development of documentation systems and procedures."[26] The MDA supports three service agencies, conducts research, and provides education and training facilities. Its clients include a few art museums among many history and science museums.

When the MDA began its work, it found that most museums had paid scant attention to the first phase of object documentation: details about the item and its source, that is, registration information. Even the second stage, the creation of the master record, had often been neglected. (It should be noted that this function is usually performed in the United States by a registrar, a position little known in Great Britain.) A third stage of documentation, control of inventory, had been only cursorily pursued, leading to criticism from overseeing agencies charged with assuring accountability. Cataloging per se had barely been attempted, and union catalogs were for the most part only a theoretical possibility. The more managerial considerations of accession and control had been generally neglected when D. Andrew Roberts and his colleagues entered the scene in 1977 with the creation of the MDA.[27]

The Museum Documentation Association, working closely with government agencies concerned with museums, developed software particularly suited to the cataloging of objects in museums of almost all types. This software could be run on mainframes, mini- and microcomputers, thus giving individual users considerable flexibility. The MDA defined data standards, and created various recording forms, cards and registers, along with instructions for their use. In the early days, many museums completed MDA forms and sent them to the MDA headquarters for inputting. Although the forms are better suited for natural history and historical collections, in that they specify relatively few fields with little room for data in each category, they are significant for this story in that they have been extremely popular even outside of Great Britain, and have led to a coherence of approach among many institutions which is very unusual in this undertaking. One could see this development as cohesion through pragmatics rather than from principle.

Through the seventies, the services of the MDA changed as member museums acquired their own hardware and the ability to modify software onsite. While the services of the MDA are centralized, the records they have built and maintained have consisted of separate databases for each member institution. Even though some members now operate independent systems, they still look to the MDA for advice on technical matters and on managerial issues. The publications of the association are among the most informative in the world of museum informatics.

In Great Britain, as in Detroit, the burgeoning of computer systems for museum documentation has led to the definition of new jobs, and the recognition of the professional nature of the function of museum documentalist/cataloger.

During the 1970s in France, under the direction of the Ministry of Culture, highly centralized, coordinated planning took place for the development of a national catalog of art works belonging to France, and making up the French artistic patrimony.[28] This concept of cultural heritage made up of objects residing in a country is almost unknown in the United States, but quite common in European countries, and those countries like Canada and Australia with European roots and connections. (When we in the United States speak of the American art heritage, we usually mean not what is *owned* by institutions in this country, but what has been *produced by* artists on this soil in the indigenous tradition.)

The implications of the concept of artistic patrimony for the creation of a national database are obvious. Because all works owned by French museums are part of French cultural property, it follows that they should be listed in a union catalog. This catalog should be overseen by the national agency charged with administering cultural property. And the catalog should be a unified entity. These assumptions have led in France to the Inventaire

Général des Richesses Artistiques de la France, and its databases for graphic art, sculpture, Egyptian antiquities, Greco-Roman antiquities, and ethnographic collections. Decorative arts, prints and national monuments will be the subjects of future databases.

(It is interesting to note that the Inventaire database for painting and drawing is named Joconde, the French version of Gioconda, the Italian name for the world-famous *Mona Lisa* whose portrait by Leonardo da Vinci hangs in the Louvre.)

The databases of the French Inventaire were dependent from the beginning upon a highly developed conceptual framework and clearly defined methods for analysis and control. Data elements are divided into these categories: keyword fields, in which vocabulary may be standardized and hierarchically organized; free-text fields, such as the title of a painting; numerical fields, and fields associated with dates. For the keyword fields, lexicons or thesauri of various types have been developed over time. They consist of open lists, in which keywords are all at the same level; closed lists, in which keywords are part of a predetermined list; and hierarchically organized lists, in which keywords may relate to one another either through inclusion or synonymy. Each database was developed as a separate entity, with its own terminology, based upon a general data format. Retrieval begins with the selection of keywords, using Boolean operators, and proceeds with free-text searching among the selected set. Considerable planning preceded data entry. Interestingly enough, the French differentiate between the "system," which is a conceptual construct, and the "realization" of a database, which consists of programming and data entry.

Italy in the 1970s, like France, assigned the cataloging of the nation's cultural heritage to a national Ministry of Culture and Environmental Property.[29] All cultural property in Italy is legally protected, including that belonging to the state, to religious groups, and to public institutions. Even private cultural property is legally controlled. According to Oreste Ferrari, director of the Istituto Centrale per il Catalogo e la Documentazione, "Cataloguing applied to the entire existing cultural patrimony." Designed for purposes additional to intellectual pursuits, it aims to improve planning and execution of curatorial activity, of both administrative/legal and technical character. Ferrari defines this cataloging of art properties as consisting of: (1) the detailed collection and verification of historical and philological data drawn from archival sources, bibliographies, and new research, (2) ascertaining the ownership of cultural property, and (3) determining the state of conservation and indicating needed conservation.

Founded in 1969, the Italian Istituto was later joined with the National Photographic Collection and the Collection of Aerial Photographs for these purposes: to maintain contact with various administrative officials, to prepare programs of cataloging to define general principles for cataloging, to establish a central archive in Rome, and to promise the scientific publication of documentation. For the Istituto, the '70s were a time to develop strategies for documenting art works situated in Italy. The computerization of records was delayed until procedures were in place for administering the work of the institute.

A chief difficulty facing Ferrari and the cataloging staff of the Istituto was the sheer number of items to be considered. They developed separate methods for gathering information on the various categories of objects, and stressed the need to integrate this information, at least at the level of the object category. A major concern for property largely archaeological in nature was the description of geographical context, including concepts of urban units, archaeological sites, and natural history sites. Two types of record cards were developed: Type A for analytical and detailed data; and Type B for the logical synthesis of Type A cards. Thus we see an attempt to deal with the "part-whole" problem which bedevils art object cataloging.

From the beginning the Italian project recognized the problem of terminology that was particularly difficult owing to the age of the Italian language, its divisions into regional dialects, and its varying levels of formality. To address these problems the project is creating a series of Terminological Dictionaries, with terms drawn in part from archival and historical documents. Some of this work was done by computer, at the Scuola Normale Superiore in Pisa.

Even though the existing catalog cards forming the source documentation for the Italian system contain a considerable amount of free-text and subjective comment, they nonetheless are susceptible to computerization. With the help of the Computing Institute of the Italian National Research Council in Pisa (CNUCE), the automation of these records is underway. Following the received wisdom of the late '70s, the Istituto is inputting a limited amount of information from each record in order to meet the practical aims of the program. Using STAIRS/VS on the CNUCE computer, the Istituto began inputting data, only to find that standardization was a severe stumbling block. Another problem was the lack of relational capability in the STAIRS package, and the inability to check data against authority files automatically at the input stage. Ferrari stated in 1986 that the Institute concluded that the most significant problem was the lack of thesauri. Reflecting that thesauri cannot be compiled completely a priori, Ferrari anticipated a period of experimentation and development of terminology in the following years.

The last significant work on computerization of art records in the 1970s reviewed here took place in Canada, at the Canadian Heritage Information Network, already introduced. The original system, designed to run a mainframe computer through batch processing, was devised with the assumption that museum data were relatively static, and need for updating was minimal. This proved not to be the case, and participating institutions found the system unusable for collection management.[30] In addition, the centralization of the database seemed to serve no particular purpose since individual museums were interested almost exclusively in their own records, and others who might want inclusive information did not have ready access to the data. A third problem, encountered also by Ferrari in Italy, was the lack of cataloging information in the participating institutions. The conception of the problem changed, from one of computerizing collection records, to one of creating useful records from available data. In December of 1980, a government agency, the National Museums of Canada, reviewed the project, and decided to continue the program with redefined goals, emphasizing issues of information management and its contribution to museum management.

Not all computerization of art object records in the 1970s was centered in museums. Among projects designed for purposes other than collection management was, for example, a computerized catalog of the work of William Merritt Chase, leading in part to a catalogue raisonné for this artist. Data were divided into three categories in this application, including emphasis upon documentation as is suitable for this purpose: (1) physical information, (2) primary documentation including contemporary literature, contemporary exhibition records, and auction records, and (3) secondary documentation. Another notable project begun in these years is the catalog of Italian art with iconographical analysis represented by the Catalogue of Italian Painting, housed at the Villa I Tatti in Florence. The project staff worked with CNUCE, and with staff at the Scuola Normale Superiore in Pisa, as did the project staff for the Catalogo under Ferrari's direction.

Thus in the seventies the quest for a cataloging code to allow universal access to information about art objects was diverted to concern for gaining control over information within single projects, and institutions, and national units. Solutions seemed not to translate readily across national borders; one can only speculate that patterns in funding, administration, and working habits inhibited ready transfer of methods. It was perceived that the major hurdle to computerization was not a technical problem, but one of lack of reliable documentation in the first place, and lack of systematic approaches to recording documentation as an attendant difficulty. To solve these problems, staff were needed with backgrounds in art history and skills in computerization, but such people were in short supply. And finally, the need for considering the managerial implications of computerized record keeping became apparent as systems, by now online, intruded themselves into institutional operations.

THE 1980s: HARMONIZATION

Harmonization, a term one finds in recent UNESCO documents on informatics, is applicable to developments in the 1980s in automated art object cataloging. Moves toward harmonization of systems have taken place in these areas: the integration of systems across departments and functions within individual institutions, the construction of authority lists including thesauri, and the identification of a core of useful data elements. In the interests of accuracy, it should be stated that these efforts are still largely in the planning and early developmental stages.

But what of the grail? What of a universal cataloging code? Like most quests for most grails, this one has led not to the anticipated prize itself, but to a redefinition of the goal in light of an improved understanding of its meaning. The original objective, the pursuit of a single cataloging code for art objects, suitable to automation, has come to be seen as impractical, to some even unnecessary, but in any case unlikely soon, in order to achieve the greater goal of access to data. An acceptance of multiple formats is growing. Some technical problems of integration or communication can be solved other ways: with harmonious vocabulary and syntax, with improved communications devices, with mapping to a standard communication format and with intelligent "front ends." These techniques are not yet developed, but they are possible. The more fundamental difficulty in gaining access to art data is one of policy: the data of museums and other research projects dealing with art objects are not seen as a public resource even in some publicly supported institutions. This issue has barely been raised in the professions of art history and museology. One might see as a preliminary step to policy setting the relatively recent application of managerial techniques to the control of data on an institutional level.

The redefining of the problem has been due not only to more sophisticated understanding of art data, but also to several recent technological advances: the hard disk, which allows convenient local storage and retrieval of large amounts of data; improved communications modes, including local area networks; fairly standard off-the-shelf software packages with flexibility in field definition and manipulation, including repeatability for mass inputting; and relational databases, allowing the intersection of authority files with part of the object record, a feature which insures control of vocabulary at the inputting stage. The concept of relational files is altering the fundamental idea of a record as a fixed unit, as one sees in OCLC and RLIN applications of the MARC record, and it is shifting attention from the structure of a record to the construction of authority files supporting the data elements of the system. With relational files, for example, one could consider "the record" to consist not only of information relating directly to a single work of art, but also all of the information in an authority file relating to the artist, and all of the authority information pertinent, for example, to the donor of the piece as well. Another significant technical factor has been the development of high-quality printers, allowing computer printout to serve directly as scholarly output. This development has caused a growing interest in software with sophisticated report capabilities. Still to come are workstations which allow the integration of files and interaction with these files, and artificial intelligence to assist retrieval. While these concepts are not part of present projects, they are known to planners (specifically at the Research Libraries Group), and they will fit naturally with the other technological devices now being adopted.

The experience of Canada in the 1980s is illustrative. In 1980, the government agency charged with responsibility for four national museums and various museum services, the National Museums of Canada, began a major review of the National Inventory Programme which had consisted of the creation of one national database which provided various reports and printouts to member museums. In 1981, the commission declared that the original mission of sharing information was appropriate, and should be pursued along with efforts to use computerization "to help museums in their daily management of collections."[31] The project renamed Canadian Heritage Information Network was seen as important for recording Canadian heritage; it should do so through collections management, exhibition planning, research and education. To achieve its mission, the CHIN headquarters continues to operate large-scale computers with which individual institutions can now interact directly. It also provides training and it facilitates the use of glossaries and other standard tools.

On the technical level, CHIN has developed lists of data categories with the help of specialists from various disciplines. Every museum has its own database, composed of portions of a common set of data fields. The fields have been greatly expanded to reflect not only the values, but also the functions of data. For example, address has been divided into mailing address, location, city, province, country, postal code, etc. Of these many fields, about twenty will probably be isolated as suitable for a combined, national database of all museum objects, some of which deal with art. While thesauri produced by CHIN staff are appropriate to some areas of the records, other thesauri are considered better defined by experts in disciplines, and some by individual museums. Some previously uncontrolled data have been brought into conformity through frequency counts and corrections, but considerable data remain uncontrolled.

In general, the Canadian Heritage Information Network has moved in the 1980s from a cataloging service to a utility that provides guidance in the construction of databases, specifies standards for transmission, and distributes databases of various kinds, including a number of conservation files, through its communications facilities.

The Smithsonian Institution, too, has seen a switch from purely technical system development to managerial considerations. Building upon their experience with SELGEM, and affected by their connection to the recently formed Smithsonian Office of Information Resource Management, the staff of the newly formed Collections Information System (CIS) began "a structured process of information analysis to develop a graphic model of art data."[32] An analysis was made of the functions performed at the Smithsonian and the data required to support these functions. Included in the summary are references to "information stores" such as filing cabinets, physical collections, computer systems and more. Thus the system has addressed the question of how to create a practical, economical, integrated automated system, and still connect with the vast informational resources housed in curatorial offices, the library, and storerooms.

An interesting contribution to cataloging theory in this field is the Smithsonian's concept of the primary entities of role player and role. For example, a specific person, Mr. Jones by name, might have painted a picture in the Smithsonian, and he might have donated a picture by someone else. The data for Mr. Jones could be stored only once, and intersected with both the artist and the donor fields, according to need. Some theorists have suggested that the files for individual persons might include enough information to function as biography files, not just authority files to identify the person and indicate the preferred form of name as is common in library circles.

A small international project, Thesaurus Artis Universalis (TAU), under the auspices of the Comité International d'Histoire de l'Art and supported by the J. Paul Getty Trust, has begun to investigate the possibility of creating complex biographical databases of this sort for exchange.[33] Thus similarity in databases would come about as much from shared files – one could call them enhanced authority files – as from the uniform definition of fields of full records.

The Thesaurus Artis Universalis project has pursued questions of vocabulary in part as a result of conclusions reached at the Second International Conference on Automatic Processing of Art History Data and Documents, held in Pisa in 1984. This conference was sponsored by the J. Paul Getty Trust and the Scuola Normale in Pisa. The conference and an attendant census revealed the existence of – or at least plans for – hundreds of computer projects in art history consisting of general national catalogs; and catalogs of architecture, sculpture, painting, prints and drawings, manuscripts, coins, and pottery. Also identified were thesauri and lexicons, documents and sources, iconographical indexes, bibliographies, biography, and photoarchives. Also discussed was the use of the computer as a tool for research. In many languages and in many contexts, the need was expressed for a better understanding of vocabulary problems, and concerted efforts to solve these problems.

Another significant activity supported by the J. Paul Getty Trust was the initiation of the Museum Prototype Project in 1982, developed originally "to build an integrated research system which merged various Getty trust sponsored projects with selected external databases.[34] Rather more modest goals were described for the eight-museum project in 1984: to establish a standard cataloging format for painting, to provide a merged shared catalog of Western paintings, and to build a database of artists represented in that catalog. While the overall goals did not meet with general agreement, some sub-goals served as guides to the project: among them to "strive for agreement" on record formats with other projects, to define data elements usual to the files of museum curators and registrars, to consider extending these data elements to other types of objects, and to plan for flexible retrieval. Other sub-goals specified the adoption of controlled vocabularies, shared cataloging, and linked collection management and cataloging systems.

During planning for the Museum Prototype Project, some discussion of using the Research Libraries Information Network to carry data, and to employ the MARC record, was introduced by William Arms, the project head who had been a consultant to the Research Libraries Group and therefore knew RLIN, but museum staff were not convinced that this solution would accommodate the complexity of their information needs.

For the Museum Prototype Project, as for others, vocabulary caused some of the biggest problems. Comparison of terminology from records input was performed, using frequency counts, but the *sense* in which the words were used could not be adequately tested. Nor could the terms be practically compared to scholarly usage. The project was terminated in 1985. Although the interest of the J. Paul Getty Trust, specifically the Art History Information Program, in shared catalogs seems to have diminished, work on terminology continues. A vocabulary coordination group has recently been formed by the Art History Information Program as part of its regular program.

In this decade it seems more useful to look to umbrella organizations rather than to individual museums and projects for advances in art object cataloging. By following the Museum Computer Network's newsletter *Spectra*, for example, one learns among other things of the several commercial cataloging software packages available to museums.[35] The Getty Art History Information Program is doing valuable work in this area in its support of individual projects such as the Art and Architecture Thesaurus. *Archival Informatics*, a journal published by the privately owned Archives and Museum Informatics in Pittsburgh, contains discussions of technical matters, and reviews conferences dealing with the issues of computerized cataloging of art objects and archival materials.[36] And the newsletter *H.A.M.I.: Histoire de l'Art et Moyens Informatiques* discusses pertinent issues and systems.[37] The Scuola Normale Superiore in Pisa, supported in part by the J. Paul Getty Trust, is endeavoring to establish a clearinghouse of international database projects of general interest to art historians. The Library of Congress is potentially a useful source of information; as an example one could cite the publication *Graphic Materials: Rules for Describing Original Items and Historical Collections*,[38] but so far art object catalogers outside of the library context have shown little inclination to borrow library terminology and techniques. The Art Libraries Society of North America, with international affiliations, publishes material generally useful for art cataloging of all kinds;[39] see for example the papers from the Authority Control Symposium, published in 1987. Both ICOM/CIDOC and the Museum Documentation Association hold conferences and publish proceedings. The American Society for Information Science (ASIS) has an active subgroup dealing with humanities issues; ASIS conferences often include the discussion of art databases. The American Association for State and Local History publishes material on museum object cataloging, and they have recently been instrumental in establishing the *Common Agenda for History Museums*, a project housed at the Smithsonian Institution. The Research Library Group is showing interest in mounting databases for art object information in its RLIN system. A clearinghouse in the Watson Library of the Metropolitan Museum maintains information on art museum computerization.[40] And finally the Smithsonian Institution conducts workshops to introduce museum professionals to issues of automation.

Even though this chapter of the tale, the harmonization of databases, is far from complete, the outlines of the next chapter are becoming clear already. The tendency for catalogers of art objects to look beyond their institutions is expanding to include looking at other fields and other approaches. One finds in the literature and in presentations at scholarly meetings, for example, discussions of archival approaches to describing collections, the linguistic concept of "frames" and its implications for faceted classification, nonverbal classification and retrieval of visual imagery, novel applications of the *Art and Architecture Thesaurus,* and – coming full circle to linking again with librarianship – increasingly frequent references to the MARC format as a suitable framework for art object information.

There is no doubt that a quest is taking place. Great amounts of activity and publication attest to that. But what is being sought is not as clear as it was twenty years ago. There is still talk of a standard approach to description – a cataloging code if you will – but there is more talk of the larger issues served by catalogs and standards, that is, the recording, control, and communication of information. The grail is described in less specific terms – and sometimes less comprehensible language – as its pursuers become more familiar with theoretical concerns and vocabulary. Though harder to grasp, the elusive grail of automated art object cataloging should still be of interest to the library community for reasons of imaginative if incomplete design, and utterly beguiling content.

NOTES

1. These ideas are developed in greater detail in the author's essay "Choosing Our Words: Reflections on Authority Control in Art Information Systems," in *Authority Control Symposium*, edited by Karen Muller, Occasional Papers no. 6 (Tucson, Ariz.: Art Libraries Society of North America, 1987), 55-67.

2. Everett Ellin, "Information Systems and the Humanities: A New Renaissance," in *Computers and Their Potential Applications in Museums*, published for The Metropolitan Museum of Art by the Arno Press, New York, 1968, 325-27.

3. *Computers and Their Potential Applications in Museums*, 23.

4. *Computers and Their Potential Applications in Museums*, xi.

5. Robert G. Chenhall, *Museum Cataloging in the Computer Age* (Nashville, Tenn.: American Association for State and Local History, 1975).

6. Chenhall, 7-8.

7. Chenhall, 8-9.

8. This work is now in its third edition: Dorothy H. Dudley, Irma Bezold Wilkinson, and others, *Museum Registration Methods* (Washington, D.C.: American Association of Museums, 1979).

9. Lucy A. Tedd, "Progress in Documentation; Computer-based Library Systems: A Review of the Last Twenty-One Years," *Journal of Documentation* 43, no. 2 (June 1987): 147-50.

10. David Vance, "The Museum Computer Network in Context," in *Museum Documentation Systems; Developments and Applications*, ed. Richard B. Light, D. Andrew Roberts, and Jennifer D. Stewart (London: Butterworths, 1986), 38.

11. Vance, 39.

12. Originally issued as *Museum Data Bank Research Report*, Number 7, in 1976; David Scott's essay has been revised and published as "The Yogi and the Registrar" in the issue of *Library Trends* 37, no. 2 (Fall 1988), edited by Deirdre C. Stam and Angela Giral and entitled "Linking Art Objects and Art Information."

13. *Computers and Their Potential Applications in Museums*, 343.

14. *Computers and Their Potential Applications in Museums*, 60.

15. *Computers and Their Potential Applications in Museums*, 121f and 112.

16. Vance, 40.

17. See note 12.

18. T. Gary Gautier, "National Museum of Natural History, Smithsonian Institution," in Light, Roberts, and Stewart, 48-54.

19. Paulette Olcina, "The Development and Coordination of Museum Documentation by International Agencies," in Light, Roberts, and Stewart, 310.

20. Jane Sledge and Betsy Comstock, "The Canadian Heritage Information Network," in Light, Roberts, and Stewart, 7.

21. D. Andrew Roberts and Richard B. Light, "The Cooperative Development of Documentation in United Kingdom Museums," in Light, Roberts, and Stewart, 115.

22. David Vance, "The Museum Computer Network in Context," in Light, Roberts, and Stewart, 37.

23. Robert G. Chenhall, *Nomenclature for Museum Cataloging: A System for Classifying Man-Made Objects* (Nashville, Tenn.: American Association for State and Local History, 1978).

24. Eloise Ricciardelli, "The Museum of Modern Art," in Light, Roberts, and Stewart, 68-70.

25. Judith L. Schulman, "The Detroit Art Registration Information System (DARIS)," in Light, Roberts, and Stewart, 77-88.

26. D. A. Roberts, "Computerized Inventories, Catalogues and Indexes of Museum Collections," in the Proceedings of the International Seminar on Information Problems in Art History, Oxford, 20-22 March, 1982, *Art Libraries Journal* 7, no. 2 (Summer 1982), 35.

27. Roberts and Light, 118f.

28. Michel Aubert and Dominique Piot, "Documenting French Cultural Property," in Light, Roberts, and Stewart, 233-40.

29. Oreste Ferrari, "Documentation of the Italian Cultural Heritage," in Light, Roberts, and Stewart, 244.

30. Sledge in Light, Roberts, and Stewart, 7.

31. Sledge in Light, Roberts, and Stewart, 8.

32. Patricia Ann Reed and Jane Sledge, "Thinking About Museum Information," in *Library Trends* 37, no. 2 (Fall 1988): 220-31 (see note 12).

33. Deirdre C. Stam, "Factors Affecting Authority Work in A;rt Historical Information Systems: A Report of Findings from a Study Undertaken for the Comité International d'Histoire de l'Art (CIHA), Project: Thesaurus Artis Universalis (TAU)," *Visual Resources* 4, no. 1 (Spring 1987): 25-49.

34. Nancy S. Allen, "The Museum Prototype Project of the J. Paul Getty Art History and Information Program: A View from the Library," in *Library Trends* 37, no. 2 (Fall 1988): 175-93 (see note 12).

35. *Spectra*'s new address is The Museum Computer Network, School of Information Studies, Syracuse University, Syracuse, New York 13244.

36. Archives & Museum Informatics, 5600 Northumberland St., Pittsburgh, PA 15217.

37. *H.A.M.I.* can be obtained from the editor, Jacques Thuillier, Collège de France, 11, Place Marcelin Berthelot, Paris, Cedex 05, 75231, France.

38. Elisabeth W. Betz, compiler, *Graphic Materials: Rules for Describing Original Items and Historical Collections* (Washington, D.C.: Library of Congress, 1982).

39. See particularly *Art Documentation: Bulletin of the Art Libraries Society of North America.*

40. Deirdre C. Stam, "For Data Based on Art, Call . . .: A Computer Information Clearinghouse," *Museum News* 65, no. 5 (June 1987): 67-74.

BIBLIOGRAPHY

Listed here are significant publications dealing with the automated cataloging of art objects. Many include extensive bibliographies. They are arranged chronologically.

Metropolitan Museum of Art. *Computers and Their Potential Applications in Museums*. New York: Arno Press, 1968.

Chenhall, Robert G. *Museum Cataloging in the Computer Age*. Nashville, Tenn.: American Association for State and Local History, 1975.

Chenhall, Robert G. *Nomenclature for Museum Cataloging: A System for Classifying Man-Made Objects*. Nashville, Tenn.: American Association for State and Local History, 1978.

Chenhall, Robert G., and Homulos, Peter. "Museum Data Standards." *Museum News* 56 (July/August, 1978): 43-48.

First International Conference on Automatic Processing of Art History Data and Documents. Pisa. Scuola Normale Superiore. 4-7 September 1978. [Conference transactions.]

Orna, Elizabeth, and Pettitt, Charles. *Information Handling in Museums*. New York: Saur, 1980.

Roberts, D. Andrew, and Light, Richard B. "Progress in Documentation: Museum Documentation." *Journal of Documentation* 36 (March 1980): 42-84.

Paijmans, J. J., and Verrijn-Stuart, A. A. "A New Approach to Automated Museum Documentation." *Computers and the Humanities* 16 (1982): 145-55.

"Proceedings of the International Seminar on Information Problems in Art History. Oxford, 20-22 March, 1982." Compiled and co-edited by Jill Heberden and Michael Doran. *Art Libraries Journal* 7, no. 2 (Summer 1982). Entire issue, including essays by T. Fawcett, M. Rinehart, D. A. Roberts, J. Sunderland, T. H. Ohlgren, I. Aleksander, and M. Greenhalgh.

Sarasan, Lenore, and Neuner, Alan M. *Museum Collections and Computers*. Nashville, Tenn.: American Association for State and Local History, 1983.

Corti, Laura, ed. *Census: Computerization in the History of Art*. Pisa: Scuola Normale Superiore, and Los Angeles, The J. Paul Getty Trust, 1984.

Corti, Laura, ed. *Automatic Processing of Art History Data and Documents: Papers*. 2 vols. Pisa: Scuola Normale Superiore, and Los Angeles, The J. Paul Getty Trust, 1984.

Corti, Laura, and Schmitt, Marilyn, eds. *Automatic Processing of Art History Data and Documents: Proceedings*. Pisa: Scuola Normale Superiore, and Los Angeles, The J. Paul Getty Trust, 1984.

"Computers and the Future of Art Research." [Entire issue of] *AICARC: Bulletin of the Archives and Documentation Centers for Modern and Contemporary Art* 2 (1984) and 1 (1985). [Edited at the Swiss Institute for Art Research, Zurich.]

Roberts, D. Andrew. *Planning the Documentation of Museum Collections*. Duxford, Cambridge: The Museum Documentation Association, 1985.

Samuel, Evelyn K. "Developing Computerized Information Systems for Art Museums." Diss. New York University, 1986.

"Computers and the Future of Art Research: Visions, Problems, Projects." [Entire issue of] *AICARC* 2 (1986) and 1 (1987). [See AICARC citation above.]

Abell-Seddon, Brian. *Museum Catalogues: A Foundation for Computer Processing*. London: Clive Bingley, 1987.

Stam, Deirdre C., and Giral, Angela, eds. "Linking Art Objects and Art Information." [Entire issue of] *Library Trends* 37, no. 2 (Fall 1988).

Chenhall, Robert G., and Vance, David. *Museum Collections and Today's Computers*. New York: Greenwood, 1988.

■ The Inventory of American Sculpture: MARC-ing Realia

CHRISTINE HENNESSEY

Despite a long tradition of object cataloging going back to detailed inventory lists of precious objects and artwork found in the tombs and palaces of the Egyptians and Mesopotamians, collection documentation has been a low priority for museums until recently.[1] Most cataloging, where it exists, is reflective of the concerns and personal idiosyncrasies of individual registrars or curators. With museum computerization, however, documentation practices have assumed a new role and importance; in recent years, there has been growing recognition that the successful retrieval of information (especially on a national and international level) is dependent on shared standards, syntax, and vocabulary.[2] As part of that awareness, several museum and visual resource curators have begun to experiment with the MARC format for cataloging their collections.[3] This paper will focus on the development and subject retrieval needs of one such MARC museum application – the National Museum of American Art's Inventory of American Sculpture.

HISTORY AND SCOPE OF THE PROJECT

Plans for a comprehensive inventory of American sculpture date back to May 1983, when leading scholars in the field and interested museum professionals met to discuss the feasibility and logistics of such an inventory.[4] The need for an inventory was clear. Whereas considerable critical and scholarly attention in recent years has been focused on American painting, architecture, and the decorative arts, sculpture remains largely undocumented.[5] Its size, weight, and fragile nature often preclude its comprehensive documentation or inclusion in exhibitions. Only a small number of museums has published sculpture collection catalogs. Moreover, many significant pieces are located in private collections or are in outdoor sites inaccessible to the scholar or historian unaware of their existence.

In response to this need, the Smithsonian's National Museum of American Art has begun a comprehensive Inventory of American Sculpture. The Inventory references works of art from the earliest European settlement of the states up to the present. Item-level records are being created for all types of sculpture, including historical busts and war memorials, modernist assemblages, and earthworks.[6]

In concept and intent, the Inventory of American Sculpture functions much like a national union catalog in that it is being built upon information others provide. Museums and historical societies are contributing checklists, photocopied registration cards, and photographs. Private collectors are sending reports of works they own. In addition, information is being culled from a variety of published sources, including theses, dissertations, catalogues raisonnés, and pertinent exhibition and auction catalogs.

Over twenty-six thousand records have been entered (see Figure 1).[7] Essential information recorded for each sculpture includes artist, title, creation dates, dimensions, medium, foundry, cast numbers and other markings, owner/location information, provenance (or past ownership), subject description, and historical and exhibition notes. Plans are also under way, in conjunction with the National Institute for the Conservation of Cultural Property and other cooperating national agencies, to conduct a comprehensive survey of outdoor sculpture in America, recording basic condition assessment and conservation treatments for each outdoor-sited work.[8]

As a research database, the Inventory of American Sculpture holds answers to questions as general as "What themes from literature have been depicted by American sculptors?" and as specific as "Are there any works by Louise Nevelson in Minneapolis?" Curators, conservators, historians, scholars, educators, and publishers from all disciplines can use the Inventory to locate works for exhibitions or comparative studies or as a starting point to locate images pertinent to the particular themes they are researching.

In contrast to the limited search types available for most library book materials (author, title, subject), the Inventory of American Sculpture provides greater flexibility through a range of access points. The database may be queried for artists, associated creators (including foundries, architects, and engineers), titles, subject, object types (e.g., fountains, memorials, mobiles), medium, specific owner or location, generic location type (e.g., park, state capitol), and exhibition history information. Providing suitable access to these fields challenged and extended the MARC format.

Figure 1   Sample Record from the Inventory of American Sculpture

ARTIST:	Manship, Paul Howard, 1885-1966, sculptor.
TITLE:	Lyric Muse (sculpture).
DATES:	1912.
MEDIUM:	Bronze.
DIMEN.:	11 3/4 x 6 15/16 x 5 9/16 in.
FOUNDER:	Roman Bronze Works, Brooklyn, New York, founder.
MARKS:	(Inscribed on top of base) PAUL MANSHIP ROMA C 1912 (Right side of base) ROMAN BRONZE WORKS N-Y-signed, founder's mark appears
OWNER:	Cincinnati Art Museum, Eden Park, Cincinnati, Ohio
SUBJECT:	Mythology – Classical – Muse Performing Arts – Music
SOURCE:	Index of American Sculpture, University of Delaware, 1985
REC ID:	ias 75006670

MARC-ING SCULPTURE DATA

Concurrent with the initial development of the Sculpture Inventory, the Smithsonian Institution implemented a MARC-based system – the Smithsonian Institution Bibliographic Information System (or SIBIS) – intended to link and serve Smithsonian Institution libraries, archives, and research projects.[9] Intrigued with the potential of using MARC for dissemination of information, the Smithsonian decided to enter the sculpture data into SIBIS, and, in 1985/86, a pioneering project was initiated to map sculpture data to the Visual Materials (VM) Format.

Because VM was designed initially for two-dimensional graphic materials, rather than three-dimensional realia, many of the needed data elements did not "fit." Particularly problematic, yet essential to the Inventory, were the fields needed to capture information about the specific owner and location of the object and its physical characteristics, especially medium, dimensions, and conservation actions. No suitable fields for recording these kinds of information had yet been defined in the VM Format. To solve the Inventory's needs, therefore, applicable fields were "borrowed" from other MARC formats. The 851 (Owner) and 561 (Provenance) fields were adapted from the Archival and Manuscripts Control (AMC) Format, with new local subfields defined to record specifics, such as street address and type of location (e.g., battlefield, cemetery, state capitol). The AMC Format also provided fields to record detailed media and date information. Similarly, the 247 (Former Title) field was borrowed from the Serials Format to capture previous titles associated with an artwork.

In some cases, completely new fields and subfields had to be defined. In the artist/creator fields, for example, a qualifying subfield to designate "attributed to" status was added; to trace the exhibition history of an artwork, a 585 (Exhibitions Note) field was defined to record name, location, and dates of an exhibition.

Many of these redefined or newly created fields and subfields subsequently were incorporated into the VM Format as a result of meetings held at the Library of Congress to expand the format to accommodate three-dimensional artifacts and realia.[10]

Admittedly, the museum's approach to the MARC format is experimental, but the decision to integrate and adapt formats was done with the ultimate goal of providing better retrieval for the art researcher.

SUBJECT ACCESS

While the use of the MARC format provides a basic structure for the potential exchange of information, access is also dependent on the standards determining the content of individual fields. Controlling the subject vocabulary to be used is especially critical for the Inventory of American Sculpture because all information is received secondhand from a variety of reporting institutions. To facilitate retrieval by providing consistency in terminology, a number of authority files and thesauri are utilized, including a *Subject Term Guide* developed at the National Museum of American Art.[11]

Subject terminology is of concern because at least 20 percent of the incoming queries received by the museum's database projects are topical or thematic in nature.[12] To accommodate these needs, subject information is entered in three places within a record: a 520 Descriptive Note Field, the 655 Form/Genre Field, and the locally defined 659 Topical Heading Field.

The 520 note field is used to enter a free-text description of the imagery depicted. For example, an Alexander Calder sundial in the database is described as: "Dial table supported by four seated figures of young women, representing the four seasons, grouped around its edge. Spring holds a rose; Summer is decorated with poppies; Autumn bears grapes; and Winter carries a branch of pine. Each holds aloft an apple bough, a suggestion of the full opulence of the year. Each season turns her head to face the next season. The signs of the Zodiac decorate the outer edge of the dial table."

Descriptions may be excerpted from those provided by the reporting source, or, if a photograph of the work is available, supplied by the cataloger. For figurative works, the narrative description may reference people, things, events, or actions taking place. For nonfigurative, abstract works, the description may reference the object's shape, color, or texture.

Although guidelines are provided for capturing subject information, no attempt is made to control vocabulary in the 520 field. The primary intent of this field is to help the researcher visualize the sculpture. The entire field is keyword searchable. To augment this free-text field, controlled subject terms are entered in several structured 65x fields.

Terms related to the overall function, shape, or type of sculpture (apart from the actual content of the work) are recorded in the 655 Form/Genre Field. Included in the fifty-five allowable terms used in the Inventory of American Sculpture are generic types such as Fountain, Mobile, and Monument. Thus, researchers may query the database for a listing of monuments done in the decade following World War I, or art historians can request a listing of all mobiles to trace the history of this genre in twentieth-century art.

Subject headings referencing the subject content or theme of the sculpture are recorded in 659 fields, so assigned because the terms are controlled locally and subfielding does not follow LC or MARC practice. Although the benefits of conforming to national standards were recognized, the Inventory chose to utilize the 659 field and enters terms from a subject guide (*Subject Term Guide*) developed specifically for the museum's extensive art database projects.

There were practical reasons for this decision. Certainly, the limitations and difficulties of applying *Library of Congress Subject Headings* (*LCSH*) are so well documented that they need not be detailed here. It is enough to say that the general nature of *LCSH* inhibits its applicability to a specialized collection of any sort. Furthermore, it must be remembered that *LCSH* is designed primarily for textual materials rather than for visual collections. Neither the terms nor the *LCSH* rule of specificity (of always assigning the most specific term applicable) provide the kind of comprehensive access needed for the Inventory of American Sculpture.

To be sure, visual materials (especially art objects) often require varying levels of subject access. As noted in Elizabeth Betz Parker's pioneering *LC Thesaurus for Graphic Materials: Topical Terms for Subject Access,* an artwork is both "of" and "about" something.[13] Artworks depict not only identifiable persons, places, or things but in addition often have underlying iconographic or thematic meanings. A woman holding a scale may represent a particular concept such as Justice. For an art database, both layers of the subject need to be referenced. General as well as specific terms must be captured; thus, subject classification lists from the library community proved unsuitable.

Nor could the handful of known museum subject classification systems be adopted.[14] Most image-based subject classification schemes in use for museum collections were developed to meet the needs of a particular institution and its collections. Indeed, the uniqueness and variability of museum collections often mandate specialized subject terminology. Medieval manuscripts, for example, have very different subjects from twentieth-century American sculpture.

To solve its needs, therefore, the Inventory of American Sculpture adopted a *Subject Term Guide* already in use for several of the museum's other art database projects. The guide employs forty-one primary headings that reference basic broad categories, among them Animal, Landscape, and Portrait. More specific secondary and tertiary headings can be concatenated with the main heading as needed (for example, Landscape – United States – Massachusetts). As illustrated in the excerpt that follows, terms within the guide are arranged alphabetically, and basic Scope Notes are included to aid the cataloger in assigning terms.

Excerpt from NMAA *Subject Term Guide*

Primary	*Secondary*	*Tertiary*
Architecture	Commercial	Name, e.g., Seagram Building
		Type, e.g., Bank Gas Station Grocery: *includes all food selling establishments, i.e.,* Bakery, Deli, Grocery, Butcher, Fish Market. Hotel: *use for any inn, auberge, hostel, motel, etc., used for sleeping purposes.* Restaurant: *use for any eating establishment.* Store: *Use for any shop in place of word* shop.

As with any subject terminology listing, the National Museum of American Art's *Subject Term Guide* has its strengths and weaknesses. One of its strengths is that it was designed primarily for American art materials, with headings relevant to our databases. Moreover, its format accommodates generic searches for broad topics as well as for specific precision matches. For example:

"Give me a listing of all scenes with dogs."

"Which twentieth century sculptures depict dalmatians?"

Not all broad topics can be referenced, of course. For example, a researcher interested in the trade history of early Florida would have to know which Indian tribes were then active in the state as well as which site names to look under. Since the guide does not have a thesaural format, nor does it include cross-references, researchers must match their queries exactly against the language in use.

Another apparent weakness is the guide's expandability. At the secondary and tertiary levels, terms are often suggested through representative examples rather than prescribed per se. For example, under the heading ARCHITECTURE – COMMERCIAL, illustrated earlier, one is advised to add the specific type of building (BANK, GROCERY, etc.). Although this ability to expand allows the addition of new terms as needed, it does little to control terms. As a result, inconsistent classifications, variant spellings, and synonymous terms may find their way into the database. Periodic reviews, either online or through printed subject frequency reports and regular staff cataloger meetings, help control terms and limit these "et cetera" categories.

Once the decision was made to use a local subject authority list, the question then arose as to how best to format these headings in MARC. The current MARC structure, designed presumably to facilitate authority control of terms, artificially separates personal, corporate, geographic, topical, and occupation terms into discrete fields – the 600, 610, 651, 650, and 656 fields, respectively. This structure does not reflect the mix of primary, secondary, and tertiary terms found in our *Subject Term Guide*, nor does it allow us to maintain relationships among terms. We chose, therefore, to define local 659 fields into which our terms can be strung together as a single heading.[15] To maintain the implied hierarchy of terms within a string, particularly important for our offline print reports, subfields "a" (primary terms), "b" (secondary terms), and "c" (tertiary terms) were defined. For example:

$aHistory$bFrance$cNapoleon

The SIBIS system allows searches on the entire string, on each subfielded portion, and on any keyword within a subject phrase. By adopting 659 fields, we were able to keep redundancy of terms to a minimum while retaining relationships among terms. This use of the MARC format improves subject access so critical in an art database.

CONCLUSION

Unfortunately, unlike the library community where descriptive standards abound and nationally accepted subject classification lists have been in existence since 1895, the museum community has few agreed-upon standards and even fewer shared vocabularies.[16] Given the specialized nature of most museum collections, it is not surprising that such a situation exists. But with computerization and prototype MARC applications, such as the Inventory of American Sculpture, it is hoped that museums will begin to see the possibilities of adopting formats and standards that facilitate the exchange and dissemination of information. One might speculate that the integrated MARC format of the future, with some adaptations, will be a good vehicle to accommodate the array of museum objects.

NOTES

1. These early inventory lists are cited in Marilyn Pink, *How to Catalogue Works of Art* (Los Angeles: Los Angeles Museum Systems, 1972), 4.

2. D. Andrew Robert's article, "Progress in Documentation," *Journal of Documentation* 36 (March 1980): 42-84, provides an excellent overview of trends in museum informatics. In the last decade, five major museum networks have been organized and at least three comprehensive surveys have been undertaken to assess museum documentation practices. In 1983, reflective of the increasing awareness of the importance of terminology, the Comité International d'Histoire de l'Art (CIHA) created a working group called Thesaurus Artis Universais (TAU) to explore problems of automating art-historical information. Similarly, in 1987, CIDOC (Comité International pour la Documentation), part of ICOM (International Council of Museums), established a Working Group for Terminology Control. The issues of standards and terminology were also the focus of the International Conference on Terminology for Museums (cosponsored by the Museum Documentation Association and the Getty Art History Information Program), held in Cambridge, England, 18-24 September 1988. Finally, here in the United States, standardization is also one of the central concerns of the Common Agenda History Museums Database Task Force.

3. Indicative of the growing awareness of the possibilities of using MARC, the Visual Resources Association presented a session on "MARC-ing the Visual Document," at the fifteenth annual conference of the Art Libraries Society of North America, held in Washington, D.C., February 1987. The same year, the Society of American Archivists approved the establishment of a MARC-VM Users Roundtable. In 1988, with funding

from the National Historical Publications and Records Commission (NHPRC), staff members of the Chicago Historical Society and Gallaudet University conducted a Conference on the Use of MARC Records for Archival Visual Materials at Gallaudet University in Washington, D.C., and have subsequently published a report of the proceedings and a compendium of practice titled *MARC for Archival Visual Materials: A Compendium of Practice*, by Linda J. Evans and Maureen O'Brien Will (Chicago: Chicago Historical Society, 1988).

4. The conference was held at the National Gallery of Art's Center for Advanced Study in the Visual Arts in May 1983. It was the consensus that the Smithsonian's National Museum of American Art, with its extensive computerized art databases, should undertake the project. In addition to the Inventory of American Sculpture, the Office of Research Support at the National Museum of American Art implemented and maintains the following art research databases:

- The Inventory of American Paintings Executed before 1914 (indexes 252 thousand paintings in public and private collections).

- The Permanent Collection Database (references 33 thousand objects in NMAA's collection).

- The Pre-1877 Art Exhibition Catalogue Index (has 150 thousand records).

- The Smithsonian Art Index (lists 200 thousand works in nonart Smithsonian Institution collections).

- The Slide and Photographic Archives (has 38 thousand slides, photographs, and negatives).

- The Peter A. Juley & Son Collection (has 127 thousand photographic negatives).

5. Paraphrased from Wayne Craven, *Sculpture in America*, new and rev. ed. (Newark, Del.: University of Delaware Press, 1984), preface.

6. Minor architectural ornament, decorative arts, and gravestones are generally excluded from the Inventory of American Sculpture, unless of major artistic or historical significance.

7. A substantial core of records came from the University of Delaware's index of American sculpture. These manual files represent the research accumulated by Professor Wayne Craven for his survey text, *Sculpture in America*, and have since been augmented with graduate student research findings.

8. This collaborative effort, SOS! (Save Our Sculpture), is being done in cooperation with the American Association for State and Local History, the National Conference of State Historic Preservation Officers, the United States National Park Service, and the Smithsonian Institution's Conservation Analytical Laboratory.

9. The Smithsonian Institution Bibliographic Information System includes an integrated library system composed of modules that support acquisitions, circulation, cataloging, and authority control functions for library materials; an archives catalog for the control of institutional records and manuscript papers housed at the Smithsonian; and a research catalog designed for research bibliographies and specialized research inventories. The system currently numbers over 1.2 million records with more than 130 terminal connections to Smithsonian sites throughout the United States and Panama.

10. Phyllis Bruns from the Network Development and MARC Standards Office at the Library of Congress coordinated a series of meetings beginning in the fall of 1985 regarding adding specifications for three-dimensional artifacts and realia to the USMARC Visual Materials Format. Many of the additions and modifications proposed at these meetings were subsequently approved by MARBI and officially incorporated into the VM Format in the spring of 1987.

11. Initially developed in 1973/74 by Eleanor E. Fink for the museum's Slide and Photographic Archives, the guide is now used by six of the museum's art resource or database projects. In addition, for the Inventory of American Sculpture, authority files or controlled vocabulary lists are maintained for artist/creator names, foundries, media (or materials), owners, specific site locations, and exhibition titles.

12. Over 895 queries were tracked between 1 October 1987 and 30 March 1988. Of the incoming queries, 70 percent were for artist, 20 percent were for subject access, and 10 percent were for other (title, owner, etc.). These statistics, although useful, may not accurately reflect researcher needs because those familiar with our inventory projects, are often repeat users and may therefore structure their queries to fit the kind of output indexes they know we can currently provide.

13. Elisabeth Betz Parker, comp., *LC Thesaurus for Graphic Materials: Topical Terms for Subject Access* (Washington, D.C.: Library of Congress, Cataloguing Distribution Service, 1987).

14. For an overview of subject classification schemes in the art history community, the reader is advised to read Thomas Ohlgren, "Subject Indexing

of Visual Resources: A Survey," *Visual Resources* 1, no. 1 (Spring 1980): 67-73.

15. The 653 MARC-defined field for uncontrolled terms is used by the Inventory of American Sculpture to record new candidate terms not found in the existing NMAA *Subject Term Guide*.

16. Lois Mai Chan, *Cataloging and Classification* (New York: McGraw Hill, 1981), 127.

■ What's the Purpose?
Functional Access to Archival Records

ALDEN N. MONROE
KATHLEEN D. ROE

Providing access to records is one of the most important services of an archival institution. Access to archival records poses special problems because of the way these records are created and used. Books and journal articles are the intentional product of an author made to stand alone as coherent pieces. Archival records are the result of the activities of an individual or an organization. As such, they are not intended as a final product and often lack focus or comprehensiveness. To provide effective access to such resources, techniques of description and indexing must go beyond those of traditional library practice.

An intimate relationship often exists in archival records between those who created the records and the actual informational content of those records. One of the essential elements archivists need to supply is information on the context in which the resources were created. From the context, a researcher can understand the contents and character of information in the records. An important key to context is understanding an organization's functions and activities. By clearly identifying the functions and activities of governments, private institutions, and business organizations, archivists provide information that helps explain why records were created. This explanation, in turn, is essential for interpreting and evaluating correctly the content of archival records. To provide indexing to this kind of information, the MARC AMC Format contains a field for Function Term (657).

The focus of this article is on the possibilities for enhancing access to the archival records created by institutions such as governments, universities, corporations, labor unions, health care institutions, and any other organizations with a formal structure by detailing their functions. The MARC Format for Archives and Manuscripts Control (AMC) may be unfamiliar to some readers, so a brief summary of the format will be given as a general context for the more specific discussion of functional access. A clear understanding of the term *function* is necessary for it to be used effectively; therefore, this essay will give a detailed definition of function and will discuss why functional access is useful.

Following this, the uses of function in various archival activities will be discussed. Function can be a significant access point for archival researchers, as well as for archivists themselves as they appraise and describe records. It allows archivists and researchers the opportunity to "browse" among groups of records that may not have been brought together by a corporate-name or subject search.

Methods for providing access to functional information using the MARC format will also be suggested. Despite a long history of emphasizing the role of function in archival description, guidelines and examples for specifically addressing this have not appeared in archival literature. This essay will make an initial attempt to do. It will also discuss recent efforts to design controlled vocabularies for functional access.

THE MARC AMC FORMAT: A GENERAL SUMMARY

Archival and manuscript materials are the permanently valuable records produced by individuals, groups, organizations, or governments in the process of conducting their daily activities or business. These may include letters, deeds, diaries, business ledgers, maps, photographs, films, or machine-readable records. These various forms of material all share a common emphasis on their archival nature over their distinguishing features of format or medium. The *USMARC Format for Bibliographic Data* accommodates the needs of archival records through the MARC Archives and Manuscripts Control (AMC) Format. The AMC Format combines a number of traditional fields – author, title, and subject terms – with several distinctive fields oriented toward the special needs of archival materials. Archival bibliographic records, for example, commonly contain extensive descriptive information in Scope and Contents Notes (520). As a result, they often have many more Subject terms (650) than traditional library materials have and make more extensive use of such indexing fields as Genre/Form (655), Geographical Name (651), Occupation (656), and Function (657). The MARC AMC Format also allows recording of important information about the history of a collection of records, namely, Historical/Biographical Notes (545) on the creator of the records; what has happened to the collection over time, that is, its Provenance (561); and the source of the collection, its Source of Acquisition, (541); and Actions (583) taken to preserve and describe the materials (i.e., fumigating, weeding, or flattening). The information in a MARC AMC record will commonly, then, describe the physical characteristics, the informational contents, the context of creation, and the history of the records themselves.[1]

DEFINING FUNCTION

Although the term *function* historically appears in the archival literature of Europe and the United States,[2] there has been limited effort to describe how it is being used, much less how it should be used. A more complex discussion of the use and role of function cannot be accomplished, however, without an understanding of the parameters of the term. Based on detailed research into archival use and application of this term, we suggest here the following definition: *Function is an area of responsibility in which an organization conducts activities to accomplish a purpose.* Examples of common functions for various kinds of organizations are:

State Government Agency

Promote health
Regulate business
Preserve environment
Assist agriculture

University Department

Socialize students
Assist students
Research science
Matriculate students

Health Care Institution

Research disease
Treat patients
Educate patients
Educate health care professionals

Understanding function helps one understand the actual records created by the organization. For example, a city government will likely have as one of its functions the responsibility to protect the public's safety. One of the activities by which it accomplishes this is to arrest lawbreakers. From this activity, records such as police blotters, arrest logs, and case files are created. Those records may cover a variety of subjects, ranging from drug sales to shop-lifting to child abuse. Although subject content is important, why the information was created is also significant. Records on child abuse created in the process of arresting lawbreakers will vary significantly from those created by a lawyer defending the accused, from those created by a children's advocacy group, and even from a hospital's examination files for an abused child. In each case, the function of the creating organization will have an impact on what information is collected, how it is collected, what depth of coverage is provided, and what perspective it provides on the subject. It is essential for users of archival materials to understand the relationship of an organization's function to the materials it creates if they are to use and interpret those records meaningfully.

THE NEED FOR FUNCTIONAL ACCESS

The kinds of access points that archivists and librarians currently use and that traditionally have been in all the MARC Formats answer most of the basic journalistic questions. Personal and corporate names supply the *who*; subject terms supply the *what*; chronological periods supply the *when*; geographic terms tell *where*; and form/genre terms show *how* the information was recorded. Although *why* may be implied by or extractable from subject, forms terms or agency name, there is no exact correlation. There is a clear need to identify function separately. Function terms round out the picture by providing access to *why* records were created. The reason for records creation is too important to be left to guesswork or personal interpretation. The originating organization itself should provide the explanation.

Access by provenance essentially relies on function because knowledge of an organization's history and responsibilities provides information on the purpose for which the records were created. This is an oblique approach to function, however. It is not always immediately evident from the name of an organization's departments or a government's agencies what functions may have been assigned to it. Furthermore, those functions may change over time or be transferred to another department or agency. For example, government agencies dealing with the control of water pollution vary considerably from state to state. In Alabama, the Department of Environmental Management is responsible for this function. In Michigan, it is the Department of Natural Resources. In Utah, it is the Department of Health. In New York, controlling water pollution has been the responsibility variously of the Department of Health and the Department of Environmental Conservation. To counteract this vagueness, archivists have relied heavily on extensive organizational background information. This requires either having an intimate knowledge of administrative history or having to pore over extensive narrative histories to identify that information. Functional access is a much simpler way to bring together information that reflects the reasons organizations conduct their business.

A function may also be split between subdivisions of an organization, or several organizations may either simultaneously or over a period of years have responsibility for the same function. They may attempt to accomplish this function by a variety of different activities. For example, the function to protect the public's safety is undertaken by a variety of agencies within state government, including potentially a department of state police, a department of prisons, a department of health, and a department of human rights. The state police protect the public by activities such as arresting lawbreakers. A department of prisons protects the public by incarcerating convicted offenders. A health department protects the public by testing food and drug quality. A department of human rights protects the public by monitoring affirmative action laws.

Identifying *why* an organization is doing a certain activity provides important contextual information. Context is particularly significant in archival records because they are the unconscious results of activities. These records are not created with the intention of making a complete, objective human record. They are created in the process of accomplishing activity. Users of these resources must have every possible contextual clue to help them interpret and understand the content and uses of archival records. Without that information, users are likely to take information in archival records at face value and from a twentieth-century perspective. Doing so is a misuse of the archival record.

THE USES OF FUNCTIONAL ACCESS

For researchers in archival repositories, functional access potentially can allow more accurate location of relevant records. Researchers of organizational records are often hampered in their search by their unfamiliarity with a particular institution's activities and history. In some cases, their research projects may warrant an in-depth study of administrative history, but in most cases, they do not. For example, because a researcher does not have a comprehensive knowledge of the intricacies of a government agency's responsibilities over time, he or she may find it hard to identify relevant agency records. The researcher must rely on the availability of an archivist and on the ability of that archivist to provide a guiding path through administrative history. Staff that does not have comprehensive knowledge is seriously impeded from providing researchers with access to records. Many archives rely heavily on the "institutional memory" of a few key individuals, and many repositories have experienced problems with reference when these staff members retire or leave the institution's employment.

The difficulties become more intense as increasing numbers of archives enter their records into online databases. Databases do make information available more quickly and easily, but the same information most certainly will be accessed by persons without the necessary knowledge of administrative history and its implicit, but often unstated, relationship to function. This will hinder their ability to accomplish meaningful retrieval. In some cases, archives are participating in institutional library databases from which librarians and students are accessing information on archival holdings. In other cases, archives are sharing their descriptions in regional and national databases, from which archivists, librarians, and researchers in different institutions are accessing these descriptions. The increasing public nature of archival description demands that the information be able to stand alone, without the need for a knowledgeable archivist to act as intermediary and to use personal recollection to explain the context provided by function.

Subject or name is not enough to reflect contextual information. For example, see how the following records description is enhanced when a functional statement is added:

Without function statement:

Northeastern Research Group.

Reports on the PCB level in brook trout, 1960-69.

These reports summarize laboratory tests conducted on samples of brook trout taken from five streams: East Creek, Mud Creek, Emerson Creek, Red Creek, and North Creek. Charts provide a yearly summary of PCB level and comparative figures from the previous year.

With function statement:

Northeastern Research Group.

Reports on the PCB level in brook trout, 1960-69.

The function of this not-for-profit organization is to preserve the environment. One of its primary activities is monitoring the level of pollution in regional waterways.

These reports summarize laboratory tests conducted on samples of brook trout taken from five streams: East Creek, Mud Creek, Emerson Creek, Red Creek, and North Creek. Charts provide a yearly summary of PCB level and comparative figures from the previous year.

The function statement shows clearly why the records were created and gives a researcher more precise information by which to determine whether the records are relevant for a particular research need. Functional access lessens the need to undertake exploratory visits to archives, to look at the actual records, or just to request additional assistance or research from archives staff.

In addition to assisting researchers, functional access can be useful to archivists for their own retrieval needs. In records appraisal, it would be useful to be able to identify records that accomplish the same function. Comparing functionally similar records could allow more consistent scheduling of records for disposal or permanent retention. This will assist in ensuring coverage and in identifying duplication between organizations and subdivisions.[3] With the increasing bulk of records to be appraised, functional access may prevent repetitive information from being preserved. Archivists can bring together all the records that accomplish the same function, even if they have been created by several parts of an organization. Once records documenting a function are collated, the archivist can more accurately assess the adequacy with which that function has been documented.

Functional access also may be used to locate information about appraisal and scheduling of records in similar organizations. For example, records documenting federal efforts to assist health care exist at the local, state, and federal government levels. Identifying the records at each level may cause a local government archives to determine that they do not need to retain their copies because the information is already well documented at the state or federal level. Conversely, sufficient documentation may exist at the state or local level to relieve the National Archives of the responsibility of documenting all federal functions. Efforts to share such data and to use records appraised and scheduled by other state governments have been undertaken by two successive cooperative projects, the Research Libraries Group Seven States Project and the Research Libraries Group Government Records Project.[4]

Functional access may also be useful in the area of long-term archival description. Rarely will an organization's archives have the opportunity to describe all of the holdings of a division or an office at one time. This is particularly true of organizations still in operation, which continue to create records that are transferred to archival custody on a regular basis. Because different staff may describe portions of the accessions at various times and over a range of years, certain staff members may be unaware of functional relationships between records and may lose some of the contextual information that could enhance descriptions. This is especially true if over the years functions are transferred or split among organizations or subdivisions within organizations. In some cases, having functional information available may prevent duplication of research in the process of conducting descriptive work. Considerable consistency in historical background information and in indexing practices can be achieved by identifying records with the same function.

FUNCTIONAL ACCESS IN ARCHIVAL PRACTICE

For most of the history of archives, archivists have been seriously interested in methods to expand access. These methods traditionally have been highly labor intensive, and many options have not been available simply because they were prohibitively costly. Unlike library materials, archival records, particularly those of institutions, often take up a hundred or more cubic feet of space. This size and complexity have long defied detailed content analysis such as that provided in library settings.

Historically, discussions of the role of provenance in archival literature include references to function as part of the information to be identified. A number of European manuals influential in the United States, such as Sir Hilary Jenkinson's *A Manual of Archive Administration*, and the *Dutch Manual for Archival Description* by Muller, Feith, and Fruin, note the significance of function to an understanding of provenance. American archivists – including Waldo Gifford Leland, Margaret Cross Norton, and Theodore Schellenberg – also acknowledge the need to understand an organization's function. Schellenberg is the only author to provide a substantial definition of *function*, although it amounts to only a few pages.[5] Otherwise, neither the European nor the American archivists have provided their colleagues with a definition of *function*, examples, or guidelines for incorporating function into description and access.

A colleague of Schellenberg at the National Archives, E. G. Thompson, saw a role for function in the arrangement of archival records. He proposed that archival records be classified by function rather than arranged by the creating organization.[6] He felt this would remove the necessity for archivists to know and prepare detailed administrative history information for archival records. Notes of discussions held by the National Archives Finding Mediums Committee indicate that staff members were sympathetic to the idea of function but found arrangement by organization more practical for physical control of the records.[7] The complexities of providing functional access on paper were perceived as too demanding at that time to merit further pursuit.

Archivists began seriously to reconsider access to archival materials when automation became available as a tool to facilitate and increase the capacity for access. David Bearman, as director of the Society of American Archivists' National Information Systems Task Force (NISTF), especially called attention to functional access. In an article on intellectual access to archives, Bearman emphasized the need for archivists to give more concentrated attention to where, under what circumstances, and why materials were generated.[8]

The potential for providing access by function was recognized by NISTF as it worked on the MARC Format for Archives and Manuscripts Control (AMC). Among the unique characteristics provided in this revision of the earlier MARC Format for Manuscripts was an indexing field for function. While the possible uses of this field were recognized, the lack of guidelines for including function in descriptive practice, the absence of a specific vocabulary, and the lack of a clear, common understanding of the concept generally have hampered implementation.

In the past few years, several efforts have been undertaken to further clarify functional access and to provide a vocabulary for practical use. David Bearman coordinated a meeting of an ad hoc group of archivists to initiate the development of a vocabulary of function terms.[9] Terms were selected initially by reviewing a dictionary, identifying potential candidate terms, and then providing Scope Notes.

That list was taken by the RLG Seven States Project for implementation with government records. The RLG Seven States Project was a cooperative endeavor among the states of Alabama, California, Minnesota, New York, Pennsylvania, Utah, and Wisconsin funded by the National Historical Publications and Records Commission (NHPRC). The purpose of the project was to test the feasibility of creating bibliographic records for government records using the MARC AMC Format, entering them into the RLIN AMC database, and using the information for archival appraisal, scheduling, description, and reference. One of the major objectives of that project was to develop a function vocabulary to provide access to these records. To accomplish this, the project members took the previously mentioned function vocabulary, expanded it, and refined it. It was then applied to several specific kinds of government records.[10] No formal testing was conducted on the usefulness of the terminology, however.

In a related development, the Research and Evaluation Section of the National Archives undertook an investigation of function as part of its Life-Cycle Tracking Study.[11] Maintaining contact with the RLG Seven States Project, the staff of Research and Evaluation adopted the project's vocabulary lists, making additions and changes based on what it felt were terms needed at the national level. A discussion of functional access was also included in the *Life Cycle Tracking Report,* and recommendations were made   that the National Archives incorporate the use of functional access in future descriptions.

The lack of clear guidelines for including function in descriptive practice and the need for an assessment of the extant vocabulary list prompted two of the original RLG Seven States Project members (the authors of this article) to conduct further research in 1988 by a Research Fellowship Program for Study of Modern Archives, sponsored by the Bentley Historical Library. This paper, outlining the definition of *function*, was prepared, and guidelines for and examples of function in descriptive practice were identified. The function vocabulary as applied by the RLG Seven States Project was analyzed, and recommendations and initial efforts at revision were made.

More recently, discussions and collaborative efforts with the *Art and Architecture Thesaurus (AAT)* have resulted in merging the original function vocabulary with the *AAT* Functions hierarchy. This vocabulary will be further tested by the RLG Government Records Project, the successor to the Seven States Project.

PROVIDING ACCESS TO FUNCTION

When archivists describe a body of organizational records, they commonly include historical information on the creating organization. At this initial phase of research, information relating to the functions and activities of the organization should also be identified. There are several sources of that information. Basic documents produced by an organization often discuss their function or functions and activities. Government executive budgets are a common resource for such information. Annual reports, mission statements, and planning documents generally provide the organization's own statement of its functions.

This kind of information must be stated specifically in a description of archival records. For example:

Department of Health.

Reports of tuberculosis cases, 1911-1920.

5 cubic feet.

A major function of the department was to protect the health of the state's citizens. Among the activities used to accomplish this was the monitoring of incidents of communicable diseases.

This series consists of monthly statistical reports submitted by each county board of health. The reports contain the following information: city in which cases were reported; number of cases; number of cases resulting in death; actions taken to prevent spread of disease.

Functional index terms: protecting health; monitoring communicable diseases.

Once a functional statement is present in the records description, a controlled vocabulary can be used to provide common terminology to facilitate access. As the *Art and Architecture Thesaurus*[12] Functions hierarchy for function is the only extant published vocabulary for this purpose at present, its potential for identifying indexing terms will receive primary attention in the following discussion of application guidelines.

Using the records description function statement as a point of departure, a term (or terms) is located in the *AAT* Functions hierarchy to represent the function and/or activity that the archivist determines should be an access point (or access points). Some of these terms may be sufficient when used alone to describe the function. In a MARC-based automated system, the term may be entered in the 657 field, Function Term. In RLIN, this field is indexed separately. In other systems, it is incorporated into the general subject searches. Following are some examples of terms from the *AAT* Functions hierarchy:

accrediting
arbitrating
censoring
condemning
confiscating
diagnosing
disbursing
enforcing
evicting
extraditing
impeaching
lobbying
naturalizing
preserving
publicizing

In other cases, the archivist may feel it is essential to provide the object of the function for clarification. At this point, an indexing string is constructed consisting of a function term and an object term. The object term may be a thing, an organization, a person, or a sphere of activity. The object terms may be found in other *AAT* hierarchies. Two options exist for users of MARC-based systems. A newly approved faceted indexing field, 654, permits the segmentation or subfielding of the terminology into discrete facets of information. For example:

654 $a assisting $bagriculture
654 $a promoting $bhealth

If there is no need to separate the terms for indexing or if the system in use has a separate function term search, the entire string may be entered in the 657 field. For example:

657 $a assisting agriculture
657 $a promoting health

Considerable discussion may be necessary over the next few years to determine guidelines and practices for further implementation and vocabulary development. At present, the *AAT* provides the most consistent, workable structure for a functions vocabulary. Its organic nature, comprehensiveness, and the willingness of staff to work with the archival community suggest that it should be pursued for further design and implementation of functional access.

CONCLUSION

Archival and manuscript materials are unique and valuable resources for a variety of researchers from scholars to students to government officials to businesspeople. Traditional library access methods are insufficient for accurate access to archival records. Library-oriented indexing is adequate for access to information on the creation, content, and even physical character of materials. It fails, however, to provide explicit access to the context in which archival records are created, and that contextual information has significant impact on the content, character, and comprehensiveness of information in archival records. Neither researchers nor archivists themselves can hope to use and interpret accurately information in archival materials without an understanding of the context of creation and use. Furthermore, for many researchers, the process of the creation and use of archival records, not the literal subject matter of the records, is in fact the topic of their research.

Function is an additional and significant potential route of access for researchers as well as for archivists. Archival descriptions traditionally contain a significant amount of narrative information in an attempt to provide an adequate summary of records for researchers. When access to function is not provided, researchers are forced to read through that narrative and perhaps even try to determine on their own why those records were created. Despite the expectation that primary research will be demanding, it should not be necessary for the researcher to make this extra effort. Perhaps this is one of the deterrents to greater use of archival materials. By clearly describing the functions and activities that lead to the creation of archival records, archivists can provide users good descriptive information that will make searching easier.

NOTES

1. For further information on the MARC AMC Format, consult Nancy Sahli, *MARC for Archives and Manuscripts: The AMC Format* (Chicago: The Society of American Archivists, 1985).

2. Discussion of function appears in the writings of the British archivist Sir Hilary Jenkinson; the Dutch archivists Samuel Muller, J. A. Feith, and R. Fruin; and United States archivists Theodore Schellenberg, Margaret Cross Norton, and Waldo Gifford Leland.

3. A study using this functional approach to documenting university records is under way at the Massachusetts Institute of Technology Archives.

4. The Research Libraries Group Seven States Project and the Research Libraries Group Government Records Project are cooperative projects in which government records repositories enter records into the Research Libraries Information Network database and investigate various elements of description and appraisal.

5. Theodore K. Schellenberg, *Modern Archives* (Chicago: The University of Chicago Press, 1956), 15, 22, 170-74.

6. E. G. Thompson, "Functional Classification of Archival Material," *Library Quarterly* 11 (1941): 431-41.

7. Records of the National Archives RG64, Minutes of the Finding Mediums Committee, 1940, Box 353.

8. David Bearman, "Who about What or from Whence, Why and How: Implications for National Archival Information Systems." Paper presented to the Conference on Archives, Automation, and Access, University of British Columbia, Victoria, B.C., 1985.

9. David Bearman, "Functions Vocabulary." Working paper of an ad hoc meeting at the Smithsonian Institution, November 1985.

10. RLIN Seven States Project, "Spheres of Activity and Processes Lists," Research Libraries Group, 1987.

11. *The MARC Format and Life Cycle Tracking at the National Archives* (Washington, D.C.: National Archives and Records Administration, 1986).

12. *Art and Architecture Thesaurus* (New York: Oxford University Press, 1990).

■ Recent Trends in Access to Music Materials*

BRAD YOUNG

This paper identifies three recent developments that represent important new directions in subject access to music materials. For each, something of its history, its most basic concepts, and some simple examples of its potential for improved access are given. In conclusion some fundamental principles, common to all three developments, that represent the overall direction being taken toward the future of subject access to music will be enumerated.

PHOENIX 780

History of Revision

The first development to be considered is the Phoenix 780 schedule of the Dewey Decimal Classification. A Phoenix schedule is reconstructed without regard to previous divisions. Integrity of numbers is suspended, and massive relocations may occur. The recently completed revision of the Dewey Decimal Classification's music schedule is one of the most radical Phoenix schedules ever prepared. Whereas the basic arrangement of numbers does not vary greatly from that of previous editions, the amenability to synthesis – that is to say, number building – is greater than that of any ever introduced to Dewey. The new music schedule has been a largely British effort, and it reflects the widespread development of faceted classification in the United Kingdom and the work of the Classification Research Group

---

*This paper was originally presented at the American Library Association's Annual Conference in New York in 1986.

(1955), formed in 1952 to review the basic principles of bibliographic classification.

Music was among the Dewey classes suggested by the Library Association for major revision in 1973. A revision project team, Russell Sweeney and John Clews, began work at Leeds Polytechnic in 1974. In 1975 a draft revision was submitted to the Decimal Classification Editorial Policy Committee, an independent body that advises Forest Press, publisher of Dewey. After considerable discussion, a revised text (Sweeney, 1980) was approved for separate publication in 1979. Review continued, and, in 1985, with further revision, the new schedule was accepted for inclusion in the twentieth edition of Dewey Decimal Classification (1989).

The Phoenix 780 has not yet been implemented in the United States. The proposed revision, however, has been used since 1982 for the *British Catalogue of Music* (BCM 1957-), a bibliography of printed music currently published in the United Kingdom. It is a classed catalog that previously employed a faceted classification devised for it by E. J. Coates (1961). The construction of the new schedule has been based on Coates's analysis of the subject although the arrangement differs in many areas.

Its Faceted Character

The Phoenix 780 is most similar to Coates's classification in its faceted character (Philp, 1982, Wursten, 1984). This is its most striking and radical feature. Previous Dewey schedules have made use of synthesis to varying degrees, with the standard subdivisions found in Figure 1 being the best known example. Here the digit *zero* is used as a facet indicator to identify the addition of a standard subdivision. The Phoenix 780 also employs the digit *one* as a facet indicator. This is accomplished by reserving 780.1-780.9 for standard subdivisions and 781.1-781.9 for general principles applicable to the rest of the schedule. This allows numbers from different parts of the schedule, each expressing a discrete concept, to be joined together with great flexibility for the representation of complex topics. Numbers follow a specified citation order for the concepts present according to the facet of music represented by each. Thus the classification of a score would begin with the medium of performance. To this would be added a number for the form of composition. Other facets would be added as applicable in accordance with the citation order expressed in the schedule. Although the classification would permit synthesis of all the characteristics present, it is recommended that no class number contain more than three. In building numbers the classifier is instructed not to add to the base number by the use of a facet indicator more than twice; however, it is optional to continue to add as many times as desired.

Figure 1

Pentecost cantata for mixed voices with strings -- Scores.

7   8   2.   5   5'   2   4'   1   6   3   2'   9   9   3'   0   2   7

7

             Fine arts

  8

             Music

   2.

          Vocal music
       [782.5-782.9 Vocal executants]

    5

          Mixed voices

MEDIUM   5

           Accompanied

      2

        Nondramatic vocal forms
     [782.23-782.29 Specific sacred vocal forms]

FORM   4

          Sacred cantatas

       1

         General principles;
    Add to 1 the numbers following 781 in 781.1-781.9

        6

    Traditions of music and specific kinds of music

        3

         Sacred music

        2

       Christian sacred music

        9

     Music of the Christian church year

        9

       Pentecost and Trinity

FUNCTION   3

        Pentecost

FORMAT   027
  Standard subdivision to distinguish scores from books about music

Analyzing and Example

This number-building process can be seen in Figure 1 by examining an example based on the revised 780 schedule. A summary is given for a moderately complex topic: the score of a Pentecost cantata for mixed voices with strings. Following the citation order specified, the medium of performance is the first facet represented: 782–vocal music; 782.5–mixed voices; 782.55–accompanied mixed voices. The schedule instructs the classifier to add digits representing a specifically vocal form of composition taken from 782.2–nondramatic vocal forms: 782.24–sacred vocal forms, specifically sacred cantata. Note that no facet indicator is required. The schedule further instructs the classifier to add digits representing a general principle, in this case music for Pentecost. It is taken from 781.6 – traditions and specific kinds of music, becoming progressively specific: sacred music – Christian music – music for the church – music for Pentecost and Trinity – music for Pentecost, that is, 781.632993. The digits following 78 are added to the base number for sacred cantatas for accompanied mixed voices. Note that the facet indicator *one* is included here. The number is completed by the addition of the standard subdivision 027, which distinguishes printed music from literature about music. This includes the second use of a facet indicator, in this case *zero*.

Other standard subdivisions might have been applied, as appropriate. For geographic treatment: – 09433 for a book about Bavarian Pentecost cantatas for accompanied mixed voices. For historical treatment: – 09032 for one about Baroque Pentecost cantatas for accompanied mixed voices. It would be possible to represent another general principle: – 1256, using the digit *one* as a facet indicator, for harmonic rhythm in Pentecost cantatas for accompanied mixed voices. The schedule specifies the order for these additions. With the option of full synthesis, additional facets could be included beyond the usual limit.

Potential for Online Document Retrieval

From this example, it should be clear that Phoenix 780 is highly amenable to expressing the relationship among discrete concepts in a complex topic. With full synthesis, the resulting number would be correspondingly long and complex. Such a number would be too long to be useful for shelf location and more complex than needed for browsing. To comprehend the usefulness of full synthesis, it is helpful to recall the influence exerted on the new schedule by Coates's BCM classification. It was devised for the retrieval of documents in a classed catalog rather than for shelf arrangement. The strength of the revised 780 is this: its great potential for use in online document retrieval. This application can be employed without regard to shelf arrangement. The example just considered illustrates this. The concept of Pentecost music, falling near the end of the citation order, could not be found in browsing the shelf. However, an online search could isolate this aspect of the topic through coding techniques that permit recognition of individual facets within a synthesized number. Arnold Wajenberg (1983) has advocated the addition of such coding to the MARC formats. Scores and recordings of Pentecost music and literature about it could all be retrieved without regard to other facets present. Multiple facets could also be retrieved. These features present potential for much more flexible access than that provided by current methods of subject cataloging. Development of authority records for class numbers could also be used to support this application. An online search would employ the schedule and relative index as an interface. This would display synonymous and hierarchical relationships among search terms and link each to the digits representing it wherever located within synthesized class numbers.

Figure 2

	BCM classification for Bach's counterpoint in his organ fugues				
BBC		Bach			
AR			Organ		
A/Y				Fugues	
A/RM					Counterpoint
			Index entries produced by chain technique		
Counterpoint: Fugue: Organ: Bach				BBCAR/Y/RM	
Fugue: Organ: Bach				BBCAR/Y	
Organ: Bach				BBCAR	
Bach				BBC	

PRECIS

The next development to be considered here is PRECIS. The Preserved Context Indexing System was developed for use in MARC records produced for the *British National Bibliography*. Like the Phoenix 780, it shows the influence of the Classification Research Group. PRECIS was first applied to music in the 1984 issues of the *British Catalogue of Music*. It has been published since 1957 by the *British National Bibliography* and is now produced at the British Library, Bibliographic Services Division. Issued quarterly, cumulated annually, it is a classed catalog with two indexes – one for names and titles, another for subjects.

Subject entries were originally generated from Coates's faceted classification by the technique of chain indexing (Redfern, 1979). This method employs a string, or chain, of terms, each of which represents a different level in the classification, from the most specific to the most broad. The chain is permuted by the indexer to produce a series of entries in which each term in succession appears as the entry element, followed by the terms hierarchically above it in the classification. These broader terms serve to give the context for the more specific entry. This technique was often used to produce the subject index to a classed catalog. Figure 2 presents an example from Coates's BCM classification for Bach's counterpoint in his organ fugues. The notation for this topic is BBCAR/Y/RM. The hierarchical chain of terms is derived from the faceted classification as indicated above. The corresponding index entries produced by chain technique are given in Figure 2.

PRECIS, now used to produce subject entries although not classification based, is in no small part derived from the chain technique. Adoption of Dewey and PRECIS brought the *British Catalogue of Music* into step with the *British National Bibliography*. While a faceted classification and chain index unique to music have been replaced with systems consistent with mainstream practice, BCM's basic concepts of subject access have remained much the same. Neither technique has had widespread use in this country. They remain unknown to many American librarians.

At the simplest level, PRECIS can be explained as an indexing system based on the construction of a string of terms that summarize the subject content of a document. To preserve natural word order, connective terms and substitutions are added. The string is then coded to produce individual entries by machine manipulation. For the purpose of this discussion, there are three salient features: Entries are produced by machine manipulation of the coded strings; entry is made for each significant term in the string; each entry is coextensive with the subject content as expressed in the string.

PRECIS entries for BCM are constructed according to the *Code of Practice for the Application of PRECIS* prepared expressly for the use of its indexers by Derek Austin, principal architect of PRECIS (Austin, 1985). It presents eight paradigms for the construction and coding of strings based on the facets of subject analysis identified in the document at hand. The proper paradigm can be selected by applying a decision table to three questions: Is the form of music known? Is the kind of performer known? Is the number of performers known? Detailed guidelines are included for choice and order of terms in strings and phrases, especially those for medium of performance.

The new directions PRECIS offers for subject access to music may best be demonstrated by comparing some PRECIS strings from the *British Catalogue of Music*, the entries produced from them, and the *Library of Congress Subject Headings* assigned to the same work. In Figures 3, 4, and 5, the centered PRECIS string appears as it would in the classed portion of the catalog as a caption identifying the class number. The PRECIS entries generated from each string appear as jp187

they would in the alphabetical subject index.

Figure 3

PRECIS STRING
    Piano solo

PRECIS ENTRIES
    Pianos
        Piano solo

LCSH
    Piano music

PRECIS STRING
    Opera – Vocal scores.

PRECIS ENTRIES
    Opera
        Vocal scores

LCSH
    Operas – Vocal scores with piano.

The first item in Figure 3 represents the facet of medium – piano; the second, form – opera. In these, the structure and vocabulary of entry, but not the essential access, differ.

In the first example in Figure 4, both form and medium are present. There are PRECIS entries for each; the Library of Congress subject heading is entered under the first. This is followed by an example of medium expressed in a compound term. Again there is a PRECIS entry for each term; the Library of Congress heading is entered under the first. In both of these cases, the *LCSH* syndetic structure could, but does not, provide an explicit link from the terms not used for entry.

Figure 4

PRECIS STRING
    Sonatas for organ solo

PRECIS ENTRIES
    Organs
            Organ solo. Sonatas
    Sonatas
            For organ solo

LCSH
    Sonatas (Organ).

PRECIS STRING
    Oboe and bassoon

PRECIS ENTRIES
    Bassoons
            Oboe and bassoon
    Oboes
            Oboe and bassoon

LCSH
    Bassoon and oboe music.

Figure 5 illustrates the access PRECIS provides for a complex topic that the *LCSH* can express only by the use of multiple headings. Both the PRECIS and *LCSH* entries provide access to all three important terms. Each of the PRECIS entries is coextensive with the subject, while none of the Library of Congress subject headings expresses the complete topic. This could be achieved only by combining them in a postcoordinate search, not possible in the card files for which they were intended. To find Christmas

carols for mixed voices, the user would have to select one term and search the entire file for the presence of the other two facets.

Figure 5

```
PRECIS STRING
     Christmas carols for mixed voices with keyboard


PRECIS ENTRIES
     Carols
             Christmas carols for mixed voices with keyboard
     Christmas carols
             For mixed voices with keyboard
     Mixed voices
             For mixed voices with keyboard. Christmas carols


LCSH
     Carols, English.
     Choruses, Sacred (Mixed voices, 4 parts) with piano.
     Christmas music.
```

When only a single element is present in the subject analysis, the access provided by PRECIS and *LCSH* differs little. As the number of terms required to express the topic and the complexity of their relationship increase, the potential for greater access offered by PRECIS becomes more apparent (Gabbard, 1985).

Figure 6 demonstrates a complex example of a type not infrequently encountered with music material. Several facets–form, medium, and function–are present, and several indexable terms are required to express the medium of performance. PRECIS not only provides entries under many terms, but, unlike the multiple Library of Congress headings, preserves the context of each term among the others. When compared to other machine-manipulated index systems, such as KWIC or KWOC title indexes, each entry is readily comprehensible and elegantly expressed in the syntax of natural language. Although developed for machine manipulation in the production of offline products, PRECIS has a potential amenability for online searching that could incorporate its capacity for clarity and attractive display.

Figure 6

PRECIS STRING
    Whitsun cantatas for soprano and bass solos and mixed voices with
    string instruments and continuo

PRECIS ENTRIES
    Bass voices
        Soprano and bass solos and mixed voices with string
    instruments and continuo. Whitsun cantatas
    Cantatas
        Whitsun cantatas for soprano and bass solos and mixed voices
    with string instruments and continuo
    Mixed voices
        Soprano and bass solos and mixed voices with string
    instruments and continuo. Whitsun cantatas
    Soprano voices
        Soprano and bass solos and mixed voices with string
    instruments and continuo. Whitsun cantatas
    String instuments
        Soprano and bass solos and mixed voices with string
    instruments and continuo. Whitsun cantatas
    Whitsun cantatas
        For soprano and bass solos and mixed voices with string
    instruments and continuo

LCSH
    Cantatas, Sacred – Scores.
    Pentecost festival music.

MARC MUSIC FORMAT

History

The last development to be considered is the MARC Music Format, which was begun by Mary Lou Little, the music librarian at Harvard, in 1969. In looking for ways to develop an enhanced music catalog, she realized that, if cataloging information were put into a computer, it could not only be readily shared but also manipulated in ways not previously contemplated. A diversity of new queries could be satisfied. She adapted the MARC Books Format for use with sound recordings.

In 1970 she sent a copy of her adapted format to the Library of Congress. In cooperation with Little, the MARC Development Office prepared the first draft of *Sound Recordings: A MARC Format*. This was presented at the Music Library Association's annual meeting in 1971. Representatives of the association were intimately involved in further developments. The format was expanded to include printed and manuscript music, and provision was made for new types of coded data not previously included in MARC formats. MLA representatives believed that encoded subject analysis was necessary to exploit the format's full potential and envisioned a faceted arrangement that these data would make feasible (Seibert, 1982).

Fixed Fields

The MARC formats were originally conceived as devices for the transmission of bibliographic data. They also carry data intended to facilitate their retrieval. As a means of storing and retrieving data about music material, the MARC Music Format is an important new direction for subject access because it offers a greater potential for searching than traditional catalogs do. This retrieval function is concentrated in the coded data carried by its fixed and control fields. Most of these coded data duplicate those contained elsewhere in the bibliographic record, such as the coded data for the place and date of publication. These fields can also carry coded information not included in the bibliographic data. They offer an enhanced capability for retrieval not only because they carry data not previously available but also because the computer can combine them in multifaceted searches better adapted to individual needs than the standardized access points of traditional catalogs.

Coded information found elsewhere in the record and that not found elsewhere are both included in the music format. Some of these types of information are also found in other formats; some are unique to music. Development of the MARC Music Format was of course strongly influenced by the book and film formats. Fields taken from these formats included a detailed coded physical description useful for retrieval of the great variety of physical formats found in music material, especially sound recordings. Others include detailed codes for the languages involved in translations and other multilingual items and for the place and date of capture for sound recordings. Additional fields unique to the music format were added. Among these are medium of performance, form of composition or musical genre, and, for printed music, format of score and presence of parts.

Music Specific Fields

Two types of coded data unique to the music format are especially important for subject access. These are the form and genre codes and those for medium of performance. Very elaborate and exhaustive lists of codes for musical form and genre were originally suggested. This was not considered feasible because their application would require so much subject analysis beyond that usually provided. Because Library of Congress subject headings were usually present, it was suggested that the form codes be drawn from them. The resulting list was found to be unbalanced and to lack some important terms. As a compromise a list was compiled of terms that are emphasized in the major histories of music, in hope of providing a consensus based on actual use. In this way the list of codes finally adopted supplements the *Library Of Congress Subject Headings* in that there are several significant variations. The MARC codes include forms not found in *LCSH* – for example, ricercar, fantasia, and divertimento. *LCSH* includes terms for many individual dance forms. The MARC codes include only the most important of these.

The codes for medium of performance provide detailed access to the type and number of voices, instruments, and ensembles present. Specific codes are provided for all the major instruments used in Western art music. Any number of these elements can be combined. In many cases this gives more information than is contained in *Library Of Congress Subject Headings*, particularly for large-scale works, large ensembles, and accompanying ensembles. The most important reason for medium of performance codes in the music format is so they can be combined with other coded data, such as form of composition, language, date of composition, and so on, in forming flexible search strategies. They also accommodate the production of elaborate bibliographies and discographies for particular instruments, voices, or combinations.

The potential value of combining these codes for document retrieval can be appreciated by comparing some possible searches with the access provided by *Library Of Congress Subject Headings*. A search for vocal scores of Italian operas of the Baroque period would require searching the entire file under a broad heading such as OPERAS – VOCAL SCORES WITH PIANO for the period and language desired. Using the codes for language, chronological coverage, form of composition, and format of score, it should be possible to retrieve a list of items corresponding to the desired topic. A more complex search for all types of chamber music including a part for the viola would require searching numerous Library of Congress headings where viola is buried in ensemble headings – for example, PIANO QUARTETS, STRING TRIOS, or TRIOS (PIANO, CLARINET, VIOLA). Music including a solo voice may have a very general heading such as SONGS WITH INSTRUMENTAL ENSEMBLE in which the presence of the viola part is obscured.

Other useful searches can be made by combining subject and non-subject codes: jazz trumpet music recorded in Memphis before 1945, piano music in braille, recordings of German songs that include English translations, or editions of Baroque keyboard music published since the Second World War. All of these would be invaluable to particular scholars, performers, or teachers.

While most of these coded data have not yet been widely used, the Rutgers University's Institute for Jazz Studies has utilized both variable and control fields in producing computer output microfiche indexes to its holdings of jazz recordings. The powerful new direction in subject access to music presented by the MARC Music Format is the possibility of online postcoordinate searching. The format's planners had this in mind from its inception. Divorcing themselves from the mentality of traditional catalogs, they sought to provide a means for more flexible subject access in the future.

THESAURI

The desire for enhancements to subject access for music materials is revealed in several efforts resulting from the use of thesauri. A thesaurus has been provided to assist in searching the descriptors used in the *RILM* bibliographic database of literature about music (*RILM Thesaurus*, 1976; Bliss, 1988). A retrospective conversion project for ethnomusicology material at UCLA has included the assignment of descriptors drawn from standard reference sources in the field (Rahkonen, 1988). Because recognized codes are already used in ethnomusicology, coded access points appear particularly attractive in that area. The *Outline of World Cultures* (Murdock, 1983), used to organize the Human Relations Area Files, provides comprehensive codes for ethnic and cultural groups. Similarly, the Sachs-Hornbostel numbers (Hornbostel, 1914) give a detailed cross-cultural classification of musical instruments according to type. By combining the code for an instrument type with that for a cultural group, one should be able to retrieve material related to a number of similar instruments, each of which may have several names. This could be invaluable for control of ethnic field recordings; otherwise, a great number of obscure names would need to be identified and searched. In 1984 the Music Library Association established a working group to explore initiating a Music Thesaurus Project similar to the *Art and Architecture Thesaurus* Project (McKnight, 1989). Interest in such thesauri shows recognition of the value standardized postcoordinate descriptors hold for subject access to music material.

CONCLUSION

This brief overview is intended to give some insight into the new directions being taken in subject access to music material. It is not possible at this point to predict which, if any, will come to be widely used either alone or in conjunction with others. There are, however, some underlying principles common to them all. These fundamental concepts may represent the future direction that subject access to music can be expected to take, whether it be through these particular projects or through others not yet begun.

The two general questions about extending MARC for improved subject access to nontraditional materials are directly addressed by these basic concepts. Do nonbook materials require different kinds of subject access than textual materials require? Based on the new directions examined here, subject access to music is seen to require two things now generally lacking in standard subject cataloging.

The first is non-topical access points (Smiraglia, 1985). A piano sonata is not about piano sonatas; it is one. This need has been recognized for other nonbook material. Word processing software is not about word processing. The need for non-topical access is coming to be more widely recognized even for books themselves. A MARC field has been proposed to provide retrieval by genre – Westerns, mysteries, Gothics, and the like – for literary works. Thesauri for bibliographic and literary form or genre and for physical characteristics have been developed for rare books (*Genre Terms*, 1983).

The other requirement is retrieval of multi-element access points. This grows from the non-topical descriptors applied to music and the frequent desire for retrieval of a work by more than one facet of its description. The necessity has been recognized for retrieval by each indexable term, or by all indexable terms, or by any combination thereof. The direction taken by information retrieval research during the last twenty years testifies to the widespread acceptance of the need for this retrieval capacity for all types of material.

Because music comprises a particular subject as well as particular types of material, it will always require a unique indexing vocabulary, but the kinds of subject access required do not differ from those required for other material, book or nonbook.

Does online access offer new opportunities to provide subject access to nonbook material? Although all the developments discussed here are capable of supporting either manual use or the production of offline products, the most effective potential for dramatic improvements in subject access to music lies in the capacity for interactive, online searching. All of these projects seem predicated on a perception that inevitably, online retrieval is the environment in which future subject access will exist.

REFERENCES

Austin, Derek. *British Catalogue of Music Code of Practice for the Application of PRECIS*. London: British Library Bibliographic Services Division, 1985. For internal use.

Bliss, Marilyn. "Indexing Policy of RILM: Present Perspectives and Future Prospects." *Fontes Artis Musicae* 35 (July 1988): 189-194.

The British Catalogue of Music. London: British Library Bibliographic Services Division, 1957-. Published by the Council of the British National Bibliography, 1957-1961.

Classification Research Group. "The Need for a Faceted Classification as the Basis of all Methods of Information Retrieval." UNESCO document 320/515, 1955. Reprinted in Lois Mai Chan. *Theory of Subject Analysis: a Sourcebook*. Littleton, Colo.: Libraries Unlimited, 1985.

Coates, Eric J. *Subject Catalogues*. London: Library Association, 1961.

Dewey Decimal Classification. 20th ed. 3 vols. Albany: OCLC Forest Press, 1989.

Gabbard, Paula Beversdorf. "LCSH and PRECIS in Music: a Comparison." *Library Quarterly* 55 (April 1985): 192-206.

Genre Terms: A Thesaurus for Use in Rare Book and Special Collections Cataloguing. Standards Committee of the Rare Books and Manuscripts Section ACRL/ALA. Chicago: Association of College and Research Libraries, 1983.

Hornbostel, E. M. von and Curt Sachs. "Systematik der Musikinstrumente: Ein Versuch." *Zeitschrift fur Ethnologie* (1914): 4-5.

McKnight, Mark. "Improving Access to Music: a Report of the MLA Music Thesaurus Project Working Group." *Notes* 45 (June 1989): 714-721.

Murdock, George Peter. *Outline of World Cultures*. 6th rev. ed. New Haven: Human Relations Area Files, 1983.

Philp, Geraint H. "Proposed Revision of 780 Music and Problems in the Development of Faceted Classification for Music." *Brio* 19 (1982): 2-13.

Rahkonen, Carl. "Databases and Networks for Archives of Traditional Music." *Notations*. 10 (Spring 1988): 11-15.

Redfern, Brian. *Organizing Music in Libraries*. 2 vols. London: C. Bingley, 1979.

RILM Thesaurus: Subject Headings for Cumulative Index of RILM Abstracts. rev. New York: RILM Abstracts, 1976.

Seibert, Donald. *The MARC Music Format: From Inception to Publication.* MLA Technical Report no. 13. Philadelphia: Music Library Association, 1982.

Smiraglia, Richard P. "Theoretical Considerations in the Bibliographic Control of Music Materials in Libraries." *Cataloging & Classification Quarterly* 5 (Spring 1985): 11-14.

Sweeney, Russell. *Proposed Revision of 780 Music: Based on Dewey Decimal Classification and Relative Index.* Albany, N.Y.: Forest Press, 1980. Prepared under the direction of Russell Sweeney and John Clews with assistance from Winton E. Matthews, Jr.

Wajenberg, Arnold S. "MARC Coding of DDC for Subject Retrieval." *Information Technology and Libraries.* 2 (September 1983): 246-51.

Wursten, Richard. "Review of Proposed Revision of 780 Music." *Cataloging & Classification Quarterly* 5 (Fall 1984): 57f.

■ Cataloging an Artifact in the USMARC Format: What Is It? What Is It About?

LINDA J. EVANS

Books are three-dimensional artifacts and are encompassed by the dictionary definition of *realia*. Library catalogers, however, rarely think of them in those terms because professional training and experience with *Anglo-American Cataloguing Rules*, second edition (*AACR 2*)[1] has separated items usually classified as published volumes from materials discussed in other chapters of *AACR 2*, particularly in chapter 10: "Three-Dimensional Artefacts and Realia." The public as well as information professionals have accepted this division. Library users are especially grateful to a reference librarian who can find the specific "large book with a green binding and silver lettering on the spine" that they are seeking because they do not consider the retrieval of a book by physical characteristics to fall within the librarian's normal responsibilities.

When catalogers and researchers deal with artifacts collected by museums, their assumptions are different. They expect catalogs to identify objects by physical characteristics, form/genre, and purpose (the object's identity) as well as by its subject (what it is about or what it depicts). For users of the *USMARC Format for Bibliographic Data* (*MFBD*), the differentiation between the identity and the subject of the item is an area in flux while new communities of MARC catalogers define their needs.

It is judicious to pause at the beginning and acknowledge that the preceding generalizations reflect boundaries that have developed between professional disciplines and types of institutions. These boundaries are not absolute. When curators speak of museum artifacts, they usually do not assume that published books are included, although catalog records for rare books may include as much detail about the physical qualities and provenance of the items as are found in other records for artifacts. Similarly, one may not expect to find cataloging of three-dimensional objects in library catalogs, but some librarians have been cataloging artifacts for years, often in MARC records. School, university, and public librarians, especially, have created many MARC records for sculpture, models, kits, games, and toys that are lent to borrowers. Furthermore, it is not uncommon for librarians to catalog equipment such as slide projectors or even book trucks because they want to be able to track them through the circulation control module that is part of their MARC-based computer system.[2]

What is new about artifact cataloging in MARC records is the need to accommodate additional data elements in these records for the organized communities of curators, museum registrars, archivists, and special librarians who expect to play roles in establishing additional standards for the content of MARC records and to accommodate the large number of artifact records that will be created in coming years as more museums invest in computer cataloging. Creating large numbers of nonstandard fields containing usage patterns that conflict with existing description practices would be counterproductive for the established community of MARC users as well as for the new groups that want to take advantage of the software and services available for MARC records. It is possible to modify old standards and to promulgate new ones, but the process of setting standards must seek a consensus that serves the entire MARC constituency.

Museum cataloging utilizes additional data elements because museums typically operate on somewhat different assumptions about their holdings than do libraries that catalog artifacts in their circulating collections. Generally, museum holdings are unique or rare and are intended to be preserved for intensive study and exhibition. Moreover, artifacts that are not rare or outstanding may be acquired because they are representative of cultures, purposes, events, or individuals. Thus, museums are very concerned with the appearance of artifacts (size, component materials, color, style, etc.). They want cataloging to provide the kind of thorough description and access points that, ideally, can guide even specialists with abstruse inquiries to relevant holdings. Also, they need to account for the unique, rare, and representative characteristics that motivated the institution to accession the artifact into the permanent collection.[3]

The MARC-VM record structure, which has served librarians well, already accommodates many of these data elements. Published and unpublished, two-dimensional and three-dimensional materials share many common data elements – main entry (artist, maker, author, etc.), title, extent, date of production (publication), to name only a few of the most obvious. The similarities are illustrated by the sample artifact record in this essay, which shows data describing a man's leisure suit from the 1960s with MARC coding (Figure 1) and as it may be displayed in an online catalog or a checklist without MARC coding (Figure 2). The sample record does not show 655 and 755 fields, which contain headings that serve as access points. These are discussed later in this article.[4]

Figure 1   Artifact Record With MARC-VM Coding

TYPE	r	REC STAT	n	BIB LVL	c
GOVT PUB	ƀ	INT LVL	ƀ	LANG	N/A
SOURCE	d	DESC	a	CTRY	itƀ
LENG	nnn	TECH	n	DATE TP	s
ENC LVL	I	MOD REC	ƀ	DATES	1969 ƀƀƀƀ
TYPE MAT	r	ACCOMP MAT	ƀƀƀƀ		

040 ƀ/ƀ/ $a   ICHi $c ICHi

099 ƀ ƀ $a   C1978 $a .0144 $a .0001 $a a-c

245 0 0 $a   [Man's leisure suit ensemble] $h [realia].

260 ƀ ƀ $c   [1969].

300 ƀ ƀ $a   1 jacket : $ƀ wool, tan.

300 ƀ ƀ/$a   1 trousers : $ƀ wool, tan.

300 ƀ ƀ/$a   1 belt : $ƀ leather, dark brown ; $c 1 1/4 in. wide.

520 8 ƀ $a   Jacket of tan wool with pointed convertible collar, long sleeves with two tan buttons at cuffs, two rectangular patch breast pockets with simulated pointed flap trim, two large patch hip pockets with pointed flaps, two vertical tucks between breast and hip pockets, large belt carrier on each side seam, center front closure with five tan buttons, horizontal yoke across back; topstitching on all seams; short slit in each side seam starting several inches above hem. Matching straight legged trousers of tan wool with set-in waistband with six belt loops, zipper fly front, two front pockets with diagonal openings, two horizontal slash pockets at back with a tan button on each.

520 8 ƀ $a   Wide belt of dark brown leather with large rectangular buckle of gold finished metal.

500 ƀ ƀ $a   Label in jacket: Rafael \ Made in Italy.

561 ƀ ƀ/$a   Purchased by the donor at Bonwit Teller in 1969.

541 b b $a   Doe, John $b 1611 Clark St, Chicago, IL 60614 $c Gift $d 1978/02/03 $e C1978.00144.0001a-c

710 2 ƀ $a   Rafael.

710 2 ƀ $a   Bonwit Teller & Co.

752 ƀ ƀ $a   Italy.

852 ƀ ƀ $c   Drawer 62 $j C1978.0144.0001a-b $3 suit

852 ƀ ƀ $c   Shelf 10 $j C1978.0144.0001c $3 belt

Figure 2 Artifact Record in a Public Display Version

DEPT	COS
CALL	C1978 .0144 .0001 a-c
MAIN	
TITL	[Man's leisure suit ensemble] [realia].
DATE	[1969].
QUAN	1 jacket : wool, tan.
QUAN	1 trousers : wool, tan.
QUAN	1 belt : leather, dark brown; 1 1/4 in. wide.
NOTE	Jacket of tan wool with pointed convertible collar, long sleeves with two tan buttons at cuffs, two rectangular patch breast pockets with simulated pointed flap trim, two large patch hip pockets with pointed flaps, two vertical tucks between breast and hip pockets, large belt carrier on each side seam, center front closure with five tan buttons, horizontal yoke across back; topstitching on all seams; short slit in each side seam starting several inches above hem. Matching straight legged trousers of tan wool with set-in waistband with six belt loops, zipper fly front, two front pockets with diagonal openings, two horizontal slash pockets at back with a tan button on each.
NOTE	Wide belt of dark brown leather with large rectangular buckle of gold finished metal.
NOTE	Label in jacket: Rafael \ Made in Italy.
NOTE	Purchased by the donor at Bonwit Teller in 1969.

A variety of other artifacts could have served as the example, but a clothing ensemble offers a challenge to the MARC format's ability to accommodate three-dimensional artifacts and art. It is about as different from a book in a circulating library as any item can be. It may contain multiple parts with different characteristics, identification numbers, and storage locations.[5]

circulating library as any item can be. It may contain multiple parts with different characteristics, identification numbers, and storage locations.[5]

It should not be surprising that description of three-dimensional artifacts fits so easily into a MARC record. The format provides a structure of fields and subfields, many of them variable in length and repeatable. Thus, it is very flexible. The sample record was created by taking data from an existing accession sheet and assigning each piece of information to appropriate MARC fields. The MARC format allows many more fields and subfields than are used in this record, but a cataloger is not required to fill in every available field. Some fields will not be relevant to a given item, and often a cataloger will not know a great deal about a particular artifact. The subfields are available, if needed, to segment the description into labeled units (e.g., Manufacturer, Place of Manufacture) that a computer can recognize. The format provides a structure to contain the data but in most cases does not specify the form of the data to be input. For example, the format provides a field to contain the title (field 245, Title Statement) but does not tell catalogers how to formulate or transcribe a title.

MARC does not oblige catalogers to follow *AACR 2* standards for the content of a record. For catalogers of unpublished, three-dimensional artifacts, however, there is little difficulty in meeting present-day content standards of the library or museum communities because the present standards are minimal. The applicable *AACR 2* chapter does little more than tell the cataloger to give basic information about the artifact with specified punctuation, also minimal. *AACR 2* is oriented, of course, to the needs of the library community. For example, in the *AACR 2* section pertaining to physical description of artifacts, it gives a few specific terms for artifacts (diorama, exhibit, game, microscope slide, mock-up, model) that the creators of *AACR 2* had anticipated cataloging. Then chapter 10.5B1 continues, "If none of the terms is appropriate, give the specific name of the item or the names of the parts of the item as concisely as possible." In a MARC record, this object term would appear in subfield $a (Extent) of field 300 (Physical Description).

The title is another very important part of an artifact description where *AACR 2* offers little guidance for naming the unpublished, three-dimensional artifacts typically found in museum collections. *AACR 2* chapter 1.1B7 says, "If no title can be found in any source, devise a brief descriptive title." Museum catalogers must rely on their own traditions in formulating titles. Because exhibition labels and the text for checklists may be derived from MARC records, catalogers will want to assign titles that can serve these collection management purposes with little or no editing.[6]

The sample record follows this practice. It describes an ensemble of items that were worn together. Therefore, it represents a group or collection record where the grouping is based on provenance. This grouping is convenient, also, because it is likely that these items will be exhibited together, and so the MARC record may provide an exhibition checklist entry. It would be permissible to catalog the belt in a separate record, but this seems unnecessary when one record can describe it within the context of the ensemble. The ensemble is given a title according to an in-house naming convention that places first the sex/age group of the clothing, tries to incorporate significant identifying characteristics of an ensemble, and encompasses all parts of the ensemble:

245 10 $a [Man's leisure suit ensemble].

The maker Rafael is given as a corporate added entry (field 710) rather than as a main entry (field 110) because it is the suit maker/manufacturer and is not responsible for the creation of the entire ensemble described by the record. This is one of many patterns for handling the role of main entry or chief responsibility. The *MFBD* allows a variety of strategies for handling the entity or entities chiefly responsible for creating the object. For example, the 1xx main entry field, which accommodates one name, may not satisfy the curator or registrar who needs to enter names of several makers or others responsible for creating the artifact. Librarians encounter this problem, too, for works of joint authorship or shared responsibility, and the MARC format provides repeatable fields for these Added Entries (fields 700-730). Included in the Main Entry and Added Entry fields are relator subfield e, where the cataloger may specify the relationship of the name to the object in a few words (e.g., editor, collector) and subfield 4, where the cataloger may assign codes for such relationships (e.g., *cst* for costume designer, *fmo* for former owner).

To review, the MARC Main Entry and Title fields offer artifact catalogers the data elements they need. The variable length, repeatable 5xx fields for notes, and other information allow catalogers great flexibility in composing descriptions. Additionally, fields 541 (Immediate Source of Acquisition) and 583 (Action Note) allow catalogers to input collection management data relating to accessioning, conservation, processing, loans, and so on. Where, then, are changes most needed in the present USMARC structure to better accommodate cataloging of three-dimensional artifacts? The fields that serve as access points when searching the records in a MARC-based computer system are an area of concern. It is essential that headings in the 6xx and 7xx fields separate the identification of the objects from the subjects shown or discussed in the artifacts. Catalogers must be able to link the name of an artifact (e.g., LEISURE SUIT) to modifying terms for associated characteristics (e.g., LEISURE SUIT – LIGHT BROWN – WOOL).

Fields 655 (Index Term – Genre/Form) and 755 (Added Entry – Physical Characteristics) were added to the *USMARC Format for Bibliographic Data* to help catalogers differentiate between attributes of an item (entered in fields 655 and 755) and the subject entries placed in the established field 650 (Subject Added Entry–Topical Heading). Fields 655 and 755 are repeatable, and each provides one subfield $a to contain the main term and repeatable subfields $x (General subdivision), subfields $y (Chronological subdivision), and subfields $z (Geographical subdivision).[7]

Catalogers may enter terms from *Library of Congress Subject Headings* (*LCSH*) in fields 655 and 755, but when these terms appear there, they identify the object (e.g., LOCOMOTIVES, CUPS AND SAUCERS, COATS) and not its subject. When these terms appear in the subject field 650, they name objects that are *subjects* of the work being cataloged. For example, an *LCSH* term like THEATRICAL POSTERS may be assigned as a topical subject heading in a field 650 in a catalog record for a book *about* theatrical posters. However, a cataloger creating a record for an original theatrical poster usually would not consider that term as describing the *subject* of the poster. Perhaps the poster shows an actor portraying a famous person, a leading actress, or other scenes and announcements. Almost certainly, the poster does not show or discuss theatrical posters.[8]

Catalogers of archives, film, photographs, rare books, and other materials have been quick to implement this distinction between the fields and to adopt new thesauri or controlled vocabulary lists of terms for form/genre and physical characteristics in fields 655 and 755. *LCSH* terms may be assigned in fields 655 and 755 as well, but, unlike the new thesauri developed for particular types of materials, *LCSH* is not a specialized thesaurus and does not offer enough specific terms to satisfy catalogers in all disciplines. One must remember that *Library of Congress Subject Headings* has developed over many decades to provide subject headings primarily for published works, mostly books. Subjects too narrow, obscure, or specialized to be the topics of books are unlikely to be found in *LCSH*. Also, terms in *LCSH* often are phrased broadly to encompass a general subject area, such as FOLKLORE AND CHILDREN or CLOCKS AND WATCHES, rather than broken apart into component concepts.

The sample record for the leisure suit is unusual among artifact records in the number of *LCSH* terms that are applicable in its 655 and 755 fields. They are:

655 ᵇ7 $a Men's clothing. $2 lcsh
655 ᵇ7 $a Belts (Clothing). $2 lcsh
655 ᵇ7 $a Coats. $2 lcsh
655 ᵇ7 $a Trousers. $2 lcsh
655 ᵇ7 $a Sport clothes. $2 lcsh
755 ᵇᵇ$a Wool. $2 lcsh
755 ᵇᵇ$a Leather. $2 lcsh

To a certain extent, fields 655 and 755 are an area of the MARC format where catalogers of three-dimensional artifacts find that the work of modifying the format and content standards has already been done for them. The separate fields have been established, and the formal thesauri have been approved. More work remains to be accomplished, however, to accommodate most artifact cataloging. As they are structured presently, fields 655 and 755 accept only terms selected from approved thesauri and, moreover carry a mandatory subfield $2 that is supposed to contain a USMARC code that identifies the thesaurus from which the term(s) was taken.

In addition to *LCSH*, this list of approved thesauri includes the new *Art and Architecture Thesaurus (AAT)*, which will provide terms for large numbers of artifacts eventually. However, the *AAT* is still undergoing development, and only some of its constituent hierarchies, primarily those relating to architecture, furniture, drawings, and modifying hierarchies (i.e., materials, styles and periods, and colors), were published in 1990. The hierarchy that will include terms for clothing is not ready yet, but the following fields show how the *AAT* may be used some day in fields 655 or 755 to describe the leisure suit in the sample record:

755 ₺b$a Belts $x Leather $x Dark brown. $2 aat
755 ₺b$a Jackets $x Wool $x Light brown. $2 aat
755 ₺b$a Trousers $x Wool $x Light brown. $2 aat
755 ₺b$a Leisure suits $x Wool $x Light brown. $2 aat

Eventually the *AAT* will contain terms for clothing and many other artifact names and characteristics of artifacts. Even when the *AAT* is complete, however, it will not attempt to provide terms for all artifacts.[9]

The Revised Nomenclature for Museum Cataloging: A Revised and Expanded Version of Robert G. Chenhall's System for Classifying Man-Made Objects, published by the American Association for State and Local History in 1988, is in the process of having a USMARC code assigned to it for use in subfield $2 in fields 655 and 755. *Nomenclature* provides several terms that would be applicable to the leisure suit in the sample record. They are:

655 ₺7 $a Belt. $2 [nmc]
655 ₺7 $a Jacket. $2 [nmc]
655 ₺7 $a Pants. $2 [nmc]
655 ₺7 $a Suit. $2 [nmc]

Nomenclature does not include modifying terms for color, component materials, place, or dates, nor does it provide a protocol for organizing such modifiers in index headings.[10]

When a USMARC code for *Nomenclature* is approved for use in these fields, catalogers face additional questions. *Nomenclature* provides a long list of terms, but it does not attempt to supply terms for everything. Rather, it is an open list. Catalogers may choose to add terms to the list as needed. These added terms must be considered local terms, unknown to the national constituency of *Nomenclature* users and of MARC users.

When one considers the universe of things that may be cataloged in MARC records in coming years, the failure of available thesauri to comprehend all of them seems inevitable. Therefore, catalogers need a field where they may enter local or nonstandard terms for the objects. The MARC format allots fields and subfields with a number *nine* in the field tag for local definition. For example, many systems and groups of users assign nonstandard *subject* headings to field 690 (one of the local option fields with a tag containing a *nine*). Catalogers of three-dimensional artifacts can adopt a similar strategy by designating one of the other 69x or 79x fields for nonstandard Form/Genre and Physical Characteristics terms. Some of the 69x and 79x field tags are already devoted to other purposes, however, and national consensus to include the major bibliographic utilities will be required if a field for nonstandard artifact headings is to achieve the de facto status accorded the use of field 690 for nonstandard topical subject headings.

In addition to fields 655 and 755, MARC records offer fields and subfields where catalogers may describe an unpublished three-dimensional artifact using text that is not controlled by a thesaurus. These include the Title (Field 245), the Alternative Title (Field 740), the Extent (Field 300), the Medium (Field 340), and the Scope Note (Field 520), among others. These fields allow a cataloger to formulate and assign a descriptive title; alternative titles (such as former titles or nicknames); a succinct identification of the item, its colors, and the materials it is composed of; and in field 520 (which is a variable-length, repeatable note field) a virtually unlimited narrative description of the artifact including as much detail as the cataloger chooses to supply.

In the sample record that appears with this article (Figures 1 and 2), field 520 is extensive and is repeated so that the suit and the belt are described in separate 520 fields. A much shorter description of the clothing ensemble would have been acceptable. Indeed, field 520 is not required at all, but note fields can grow quite long as catalogers update and improve the records. Thus, they probably will contain more detail than a cataloger will choose to assign as headings in the fields tagged 6xx and 7xx. For example, the leisure suit record mentions collars and cuffs in the 520 field, and the terms COLLARS and CUFFS are available in an officially approved thesaurus (*LCSH*), but most catalogers would not consider these characteristics of the artifact to be significant enough to justify creating 655 index fields for them in addition to mentioning them in field 520.

Free-text fields, like field 520, may not, however, be as useful as the fields tagged 6xx and 7xx for retrieving records in online searches. Most software implementations of MARC make the title fields searchable, and some implementations allow the purchaser of the system to make any field searchable. However, fields such as the Title (245) or the Scope Note (520) are not acceptable substitutes for headings in the 6xx or 7xx fields because a machine making a search of their text cannot determine the meaning of a word – that is, whether it is subject, object, or part of another concept.

To understand this situation, one can imagine searching the Title (245) and Note (5xx) fields for the word *chair* to locate catalog records of chairs in museum collections. The search would find not only chairs as artifacts but also books about chairs, pictures of chairs, persons designated as chairs of committees, works about administration techniques (How to Chair. . .), and so on. The number of false hits in this kind of search discourages researchers from using it unless other search strategies have failed. The possibilities of confusion become even greater if the researcher wishes to combine search terms. Conversely, if the term *chair* is located in a search limited to Fields 655 and 755, the computer and the researcher recognize that all hits are indeed records for three-dimensional chairs.

Besides identifying the artifact with an object name, catalogers want fields to be capable of including other characteristics that are part of the identity of an artifact, such as the style, culture, purpose, color, and component materials of an artifact. Not every heading would include all of these modifiers, but catalogers will choose to assign those that seem most significant in particular cases (as they do now in card catalogs). Again, these characteristics should not be intermingled with subjects in Field 650. A chair made in Art Nouveau style is not *about* that style. Similarly, artifacts often are identified in terms of the cultural group of their maker/user, or they are labeled by the purpose for which they were created or used. Again, these characteristics are *not* subjects of the artifacts and would be inappropriate in the Topical Subject Field 650.

Artifact catalogers as well as librarians have an interest in maintaining the integrity of the 650 Topical Subject Field. Some artifacts do possess subjects, usually depicted or written on the artifacts, and artifact catalogers will want to utilize the subject heading fields just as other catalogers do. Furthermore, researchers would feel disoriented if they sought subjects and instead found objects cataloged in subject fields – for example, if they sought works about WEDDINGS and instead found a record for a suit of clothes worn to weddings; if they sought works about FLOUR and found a flour sack; if they sought works about YACHT RACING and found a trophy; if they sought works about COOKERY and found a cook stove (as distinguished from a heating stove); if they sought works about GERMAN AMERICANS and found a German-American cupboard.[11]

The meaning of the modifying terms is clearest if the terms are included in the same field that names the object – for example, CHAIR – AMERICAN

COLONIAL – WOOD – PAINT – RED. Thus, a person searching the Objects or Artifacts file for WOOD will know that the records retrieved are for things made of wood and not about wood. It is difficult to decide whether these modifying terms should appear with the object name in field 655 (Genre/Form) or in field 755 (Physical Characteristics), however, because the modifiers may relate to genre (e.g., a style term), to physical attributes (e.g., a component material), or to both. Field 755 may be the better choice for identifying objects because fields with 6xx tags (in the MARC-VM Format) pertain to subjects, except for field 655, whereas the 700-755 fields are added entries of various types.

If the cataloger separates the modifying terms from the object name, researchers are likely to find many incorrect hits in their searches. For example, in the record for the leisure suit, if the *LCSH* terms are assigned in 655 fields (a field for COATS and a field for BELTS (CLOTHING)) and in 755 fields (a field for WOOL and a field for LEATHER), a request for LEATHER and COATS will pull up this record incorrectly.

The cataloger could have chosen to make a separate record for the belt to prevent this confusion. Creating separate records for each different component is not a satisfactory solution, however. The fact that the MARC structure allows catalogers to link records for related items is little consolation. Many artifacts are composed of separate pieces made of different materials in different colors. Consider, for example, a cup and saucer set, crystal salt and pepper shakers in a silver holder, a red wagon with four rubber tires, and so forth. It would be inconvenient and repetitive to catalog the cup in a separate record from the saucer, the salt shaker in a separate record from the silver holder, and so on. Even a separate record for the suit belt would not eliminate confusion if the cataloger wanted to create indexed headings for the metal buckle as well (i.e., 655 BUCKLE and 755 METAL). The researcher seeking metal belts would now incorrectly pull up the record for the leather belt with the metal buckle. The wool suit probably has a metal zipper and plastic buttons (or a plastic zipper and metal buttons?).

Without belaboring the point, it is clear that the cataloging of artifacts, which exist in infinite variety and combinations of attributes, challenges the MARC Format to identify which modifying terms relate to which objects. Perhaps the strategy that is simplest to implement within the present MARC structure is to combine the modifying terms with the artifact name in a single heading field. For the leisure suit, this results in fields like JACKETS – WOOL – TAN, using the kinds of terms that are (or will be) available in the *Art and Architecture Thesaurus*. Some MARC-based searching systems already allow researchers to specify that they are searching *only* for terms that appear *together* in the same field. In a search for leather jackets, these systems would not pick up a record where LEATHER appeared as

BELTS – LEATHER – DARK BROWN and Jackets appeared in a separate field in the same record as JACKETS – WOOL – TAN.

Theoretically, there are other ways to encode relationships between fields. For example, each 655 and 755 field could carry a subfield giving the number or code of the item to which it pertains. Some implementations of the MARC Format already number fields in this manner so that it is possible to link fields within a record that pertain to the *same* item when the record as a whole describes several items. This type of field numbering is not now officially part of the format, however.

This pattern can be carried out (albeit awkwardly) within the present USMARC structure because fields 655 and 755 include an optional subfield $3 for Materials Specified. For the sample record, a cataloger could assign fields that look like this:

> 655 ⁊7 $a Coats. $2 lcsh
> 655 ⁊7 $a Belts (Clothing). $2 lcsh
> 755 ⁊b$a Wool. $2 lcsh $3 coats
> 755 ⁊b$a Leather. $2 lcsh $3 belts

Besides the unsatisfactory redundancy, this version would not achieve linkage between the fields because the MARC format has not defined subfield $3 as a link between fields (as subfield $6 is defined as a link between fields written in different alphabets). Because computer systems do not automatically link fields with the same content in the subfield $3, a search for LEATHER and COATS would retrieve the record above incorrectly (unless the system searches on subfield $3 and limits the search to data that appear together in the same field).

The MARC Format does not dictate what retrieval features a software vendor will provide in an implementation. The format may facilitate, and thereby encourage, certain implementation features by making available fields and subfields that provide a computer with the information on relationships among terms in fields and subfields. This structure may be found in the new subject field 654 (Subject Added Entry – Faceted Topical Heading), which was designed to accommodate faceted thesauri such as the *AAT*. The faceted relationships among terms within 654 fields are drawn from a thesaurus that itself is structured in hierarchies. By indicating the facet a term represents in the field, the cataloger defines how that term relates to other terms. In a field that may be displayed as DARK BROWN LEATHER BELTS, the hidden facet codes would designate DARK BROWN as a physical attribute, LEATHER as a material, and BELTS as the object name. By isolating each facet code and term, the structure of the field makes possible implementations that allow researchers to narrow their searches to particular facets within fields or to a specific combination of facets.

Field 654 is a subject field, however. It tells researchers what the item described by the catalog record is *about*, not what it is. Thus, a field 654 for DARK BROWN LEATHER BELTS may appear in a record for a photograph that shows the belt or in a record for an exhibition catalog that discusses the belt, but it may not appear in a record for the actual artifact because, in that record, the belt is an object and not a subject. Basically, this is the same contrast discussed earlier in the comparison of field 650 (Subject Added Entry–Topical Heading) with fields 655 (Index Term–Genre/Form) and 755 (Added Entry–Physical Characteristics). Field 654 holds terms for the subjects of the artifacts or other items being cataloged, not terms for the objects themselves.

The cure for this omission in MARC may be as simple as petitioning the Library of Congress to create a field for use in identifying objects that is structured like the 654 field for subjects or to add the features of the 654 field to the 655 and 755 fields. The lack of such a field at present exemplifies the unsettled condition of standards for the cataloging of three-dimensional artifacts. The MARC Format provides fields and subfields capable of great precision, and the format can be amended to accommodate new thesauri and new cataloging rules. Catalogers of three-dimensional artifacts must decide what these new rules should be, and they must build consensus among their colleagues to support new standards. Far from dictating content standards, MARC has a history of responding to initiatives presented by unified professional groups.

To point out the dearth of national standards for cataloging three-dimensional artifacts is not to criticize the museum community harshly. Other professional groups dealing with more circumscribed areas of responsibility than the universe of artifacts also have moved slowly and carefully to develop standards. It will be unfortunate, however, if the lack of national consensus on cataloging standards discourages catalogers of three-dimensional artifacts from creating MARC records. The MARC Format does not require catalogers to input perfect data, and catalogers are not inclined to wait for perfection, either. They want to take advantage of the power of computers to describe and manage their collections now.

In summary, much of the *USMARC Format for Bibliographic Data* for visual materials (including three-dimensional artifacts) works well for museum cataloging. Artifact catalogers will find MARC-based computer systems to be even more satisfactory when museums are able to agree among themselves on description standards for the content of certain fields, such as how to formulate a title for unpublished artifacts. Overall, artifact catalogers benefit by entering the community of MARC users where MARC-based software and services are readily available and many useful thesauri have been developed. To offer appropriate search features for museum artifacts, MARC-based computer systems must be able to differentiate in sophisticated ways between the identity of an artifact–its name, component materials, colors, style, purpose, use–and its subjects–what it is about or what it depicts. To achieve this goal will require modifications of the format and adoption of thesauri and other content standards by the user community.

NOTES

1. *Anglo-American Cataloguing Rules*, 2d ed. (Chicago: American Library Association, 1988).

2. Usage of the MARC-VM format is discussed in the *OLAC Newsletter*, published by Online Audiovisual Catalogers, Inc., a leading organization of library catalogers of special materials.

3. Patricia J. Barnett, "An Art Information System: From Integration to Interpretation," *Library Trends* 37 (Fall 1988): 194-205.

4. In Figure 1, the record is hypothetical and does not actually exist in any MARC-based computer system. For readability, extra spaces are shown before the indicator characters, the subfield labels/delimiters, and the subfield contents. Each MARC-based system has its own rules for inputting and displaying data. Some use extra spaces, and some supply field labels rather than expect the cataloger to input the MARC coding. For Figure 2, private collection management information from fields 541, 583, and 852 does not appear in a public display version. Fields with 6xx and 7xx tags serve as headings in indexes and may or may not be displayed with the main section of the record. The fixed field codes "I" for Encoding Level and "N/A" for language follow OCLC patterns.

5. Field 852 is taken from the USMARC Holdings and Locations Format. It is a repeatable field containing subfields for identification numbers, shelf location, and so on. The title is entered in brackets to differentiate between an original title of the artifact and one formulated and assigned by the cataloger.

6. Evelyn K. Samuel, "Documenting Our Heritage," *Library Trends* 37 (Fall 1988): 142-53.

7. Library of Congress, *USMARC Format for Bibliographic Data: Including Guidelines for Content Designation* (Washington, D.C.: Library of Congress, 1988).

8. Library of Congress, Subject Cataloging Division, *Library of Congress Subject Headings* 11th ed., 3 vols. (Washington, D.C.: Library of Congress, 1989). *LCSH* is compared to one new thesaurus by Jackie M. Dooley, "Introduction" in *LC Thesaurus for Graphic Materials*, comp. Elisabeth Betz

Parker (Washington, D.C.: Library of Congress, 1987). Linda J. Evans and Maureen O'Brien Will, discuss usage in Appendix C: "Report of the Conference," in *MARC for Archival Visual Materials: A Compendium of Practice* (Chicago: Chicago Historical Society, distributed by Society of American Archivists, 1988).

9. The *Art and Architecture Thesaurus* is a project of The Getty Art History Information Program; its staff may be contacted at 62 Stratton Road, Williamstown, MA 01267.

10. James R. Blackaby, Patricia Greeno, and The Nomenclature Committee, *The Revised Nomenclature for Museum Cataloging* (Nashville: American Association for State and Local History, 1988).

11. It is not clear yet what the standard form of indexing for some of these characteristics will be. Generally, the trend in the growth of information networks favors a strategy of cataloging the item in hand very specifically and then relying on future systems of authority records, knowledge bases, and artificial intelligence to make the links between the item cataloged and the broader context in which it was created and used. Each catalog record cannot describe the entire context in which an item was made and used. David Bearman and Richard Szary, "Beyond Authorized Headings: Authorities as Reference Files in a Multi-Disciplinary Setting," in *Authority Control Symposium* (Occasional Paper no. 6) ed. Karen Muller (Tucson: Art Libraries Association of North America, 1987), 69-78.

■ Access to Diverse Collections in University Settings: The Berkeley Dilemma

HOWARD BESSER
MARYLY SNOW

What do woodpeckers and cardinals, wood bark samples, Hans Hoffman paintings, Asian clay tablets, and slides of architecture have in common? At the University of California at Berkeley (UCB), scores of object and visual collections are scattered across hundreds of acres in numerous buildings. Although these are university collections, they are not available to the academic community as a whole. Access to these materials is restricted to select faculty and researchers in each field.

The UCB Image Database Project is proposing tools, using sophisticated but available computer technologies, to open up access to the entire academic community. The intent of the UCB Image Database Project is to provide access to the objects via surrogate images and the data that identify them regardless of material format, organizational schema, or administrative structure. These objects range from collections of relatively rare original materials housed in museums of art, paleontology, anthropology, and vertebrate zoology to collections of more replicable materials housed in teaching departments and research institutes (botanical specimens, satellite images, motion picture film, insect specimens, slides of art and architecture, maps, and architectural images). This paper will describe the UCB Image Database Project, and will address critical problems encountered and solutions discovered in the pursuit of what some call a dream and others call a need. We call it policy implementation.

In the mid-1980s, UC Berkeley's Computer Center entered a period of rapid growth designed to prepare the campus for computing in the twenty-first century. Under aggressive and forward-thinking leadership, the beginnings of a high-speed computing network linking the entire campus came into place. The "campus of the future" was in its infancy, with computer-processing power distributed around the campus rather than centralized in the computer center's mainframe computers. Thousands of powerful, high-resolution workstations were promised to campus departments. Goals in those heady days included providing a workstation for every scholar and distributing computing capabilities more equally among the humanities, social sciences, biological sciences, and physical sciences. Implicit in these goals was the provision of equal access to data and information, whatever its form. Specifically, this philosophy stressed that all campus information resources and data should be available from anywhere on the campus through the campus network.

The time was right to develop an answer to Berkeley's age-old problem of lack of access to her own riches. The technological tools being developed (a campus network, high-resolution workstations, and processing distributed around the campus) were well suited to handling databases of images. Computer center goals and philosophy (availability of all campus resources through the network, more computing services to campus departments) meshed perfectly with notions of making the contents of departmental collections available as a campus network resource. After years of informal scheming and dreaming, The UCB Image Database Project had its official beginnings in 1986 as a cooperative effort among three campus departmental collections (the University Art Museum, the Architecture Slide Library, and the Geography Map Library) and UCB's Computer Center. Shortly thereafter, unfortunately, visionary thinking exceeded budgetary capabilities, forcing the university to drastically curb its pace of computing development. Still, the desire for universal access to computing, data, and information remains strong throughout the university.

THE UCB IMAGE DATABASE PROJECT

The UCB Image Database Project was designed as a uniform information retrieval system for the display of both bibliographic records and their associated images and was developed for all campus departmental collections wishing to use the system. The primary function of the UCB Image Database Project is to give all object and image collections on campus an easy-to-use online catalog incorporating text and image information accessible from any place on the campus network. Related functions include preservation and conservation, simulation, and other forms of research. The UCB Image Database Project features a user-friendly interface, image browsing, image processing, and a spatial querying system, collectively entitled ImageQuery. It is not the intention of the UCB Image Database Project at this time to provide an integrated collections management system for all campus collections, although there are some expectations that many collections' collections management systems will sit underneath the Image Database, with only those portions relevant to the general public exposed.

Figure 1 The ImageQuery query construction panel. The mouse is used to pull down a choice of fields to query. The choices vary for different databases. Shown here is the Architecture database. In this query the user has selected *Place*.

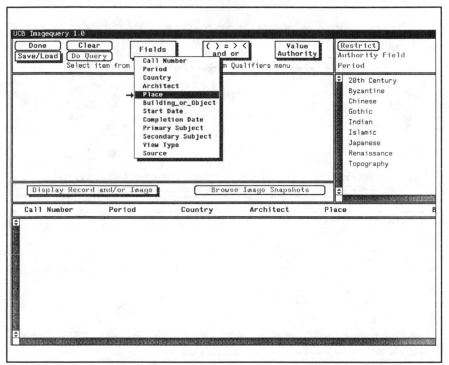

Using ImageQuery is simple. The user formulates a query by selecting options from pull-down menus in a query construction window. Boolean logic and truncated searching are supported. Lookup tables of data actually entered into the system are available by clicking on the Value Authority button. The collection manager has predetermined which fields can be looked up. Figure 1 illustrates the query construction panel. Initial choices are made by pulling down a menu off the Fields button to begin constructing a query. Figure 2 shows a fully constructed query before it has been run. When the query is completed, a list of short records is displayed in the bottom portion of the spreadsheet, and the number of hits is noted at the top. The mouse can be used to bring up a new window showing complete bibliographic information for any short record (not shown). Figure 3 shows the completed query and three short records in the display portion of the window.

Figure 2 Typing is optional in ImageQuery. The value *Venice* has been inserted into the query automatically by selecting the value from the Value Authority Field (actually a lookup table). This completed query construction has not yet been executed.

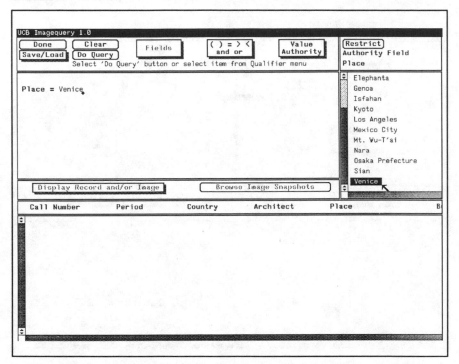

Thus far we have described a system that basically places a user-friendly interface on top of traditional textual queries. For records associated with visual elements, however, we have extended this system to include visual displays and queries. Once one has retrieved an initial hit list, one can click on the browse button (Browse Image Snapshots) and preview slide-sized images associated with the hit list. To determine which image is associated with which record, one may click on either the short record or the snapshot image for the system to highlight the matching record and image. One can also point at a given image or its record and pull down a menu asking to see the associated full bibliographic record, a high-resolution version of the image (UCB ImageView), or both. Figure 3 shows the pull-down menu and its options from the short record. Figure 4 shows a completed query, with digital snapshots and larger resolution images. It should be noted here that the images are digitized and stored in color yet may be viewed in black and white as well.

Figure 3 The query has been executed. The three resulting records are displayed in the display portion of the window, with the total number of hits noted above.

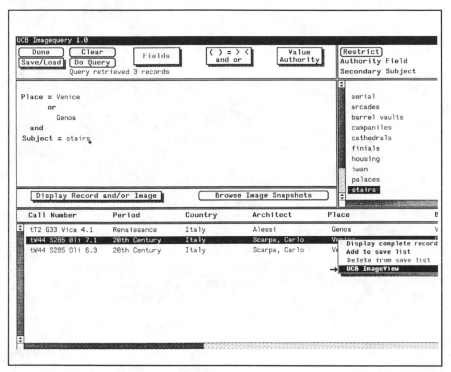

Materials that have a geographic component (where they came from, where they were discovered, where their creator lived, etc.) can have these locations electronically displayed geographically as icons on any type of map (topographical, physical features, etc.). Results of different queries can be displayed as different icons on the onscreen map, and one can see the different geographic clusterings. Figure 5 shows a coordinate-based query window. If the data were in the database, anthropologists could plot Bronze Age human bone finds alongside discoveries of arrowheads dating from the same period and see where these tend to overlap. They could display these on a map indicating elevations or stream-flow data. If they wanted to examine any particular bone or arrowhead more closely, all they would have to do is click on its marker to see a high-resolution image of it or a full descriptive record.

Figure 4   ImageQuery with browsing snapshots and the larger resolution ImageView on display.

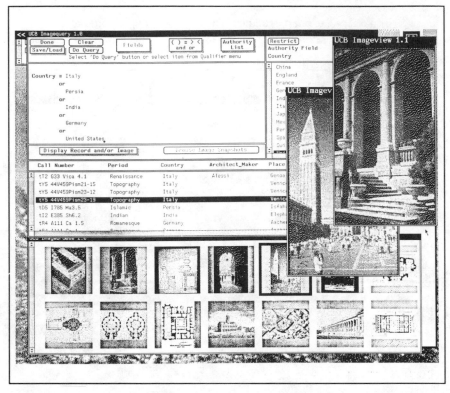

The visual browsing tools act to preserve collections by allowing users to identify exactly which objects are desired without actually removing the often delicate materials from storage. More advanced image processing tools allow users to perform analyses that would be difficult to do on the original objects. Once any high-resolution image is displayed, pull-down menus are available to invoke image processing functions (ImageView) such as zooms, brightness and contrast control, color alteration, and annotation or changing of the image through pixel-by-pixel drawing and painting. The user can see details up close and change colors to enhance poorly lit sections of the image. Patrons can simulate what slides looked like before they faded to pink, what photographs looked like before they turned yellow, and what photographs looked like before they were torn. Eventually, researchers will be able to resize and overlay images for contrast and comparison, enabling significant advances in visual research and scholarship.

Figure 5 ImageQuery with the Coordinate-based Query Window. Camera icons show the angle of photographic images, and known place names are marked with the target icons.

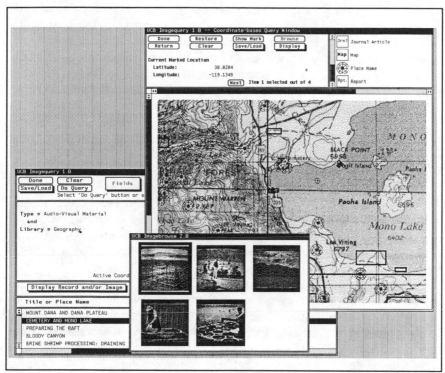

This kind of multi-image display and analysis is possible only because the images are preserved in digital, rather than analog, form. Analog systems, such as videodisc, offer the advantages of cheap mass storage and relatively cheap and readily available hardware. A videodisc system usually requires a full hardware setup of a personal computer, a videodisc player, and a separate monitor for each workstation; a digital system requires more expensive computers (workstation-sized) but only a single piece of hardware at each station. An analog system may be more cost effective in some environments, but UC Berkeley's infrastructure (with its hundreds of workstations in place and a campus network under development) and stated goals (access to all campus resources from each workstation) led to the selection of a digital system. For this digital alternative to be successful, storage costs must drop in the near future, a widely held expectation based on the mass production of optical storage media and prior computer industry experience.

ImageQuery, with its attendant views, browses, and image processing functions, was designed specifically for querying and displaying images and identifying information from the various Berkeley collections.

The interface was intended to be so simple to use that less training and documentation would be necessary than that required for traditional online catalogs. Because the interface is virtually uniform, a user familiar with one collection will be able to browse easily through other collections, even if field names and vocabularies are different. The interface was originally developed using Sun Microsystem's proprietary window management system, SunTools. (All figures in this essay show ImageQuery on SunTools.) The interface has been ported to the more open and more standard X Windows management system. This will guarantee that the software is available on all supported, Unix-based campus workstations, including the Mac II, IBM RT's, DEC's MicroVax, and Sun's entire product line.

The system was designed to sit on top of any database or information retrieval system that can be accessed from the UNIX operating system through C language subroutines. An intended design feature was that collections with existing collection management software need not recatalog or transfer data and that they would continue to use their existing software for collection management functions such as generating reports.

There are negative by-products to the ease with which this system fits over existing software. Primary among these is the possibility that previous cataloging and classification choices made by the collections could become institutionalized. The minimal cataloging in some of these collections is not likely to be expanded, and the efforts toward standardization and the linking of internal collections with one another, which usually take place when a collection begins to use new software, are not likely to happen without some kind of centralized university leadership to emphasize standards and agreed-upon minimum level record requirements.

THE DREAM

We have described the computer system and access to image and object collections in its present form in mid-1990. More capabilities are needed for an ideal image querying system in the not-too-distant future. We will first discuss these features and will then describe the possible structures to make these features possible.

A campuswide querying system should provide integrated access to all collections housed on the Berkeley campus. In addition to searching for all the images and objects described at the beginning of this essay, users should also be able to query Melvyl,[1] the University of California systemwide online union catalog of books and periodicals, and Gladis, the UC Berkeley online book and periodical catalog, through a single computer system. Because of the quirks of history and the needs of extremely specialized subject areas, each of these curated collections has its own cataloging schemes and subject vocabularies. And because of the quirks of politics and economics, these collections will continue to maintain their own idiosyncratic organizational and access methods. Regardless of these differences, access to these unique collections should be possible through one computer gateway. A researcher interested in nineteenth-century Japanese-American culture should be able to find relevant paintings in the University Art Museum or the Art History Slide Library; pictures of housing, places of worship, and community focal points in the Architecture Slide Library; maps of population concentrations and historical migrations in the Geography Department Map Collection; drawings and watercolors of cultural activities in the Bancroft Library; related ethnographic materials in the Lowie Museum of Anthropology; and related monographic materials in the university library system.

Being able to search across the numerous collections of the University of California is not a new idea. In 1974, the university determined that the "holdings of all campuses should be considered a single University collection."[2] This "one university, one catalog" idea was reiterated throughout the 1977 Library Plan.[3] Only recently, however, has the technology begun to make this dream take on a more realistic and achievable cast. Equally important, the changes taking place in the scholarly and curricular programs of the humanities make such systemwide searching far more desirable, and, some would argue, necessary. With the growing focus on historiography in every area of the humanities – whether that focus is structuralist, deconstructivist, or phenomenological – scholars are more concerned with social context than ever before. The need for a full understanding of social context will take the scholar out of one discipline into numerous related ones. The artifacts collected by one discipline as well as the particular way in which those artifacts are organized are informing the research and pedagogy of other disciplines. Cross-cultural computer searching, then, is needed for cross-cultural scholarship. Furthermore, at Berkeley we have reached a point where the student body is ethnically and culturally diverse. After several years of increasing ethnic enrollments, for the first time minorities comprised over fifty percent of the 1988 freshman class, a reflection of population trends in the state as a whole. This development has far-ranging implications for curriculum and research directions. One implication is that the hundreds of little-known collections on the campus will take on broader significance and importance. Whether cross-cultural computer searching will change the study of a subject or merely make it more convenient is not really relevant here; the increased convenience is desirable in and of itself and will in fact continue changes that are already happening.

It must be noted parenthetically that providing access to a wide range of users raises questions about how the information itself is oriented. The information needs of a museum curator differ from those of a historian in the very same discipline. Both those sets of needs differ from those of a connoisseur or a conservator. For a further discussion of these problems in the art world, see David Bearman's article, "Considerations in the Design of Art Scholarly Databases."[4]

To realize our goal of being able to search across collections, we envision three possible search scenarios. These range from minimum to maximum coordination of diverse collections and their uncoordinated cataloging, and from verbal to visual informational displays. In the minimal-level scenario, a search for Japanese-American cultural artifacts in the online catalog of any one of these collections should yield the results in that particular collection as well as a flag or note indicating that related materials exist in other campus collections. Furthermore, the user should be able to query those collections from that same workstation. In a more advanced scenario, the user could set an option to search that single collection or transparently run that same search over other collections as well, using the searching syntax of the local collection. This is similar to the goals of the Linked Systems Project of the Library of Congress, and Research Libraries Information Network (RLIN), and Washington Libraries Network (WLN). Of course, UC's online book catalogs, Gladis and Melvyl, should be searchable in the same manner as all the other collections.

Taking these scenarios one step further, we can envision keying all geographically based material in different collections to their geographic point of origin. In this way, users could display retrieved items from several collections on any relevant base map. In our earlier example of geographic plotting, we were concerned with visually displaying disparate data from a single collection. It should also be possible to display geographic data from various collections simultaneously on one map. For example, a researcher might display a map of California's Mono Basin on his or her workstation and then plot on that map the geographic origins of desired materials from various campus collections. More specifically, the locations from which Modoc arrowheads in the Lowie Museum of Anthropology were originally obtained from a particular time period might be displayed on the base map by one type of icon, while the locations of specific botanical specimens from the university's Herbarium might be represented by another icon, and origins of bones from the Paleontology Museum might be shown as still a third icon. In this way researchers can begin to see visual relationships (such as the clustering of certain objects around particular lakes, streams, or valleys) among materials in different types of university collections. Thus, the online catalog not only would provide access to heretofore inaccessible collections but also would enable researchers to use the catalog as an active research tool.

The search for a technological model or strategy that will help achieve the vision outlined above raises a number of important issues. The two most important of these are the trade-offs between bibliographic retrieval systems and relational database management systems and the adequacy of the MARC format when it is applied to nontraditional materials.

The issue of whether to use a commercial bibliographic retrieval system designed to handle MARC records or to use a generic, commercial relational database management system (dbms) is complex, and it involves economic, institutional, and cooperative concerns. Bibliographic information retrieval systems, such as those marketed by NOTIS, Carlyle, and GEAC, are highly developed for handling printed material. They are oriented around MARC records for books and serials and as such encourage internal consistency and adherence to standards. Records are easily transferable in and out of these systems (i.e., from LC MARC tapes or into national bibliographic utilities such as OCLC).

On the other hand, this software is expensive and runs on even more expensive hardware platforms. The costs involved exceed the budgets of the image and object collections, and the vendors are unknown outside the library world. Such systems tend to be proprietary and act as "closed boxes" whose only link to the outside world is through terminal queries or batch input or output of MARC records. In addition, catalogers using a bibliographic retrieval system generally require extensive training in a MARC-tagged input system. This situation creates problems for Berkeley's goal of integrating systems and ensuring access to all information from every campus workstation.

RELATIONAL DATABASE MANAGEMENT SYSTEMS AND MARC

Relational Database Management Systems (such as Ingres, Oracle, Sybase, Unify, and, to a lesser extent, the pseudo-relational dBase), on the other hand, tend to be open systems, running on common, relatively cheap hardware platforms, and are accessible across a network as well as through programming language subroutines. Relational dbms have all the benefits that come with the mass production and sales of hundreds of thousands of copies in comparison to the dozens of copies sold of the bibliographic retrieval systems: a high profile in the financial, commercial, industrial, and educational worlds; a large pool of programmers to draw upon who are familiar with the software; numerous user groups to turn to for advice; and a frequent updating of the software – to incorporate new algorithms, improve performance, and extend functionality–particularly in adapting it to work with new forms of technology, such as optical storage media. Clifford Lynch[5] argues that bibliographic retrieval applications are too specialized an area to economically support the new kinds of developments on the horizon and that, rather than constantly update bibliographic systems, we should explore adapting relational database management systems to bibliographic use. (Since this essay was written, two MARC-based systems that run on PC platforms have been released: Cactus software's Minaret, and Micromarc: AMC. If these systems prove to be as powerful and thorough as their developers claim, the financial constraints that lead collections to shun MARC-based systems would disappear.)

The advantages of relational dbms for Berkeley campus collections are particularly strong. The platform on which they run is ideal for meeting Berkeley's goals of access to all campus information from every workstation. Spreading costs across multiple uses also makes the cost of each workstation more justifiable. Because dbms run on hardware most commonly found in university departments, not only is the equipment on which to run the dbms readily available, but curators and catalogers can often find experienced users of this software and hardware just down the hall. In fact, a number of small collections has begun automating inventory-type records using less robust commercial dbms.

But off-the-shelf relational database management systems were created primarily to handle numbers rather than text and are very ungraceful with certain functions that bibliographic retrieval systems handle quite easily. Most dbms are based upon fixed-length fields. Although there are ways to simulate variable-length fields by declaring them to be very long and using only the space taken up by characters, there are limits to the number of times this can be done in any given database. Relational dbms can easily handle occasional one-to-many relationships, such as alternate titles or multiple publishers, but to do so they introduce a new level of complexity (such as an extra table lookup for every record in the database) that seems hard to justify in such infrequent occurrences. Many dbms are case-sensitive; for example, searching for De Chirico or de chirico would not find de Chirico. Alternate character sets usually cannot be reflected, and some dbms that claim to support other languages will only support one language at any given time. Sorting on fields including alternate character sets, diacritics, or mixtures of upper and lower cases will result in alphabetical lists that do not appear to be in alphabetical order (such as del Valle coming after Mendez). Many of these problems can be circumvented with sophisticated programming, but such an effort cancels out some of the major advantages of relational databases, that is, their ease of use and their generic qualities. Given the market pressure on commercial dbms vendors, one can expect that they will incorporate many of these features into future releases. In a promising sign, at the 1989 annual meeting of the American Library Association (after this essay was completed), a major vendor of the bibliographic retrieval systems and a major vendor of relational database management systems announced that they would work together to bring to market a bibliographic information retrieval system based upon an underlying commercial relational dbms.

The biggest problem with relational dbms, however, is the problem of transferring and sharing data. This is not a technical problem, but an intellectual and structural one. The flexibility that one enjoys in a relational dbms avoids the strictures of the MARC structure that the bibliographic retrieval systems require, but one pays for that in lack of consistency and transportability. The bibliographic retrieval systems are less flexible, but because they enforce MARC standards, they become important for cooperative efforts.

The adequacy of MARC for nonbook materials is a key issue in this decision-making process. MARC is an international library data communications standard for the sharing of bibliographic data. Here we are using *bibliographic* in its original and narrower focus, that is, pertaining to books and serials, materials that are read via words as compared to materials that are read visually. Although the MARC Formats are no longer limited to monographs and serials, the bulk of library data communications is concerned with those formats. The Archives and Manuscripts Collections Format (AMC) is receiving a lot of attention by professional archivists, and the Visual Materials Format (VM) has become more accepted in the world of archival visual materials, but these formats are still cumbersome and challenging.

For a variety of reasons, MARC has not yet been uniformly adopted by the museum and visual resources communities for the computer storage and sharing of nonprint materials. This is in part related to a perception that MARC is for large libraries rather than for small nonprint collections. Because many of these collection managers view MARC as foreign, they haven't put in the effort needed to adopt a MARC format more suitable to their needs, as the archives and manuscripts community did. Because they haven't tried to create a MARC format that works, saying that MARC does not meet their needs becomes a self-fulfilling prophecy. Of course, there is less incentive for those who have collections of original materials to use MARC. One of the driving forces behind the library world's acceptance of MARC was the near-elimination of original cataloging. Collections of original objects will not be able to benefit from shared cataloging. However, taking the time and making the effort to provide MARC records for original materials will eventually mean that more specialized subject cataloging will be available, as collections build upon previous cataloging efforts in similar materials. In addition, MARC authority records would be greatly enriched by the use of MARC in museums, archives, and slide libraries.

Most Berkeley collection managers are not familiar with MARC. As we will see later in this essay, collection managers usually identify with their own disciplines rather than with the world of library and information science. The general perception is that MARC cataloging would be too complex for these collections to afford. Many of their records have little more information than title, accession number, and format. Using MARC cataloging for such abbreviated records is seldom justifiable. The cost of cataloger training and increased cataloging time are prohibitive for most of these collections, which have less than a handful of employees and operate on minuscule budgets. Even collection managers with dozens of fields look at MARC cataloging as tremendous overkill for their needs.

MAPPING TO MARC

One obvious alternative to the relational dbms/bibliographic retrieval system quandary is for each collection to create, store, and query its records in a relational form and to export and import records via MARC. This means it would have the ability to accept MARC records for input and to create MARC-formatted records from dbms data for output to other collections. This would allow each collection to take advantage of the cost savings, simplicity, and availability offered by commercial relational products, to maintain its own current classification procedures, and still share MARC-formatted records with other institutions. Storing relationally and inputting/outputting in a MARC format is called *mapping to MARC*. The assumption in mapping to MARC is that the collection maintains its database in a relational format and uses a filtering program for importing and exporting records.

Mapping to MARC may not be as easy as it seems. Conceptually, a MARC record is like a hierarchical database, with one-to-one and one-to-many relationships. For any given work, there are one or more given attributes, such as publication dates, authors, and publishers. Relational dbms reflect one-to-one relationships within a given table, and one-to-many or many-to-many relationships between tables. Conversion of a MARC record with no subfields or repeating fields to a relational dbms is quite easy; it will map into a single relation (i.e., author, title, date, publisher) and the relation will map right back into a MARC record. It is the occasional subfield or repeating field – multiple authors, multiple publishers, etc. – that creates a complex relational database structure, perhaps including hundreds of linked tables, and makes the mapping to and from MARC very difficult, though not impossible. Other problems include how to handle the likely uncontrolled vocabulary in relational systems, where to place seldom-used fields (such as local information from the relational dbms or general information from the

MARC record), and how to distinguish when a MARC repeating field contains a type of data that should go into a different place in the dbms.

There has been very little experience actually mapping to MARC and even less literature on the subject. Limited mapping to MARC has been done, although few guidelines for a successful mapping project exist. It is critical that the dbms be designed with eventual mapping in mind so that data elements that will be tagged and subfielded in MARC stand alone as discrete fields in a very complex, normalized (nonredundant) dbms. The Getty Photo Archive, for example, has mapped its STAR database to MARC, although the program merely tags and subfields the STAR data elements; a program to load the converted records into a bibliographic utility such as RLIN has not been written. The National Center for Film and Video Preservation has engaged in a similar project. The Museum Prototype Project (MPP), once a project of the Getty Art History Information Program, mapped its preliminary data from collection management systems to MARC in 1984. MPP members were convinced that a library computer system could not meet museum needs, however, so the mapping was abandoned.[6] Recently, a successful mapping of the *Art and Architecture Thesaurus* to the MARC Authorities Format was achieved. A MARC tape was delivered to RLIN for mounting in its authorities subsystem in mid-1990.

If each collection was stored relationally with the ability to import and export MARC records, as outlined above, further design efforts would have to be made to permit the user to search across these collections. We would have to either establish linkages between common fields among the collections or develop a set of common fields for each collection to use. We would also have to link their assorted vocabularies. One obvious but difficult approach would be to get each collection to agree to a small set of standard fields, with controlled vocabularies or protocols for data entry for the fields that are in common. With a broad outline of standards, new collections as well as collections at the early stages of automation would have incentive to follow this standard path. Unfortunately, we do not live in an ideal world. If the eight art museum members of the Museum Prototype Project, with special funding and direction, could not agree on standard data fields, it is hard to imagine that museum scientists, curators, and advising faculty collecting in every branch of knowledge from paleontology to wood samples to architectural history could agree on a standard set of data fields without some extraordinary leadership.

Another approach would be to map certain subject-oriented terms to one another, or to and from some sort of master list. If this kind of vocabulary mapping existed, an automated system could be developed that essentially would transparently translate the vocabulary from one collection query to another, again, similar to the Linked Systems Project.

The problem of coordinating vocabulary is not easy. Each of these collections has a different vocabulary and different data elements, and some do not maintain authority lists at all. Each one has different kinds of local needs, often specific to particular faculty, and has certainly grown idiosyncratic over the years of collecting. A few of them belong to subject disciplines that already have their own sets of controlled vocabularies such as Chenhall's *Nomenclature* and the *Art and Architecture Thesaurus*. With the possible exception of the *AAT*, which has retained source information for each of its terms in an authority record, controlled vocabularies will not be easily mapped to one another.

A third possibility would be to map each record in each dbms to a MARC-formatted record stored in a bibliographic retrieval system. This way, copies of all the records would reside in a single system oriented toward MARC formatting, making searching much easier. At the same time, each collection would retain the flexibility that comes from having its own relational dbms. But such a double-system poses its own problems. A double-system like this requires careful attention to control of current data so that updates in the dbms can be reflected in the bibliographic retrieval system. This begins to impinge upon some of the flexibility that caused collection managers to turn to relational dbms in the first place. The primary argument against such a system would be the cost. Such a system would require a very fast, powerful computer in addition to each individual collection's more personalized relational dbms. At this point in time, it would be difficult, if not impossible, to find someone within the university willing to fund such a project. To realize any gain from such a double-system, one still has many sticky problems to tackle involving vocabulary control and consistency.

All these scenarios for linking together the collection data across campus must await some kind of coordinated effort or leadership from the campus. As will be shown in a later section, this has been a major problem in this project. In addition, ways to apply MARC for objects must be resolved at the national level before we begin campuswide data coordination.

THE DILEMMA

Several factors are serving to keep the dream of cross-campus computer access to all collections from being realized. These factors fall into two very broad general categories: those involving institutional, or human and political, conflicts and those involving technical, technological, and design problems. We will touch upon a number of these factors in the remaining pages.

Many institutional factors are slowing progress toward the dream of one system/one collection. Primary among these is how these collections are situated administratively within the university structure. Each collection belongs to an individual department; there is no administrative entity linking the collections with one another or with the campus library. Funding is channeled through the department, and the primary mission of each collection is to serve its own department. Although the collection managers with library backgrounds would like to see increased use of their collections by those outside their own department (either from other campus departments or from collections and scholars in their own disciplines at other institutions), this cannot really be justified from a fiscal standpoint.

Because they are rooted in their own departments, department administrators tend to look upon collection management problems as departmental administrative problems and to apply standard administrative tools to solve them. Most of these departments have already gone through their office automation stage and can supply experienced support personnel for word processing, spreadsheets, and database management systems on single-user workstations. Real collection management needs are a foreign arena. Those with decision-making power do not understand the problems, nor do they have access to the tools necessary to provide ongoing support.

The lack of an administrative entity linking the collections leaves them without coordinated long-term planning or a support group for analyzing automated collection management systems. Because they could not benefit from the economies of scale that might have been realized by gathering a number of collections together for a joint automation project and because they were forced to rely on very thin departmental funds for any activity, for many years any attempts at automation appeared hopeless.

This departmental isolation has also created a situation in which each collection finds it hard to see any benefits of the MARC format. The MARC format was created for the exchange of information, and these collections have very little information exchange with similar collections at other locations or with different collections on the campus. In commercial automated collection management systems, the MARC-based ones have capabilities the small collections have found unnecessary. Also, MARC-based systems are priced beyond the financial resources of any of these collections. Beyond these practical reasons, there has been a popular perception in the museum and archival community that MARC is really a format for books and is not appropriate for other types of materials.

Of course, the fact that these collections have no administrative relationship with the campus library has been a key factor in the failure to make information exchange through the use of MARC a priority. The library does provide its own online catalog of MARC-based records and will make its dedicated terminals available to some of these campus collections for an ongoing rental fee. At this time, it is prohibitively expensive for these collections to contribute individual records to the campus library system. One might imagine a different scenario in which the library took the lead in establishing guidelines for cataloging materials in departmental collections; in bringing managers of these collections together to talk about common problems; in creating long-range coordinated automation timetables; in suggesting suitable, specialized subject vocabularies; and in setting up task forces to look for outside funding for these collections. Despite tentative requests from a few collection managers for the library to take on a more aggressive role, the library has its own pressing concerns and has declined to exert leadership in this area.

Given the isolation of the departmental collections and the lack of higher-level coordination, the Image Database Project got underway with three "client" collections, working with the computer center as the only administrative link among them. Without participation or guidance from the campus library or any higher-level administrative unit on campus, the goals and directions of the project were subject to the changing interpretations of the individual participants. Although all the participants agreed on the basic outline of the Image Database Project, numerous differences arose regarding features perceived to be a necessary part of that software. It was also not clear at the outset what contributions each of the participants would make toward its completion. For instance, the computer center staff did not want to get involved in collections processing or data entry, which seems logical. Yet that decision caused the creation of an information retrieval system that had no data entry mechanisms. In addition, the computer center saw MARC-based systems as "old" technology, of which they wanted no part. The computer center also felt that it was not its role to suggest that the collections adhere to national vocabulary standards, although it was in these very areas that the individual collection managers required guidance and coordination. Collection managers felt that the computer center, the only campuswide unit involved in the project, should make a more coordinating effort and should step in where the library had failed to do so. The computer center expected individual collections to locate funding support from their individual departments for programming data entry mechanisms and related programming needs. The collections were by and large unable to secure contributive funding, a fact that the computer center erroneously interpreted as lack of support for the project. In addition, a considerable amount of time was spent clarifying issues of values, perceived roles, and perceptions among the participants, which slowed down the project considerably. Finally, without guidance or leadership from any higher-level campus administrative unit, it was difficult to navigate through these different issues, values, and perceptions.

Although human and personnel problems are universal, they seldom are directly transferable to other situations. On the other hand, technical, technological, and design problems – problems that rely less on human factors–are more directly replicable, if only for narrow windows of time because technological or theoretical advances may change the picture dramatically. These problems are access to existing technology, stability of technology, cost of technology, design breakthroughs, and the like. We will not discuss issues such as the obtainment of equipment, setting up, training, operation, and support; these topics should be familiar to anyone who has gone through an automation project. Instead, we will concentrate on issues that tend to be specific to those embarking upon a cutting-edge project.

A few of the problems faced by this project have been caused by using technology that had not yet stabilized as mass market products. Much of this technology tended to be expensive and to require technically literate people to make it work properly. For example, the first digitizer acquired was quite expensive, and it arrived with no user interface and very sketchy documentation.

Another major roadblock has been the cost and complexity of commercial database management systems for the workstation environment. Unlike PC-based products, which sold for under five hundred dollars and required little programming experience to set up, workstation products sold for thousands of dollars and required an experienced programmer to set up.

Another key problem has revolved around storage technology. Digital storage is very consumptive of space. The storage needs for even a small collection of one hundred thousand slides at a resolution of one-third megabyte per image would be approximately thirty thousand megabytes, without considering compression. Studies have yet to be done to determine what level of resolution is necessary for which uses. We assume that much higher resolution (perhaps as high as forty-eight megabytes per image) may be necessary for certain purposes, such as automated condition reports or very detailed studies of objects. Clearly, this poses vast storage problems that cannot be solved by commercial products that existed at the start of this project. Initial planning surmised that storage costs would tumble dramatically with the introduction of optical disks (something that has not yet occurred, although there are some promising signs of it) and that this project would not need such technology until about the time it became affordable.

Another technological limitation is the number of simultaneous colors displayable on the computer screen. When the project began, only 8-bit (256 simultaneous colors) screens were commercially available, although 24-bit (16 million simultaneous colors) displays were seen in research labs. Therefore, initial software experimentation that provided routines for detailed comparisons between close-ups of different images was eliminated from the working system design. Although there was an early desire to make the system run under a standard window management system available on a wide variety of platforms, X Windows was not yet stable enough to use for serious development. Even a year after the initial development work under

Sun Windows, the X Window tool kit was so incomplete that UCB programmers spent hundreds of hours writing their own tools.

Surprisingly few problems were faced in the design of the primary user interface. This interface was designed to work with only minor modifications on top of any commercial database management system with UNIX operating systems and addressable with C language subroutines. ImageQuery was also designed to work with flat-file databases for collections that had minimal cataloging information and/or no resources to purchase commercial dbms software. This design worked surprisingly well with test databases and pleased everyone involved.

Other design problems border on political problems, as certain design decisions reflect the perceived missions of some groups involved in the design while not reflecting others. While some librarians and collection managers feel that an attempt should be made to allow this user interface to sit on top of ADABAS-type back-ends (the kind of database found in most large library online catalogs that support MARC-formatted records), the computer programmers consider this task out of their jurisdiction, viewing MARC as a campus library issue. Thus, they see no reason to conduct preliminary inquiries as to whether this might work.

Attempts to create a design that might allow searching across different collections' records, as described earlier, have been hampered by the lack of centralized leadership, either from the library, the computer center, or, more appropriately, a higher administrative level.

CONCLUSION

The UCB Image Database Project has produced ImageQuery, the Unix-based software for composing queries and retrieval of images and associated bibliographic information. ImageQuery is in use in several campus collections, each of which is struggling to leave behind prototype development and move to a production (or volume) environment. This is Phase One of a three-part project. Phase One involves integrating images with their corresponding text records for data entry into what will serve as an online public access catalog–ImageQuery. Data structures must be developed and controlled vocabularies selected. The database structures must be complex and detailed enough to handle the needs of each collection, yet flexible enough to link eventually with other systems. Data entry and control problems must be solved. Once structure and data entry are stabilized, grants must be written for the inputting of existing manual records, or retrospective conversion (recon). Recon is seen as an advanced portion of Phase One, and clearly recon will be a very long term process, for most collections are large and complex. Phase Two involves mapping the relational database management systems that form the back end of the ImageQuery catalogs to MARC for data sharing across campus and with other institutions. Phase Two could occur before or simultaneously with Phase One. Because of the various institutional factors we have alluded to on the Berkeley campus, mapping to MARC is likely to follow Phase One, that of making Berkeley's diverse collections accessible.

We must admit to some skepticism over the speed at which the progression to Phase Two will take place; without any authority or support beyond the collection managers, it could take years before the campus prepares for data sharing. We have outlined the capabilities of the UCB Image Database Project, including some pitfalls we have encountered and some of the dilemmas and issues that continue to slow development of ImageQuery, our visual online public access catalog, as we need it today and envision it for tomorrow. The future scenario will be played out in the world of national and international scholarship. Once access to images and objects is possible via computer, we will be able to meet the often unrecognized needs of scholars, faculty, and students. In time, the linking of the bibliographic record for an object with a digital representation of its image will likely seem natural, and its benefits obvious. Also, as computer technology continues to develop, more and more institutions and individuals will use high-speed, high-resolution, bit-mapped workstations. In time, even the national bibliographic utilities may be commonly accessed from bit-mapped terminals. Some day MARC fields for digital image files may even be available on OCLC, RLIN, and other utilities. Not only bibliographic records of objects, but also their representations, will be transmitted electronically. Scholars will query systems before deciding which archives and universities must be visited, and they will be able to study closely surrogate images to weed out the pieces that must be examined on location.

We believe these efforts and capabilities will more clearly reveal the value of visual materials and objects in all levels of higher education and scholarship. The marriage of relational database management systems, MARC, and bit-mapped technology may even challenge just a bit our national addiction to education by television, the paramount visual medium.

ACKNOWLEDGMENTS

Discussions with Kody Janney, Clifford Lynch, David Bearman, and Dan Holmes contributed to the thoughts that helped formulate this paper. The Librarians' Association of the University of California at Berkeley Research Grants Program provided funding for literature searches and document delivery. Implementation of the UCB Image Database would not have been possible without the help and commitment of the other members of the UCB

Advanced Technology Planning Group: Barbara Morgan, Steve Jacobson, Randy Ballew, and Ken Lindahl.

NOTES

1. Melvyl is a registered trademark of the regents of the University of California for its online union catalog.

2. University of California, Library Policy Task Force. "University of California Library Policy to 1980-81," 1974, 2. Quoted in University of California (System), Office of the Executive Director of Universitywide Library Planning, The University of California Libraries: A Plan for Development, 1978-1988, 59.

3. University of California (System), Office of the Executive Director of Universitywide Library Planning, "The University of California Libraries: A Plan for Development, 1978-1988," July 1977.

4. David Bearman, "Considerations in the Design of Art Scholarly Databases," *Library Trends* 37, no. 2 (Fall 1988): 206-19.

5. Clifford Lynch, "Extending Relational Database Management Systems for Information Retrieval Applications" (Ph.D. dissertation, University of California, Berkeley, 1987).

6. Nancy Allen, "The Museum Prototype Project of the J. Paul Getty Art History Information Program: A View from the Library," *Library Trends* 37, no. 2 (Fall 1988): 175-93.

■ Visual Depictions and the Use of MARC: A View from the Trenches of Slide Librarianship*

MARYLY SNOW

SHOULD SLIDE LIBRARIANS USE MARC?

The only way to get slide records into the national bibliographic utilities such as RLIN and OCLC is through the use of the MARC format. If slide librarians want to have their records available on campus online library catalogs, those records must also be in the MARC format. This essay will discuss the importance of having individual slide and photograph records on the national bibliographic utilities and the obstacles that currently make this difficult. Mapping to MARC from database management systems will be discussed briefly.

Visual materials include drawings, illustrations, prints, posters, broadsides, films, videotapes, architectural drawings and blueprints, greeting cards, albums, scrapbooks, slides, and photographs. Archival visual materials, as used in *MARC for Archival Visual Materials: A Compendium of Practice*, include all of the formats listed above except for copy photographs and copy slides, which are original slides and photographs that slide and photo curators catalog as visual depictions, that is, as reproductions of objects or scenes.[1]

The term *copy* denotes images that have been photographically reproduced or copied from published materials or other originals. Copy

---

*This paper was originally presented at the Art Libraries Society of North America's Annual Conference, Phoenix, March 1989.

slides, then, have not been published, are not available commercially, are not original, and are not archival. Copy slides are a unique hybrid. The materials held by slide libraries and some photo archives are collected because of what they depict, because the materials are surrogates for either original works or specific places in time. This distinction between original materials and visual depictions presents problems for slide cataloging on the national utilities and will be addressed later in this paper.

For the sake of discussion, let us imagine some day in the future when slide libraries routinely contribute individual records to the national utilities. I am not talking about records for commercial slide sets; these are currently found on the national utilities. The power, strength, and uniqueness of slide libraries reside in their bringing together thousands of individual images into a classified arrangement and not in collections of slide sets as are found in learning and media centers. Assume that in the future slide libraries will: (1) have the necessary hardware, funding, and staffing to create and load MARC records; (2) have access to the bibliographic utilities; and (3) find individual slide and photograph records already in the utilities. What would be gained is the system of shared cataloging now enjoyed by the rest of the library profession.

Although slides are not published in the thousands, like books, there are still advantages to shared cataloging. In particular, the authority work that could be shared is significant. Access to the authority records of visual collections would save visual resource librarians from having to verify the same personal name or the same place name over and over again.

Another advantage is that slide librarians could build upon each other's subject cataloging. For a variety of reasons, most slide librarians have little or no subject access to their collections. Now that the *Art and Architecture Thesaurus* (*AAT*) is available as a controlled subject vocabulary, slide librarians can begin solving their subject access problems. Cataloging will take longer than in the past, however. This is not a critical statement about the *AAT*; it is simply a statement of fact that adding subject cataloging will increase the time needed to catalog a slide. Nonetheless, with access to the utilities and with the approved use of the *AAT* in MARC's 654 field and other MARC subject fields, slide librarians can add terms to each others' records, as is possible in OCLC, or can see which terms have been used by other slide collections and borrow any of those terms that are deemed appropriate. Over time, slide libraries could accumulate a much more complex set of terms and, eventually, a rich tradition of subject access. If one slide library had the time to use two or three *AAT* terms, perhaps another would add three more.

Slide librarians and photo curators, however, are not the only people who would benefit by the addition of these materials to the national utilities. The end users of these cataloging databases, art reference librarians and scholars, would reap benefits far beyond those gained by slide and photo catalogers. Currently, authority records in the national utilities come primarily from monographs and serials. While slide libraries contain both commercially published and original slides, the majority of images is taken from monographs and periodicals.[2] Slide librarians have gathered information on artists and architects who have not yet warranted monographic treatment and who may never warrant such treatment. Slide librarians also have information on the individual artists and architects who make up groups, schools, and movements. Books are cataloged at what seems to a slide librarian to be a rather gross level. The addition of more specialized authority records reflecting, essentially , chapters or sections of a monograph would be a boon to art and architecture reference librarians and their patrons.

Toward a National Visual Index

In addition to providing these unique authority records, the contribution of individual slide records to the national utilities could also constitute the creation of a de facto national visual index. By using the 773 Host Item Entry Field in MARC, individual slide records would be tied to the source from which the slide was derived. This index to the fine arts, architecture, and the decorative arts would change the dismal state of visual indexing in the United States and the international bibliographic communities. Pictures are important conveyors of information in our society. Our culture has been moving away from reliance on traditional forms of written-word literacy to more visual learning and visual education. Unfortunately, indexes to images have not kept pace with the use of images. Slide librarians and the faculty with whom they work closely have culled hundreds of thousands of images in art and architecture, material culture, and social history from thousands of sources. This culling has been going on in some slide libraries for more than fifty years. Most often slide libraries can retrace where a picture came from. This information is kept for copyright and publishing purposes and in case another copy of the slide is needed. How beneficial it would be if one slide library could find out from which book another slide library had made a particular slide! How beneficial it would be for scholars to be able to determine which monographs, exhibition catalogs, and serials held reproductions on their topic! Even better, how beneficial it would be for reference librarians if they could tell which artists or architects a particular book discussed! Where there is a particular image, there is usually related textual information. The linking of images and sources would create a de facto subject index to specific persons and places. Thus, we can foresee subject access to the detailed contents of monographs, exhibition catalogs, and periodicals, as well as the creation of a national visual index.

These are not insignificant contributions to the field of librarianship or to our collective store of knowledge. A recent publication of the Getty Trust, *Object, Image, Inquiry: The Art Historian at Work*,[3] is an in-depth study of the art historical research process. The importance of reproductions to the scholar's work is clearly stated in this analysis. Both originals and reproductions are necessary for art historical research. Too often librarians think of slide libraries as mere repositories of teaching materials, and they overlook the role that reproductions play in scholarly research.

It is not only scholars who rely on reproductions. How many patrons have asked you for a particular book or subject when you suspect they are really looking only for pictures of artist A or architect B? Notice how easy it is for visual resources professionals to fall prey to a deeply ingrained negative attitude toward pictures by writing, and reading, "when you suspect they are really looking only for pictures." This perception of visual images as less noble than the written word pervades our culture and our profession. It is beyond the scope of this paper to examine the causes of this discrimination, yet we see its effect reflected in many of the so-called standards for cataloging visual materials.

Another benefit of the inclusion of individual slide records is that we, as a people and as a culture, need full media representation in the national utilities. Although monographs and serials currently predominate in the utilities, more and more nonbook materials have found their way into these databases. As manuscripts, films, and other archival visual materials are added, the utilities will be representing two ends of the scale of materials: those published in quantity, such as monographs, and those that exist as unique items. Between these two extremes should be slides and photographs – not just original, historic, archival photographs but also pictures of "things." To build truly national and international library databases without representing slides and photographs of ordinary objects and common events would do our users and future users a great disservice.

How might those records look at the collection level, group level, or item level? The types of information needed to describe architectural images should help determine which level is appropriate. For any one building, we have hundreds of possible views: a variety of plans, axonometric drawings, sections, elevations, design sketches, and models. There are unlimited exteriors of varying angles, times of day, and times of year. Also included are exterior details (the door, the stair, the window), interiors, interior details, the building over time (as it ages, as it is remodeled, as it is restored, and the ways its occupants used the building from one century to the next). Certainly Louis XIV's court at Versailles conjures up a different image than a group of twentieth-century tourists at Versailles. There are named and unnamed buildings within complexes (L'Hameau, Le Petit Trianon). There are named rooms and places within a building, such as the Salon de la Guerre or L'Escalier de la Reine in the palace at Versailles.

Because there are so many possible views for any one building, the image record should group these views together, with the entire building or painting constituting a group-level record. For instance, the record might read:

Wright, Frank, Lloyd.

Kaufmann House, Bear Run, Pa., 1936.

Collection consists of plans and drawings; exteriors; interiors.

One could then explode or explore these three parts. Exploding plans and drawings, we would find, for example:

1. Plan, From Arthur Drexler's book, Frank Lloyd Wright Drawings, p. 93
   CU MCM NIC

2. Plan, From Eduardo Sacriste's book, Usonia: Aspectos de la Obra de Wright, p. 6
   CU CUSB PU

3. Plan, From Kenneth Frampton's book, Modern Architecture, 1851-1945, p. 398
   CU CUSD NjP MH

4. Plan, From Rosenthal Art Slides # 160
   CUSC AzU

This group-level, or clustered, approach is economical and sensible. It provides all the information the slide library needs, as well as what the scholar and reference librarian wants. For instance, the collection of twenty-five hundred slides of Frank Lloyd Wright in the Architecture Slide Library at the University of California at Berkeley depicts 63 unbuilt projects and 185 built buildings, yet represents only 20 percent of his total oeuvre. As long as clustering and exploding views to get to the necessary level of detail are, or could be, possible, it makes sense to cluster. Individual slide records would be clustered together and would not clutter up the databases. Slide librarians would still have access to all the data they would need, and, just as important, they would be linking these records to bibliographic data, creating the visual and subject indexes mentioned earlier.

OBSTACLES

Numerous obstacles get in the way of the realization of this dream, from high costs to the limited capabilities of the national utilities to attitudes about depictions and the way they ought to be cataloged.

The simplest obstacle to recognize is money. Most slide libraries are administered through academic teaching departments; fewer are administered through campus library systems. Slide libraries that are housed in campus library systems are fortunate, in one respect, for these systems undoubtedly already contribute their records to at least one of the national bibliographic utilities. Slide library records represent only a small increase in existing, ongoing costs, and it should not be too difficult to convince a librarian administrator to add individual slide records to the output. Slide libraries administered through academic departments will have a more difficult time securing funding because they generally report to faculty or administrators not familiar with, nor already committed to, the inputting of records in the bibliographic utilities.

In some ways, money is the least important of the obstacles. If the slide library community works on solving all the other obstacles and the entire library and scholarly community acknowledge the benefits of having slide records on the national utilities, ways will be found to get the money. "If a clear vision of what we need is developed, most barriers can be overcome. If we concentrate on the barriers, the structure will defeat us."[4]

Another perceived obstacle is MARC itself. It looks too complicated to slide librarians, with its hundreds of fields and countless indicators and delimiters. A perusal of *USMARC Format for Bibliographic Data* or *MARC for Archival Visual Materials: A Compendium of Practice* will reveal MARC's logical structure as just another system to learn, even though none of the examples in the *Compendium* show copy slides or photographic depictions.

The *Compendium* clearly points out that MARC imposes very few rules for the content of fields and that participating repositories generally choose to adhere to *AACR 2* and other standards to participate in bibliographic networks. For archival visual materials, *AACR 2* has been interpreted by two accepted documents. One is Wendy White-Hensen's *Archival Moving Image Materials: A Cataloging Manual*. The other is Elisabeth Betz [Parker]'s *Graphic Materials: Rules for Describing Original Items and Historical Collections*. Neither of these works interprets *AACR 2* from the point of view of slide libraries. Betz and the compilers of the *Compendium* say that slide libraries do not catalog their slides according to *AACR 2* and that to use *AACR 2* would mean that the artist or the architect would not be the main entry, as is often the case in slide catalogs, but the added entry. In their view, the main entry would be the person who created the photographic image being cataloged.[5] The interpretation of *AACR 2*'s statement of authorship and its application to depictions is an important cataloging debate. The question is whether slide librarians should catalog the slide or the item depicted. Although we say we are cataloging slides, we are, in fact, cataloging the item depicted. We catalog the building shown in the slide, not the photographer of the building. In 99 percent of the cases, the photographer is not important to the slide librarian or the patrons. When the photographer is important, the slide is cataloged under the photographer's name, as in Man Ray or Dorothea Lange. However, we are still cataloging the item depicted.

The difference between cataloging the original versus the depiction also shows up in the physical description. We use the size of the original item depicted in the slide, for example, a painting 80 cm-by-120 cm, and not the two-by-two-inch size of the slide itself. The MARC 300 Field for Physical Description is a repeating field. The first 300 field must denote the two-by-two-inch size of the slide to be consistent with the 007 field in the directory. The second 300 field would therefore denote the size of the original.

Slide libraries are not the only type of visual collection that catalogs depicted items. The Getty Photo Archives and the National Gallery of Art Photographic Archives, to name but two, also catalog the image depicted. The National Museum of American Art's Inventory of American Sculpture catalogs the actual sculptures. What these projects have in common with slide libraries is that none of these projects follow the traditional library practice of cataloging items in hand, or items owned. In a book library, it doesn't make sense to catalog a book not owned, but cataloging practices for books do not apply to visual materials and ought not to be forced upon the visual community. When slide libraries catalog a depicted item, they do not own the item, nor is it necessary to own the item. Information should not be censored by type of ownership. When information is compiled, regardless of property rights, the information should be shared. Because slide libraries and some art information projects catalog items not owned, most (book) librarians feel that slide libraries are not cataloging according to *AACR 2* and that therefore those records cannot be added to the national utilities. Slide libraries may indeed be cataloging according to the principles of *AACR 2*, although they may be interpreting those principles differently than do book and archival librarians, who, perforce, must catalog items in hand. It should be noted that book libraries do occasionally catalog items they do not own, such as when they catalog microfilm or microfiche of historic documents and newspapers. In 1984, when *AACR 2* did not drop the concept of main entry, Michael Gorman, one of the editors of *AACR 2*, noted that the decision was made for political reasons, not for philosophical reasons, and "that, as always, the dilemma for cataloging is the conflict between the philosophical concept of authorship versus the practical approach to access."[6]

Representatives of OCLC and RLG were both consulted in an attempt to clarify this cataloging dilemma. OCLC, while familiar with the debate, thought that the way slide librarians catalog individual slides would be appropriate for inclusion in their database. Of course, this is not a formal policy decision but an informal opinion based on my interpretation of *AACR 2*. OCLC suggests that slide librarians try to adhere to *AACR 2*'s Rule 1.0D1, which defines a first level of description. This rule cites the title proper, the first statement of responsibility if different from the main entry, the edition statement, material, publisher, date, extent of item, notes, and standard number. OCLC does not require all of these elements as a minimum-level visual record.

RLG, as well as the compilers of the *Compendium*, mentioned the long-standing debate on interpreting the main entry as the person who created the main, or original, work – for example, the architect – instead of the person who created the depiction of the work – for example, the photographer. They underscored the need for differentiating between cataloging the original object and cataloging the depiction of the object because the distinction is essential to reference users. As mentioned above, however, the repeating 300 field should be sufficient distinction. Furthermore, *AACR 2*'s Rule 21.16B allows one to enter a reproduction of an artwork under the heading for the original work, with an added entry for the person or body responsible for the reproduction.

Both OCLC and RLG suggested that the slide librarian community should agree upon and publish standards for cataloging visual depictions. This would allow slide librarians to continue to catalog images as depictions, rather than as slides. Both felt that a committee or task force should look at *AACR 2*, at Betz's interpretation, *Graphic Materials*, and at standard slide library cataloging practices to come up with an agreed-upon set of guidelines for access points and descriptive statements. If guidelines were drawn up by the Art Libraries Society of North America's Visual Resources Division and accepted by the Visual Resources Association, that would constitute sufficient review for OCLC.

If it is possible currently to enter slide records, what would be achieved by establishing and approving slide library or depiction cataloging and classification guidelines? From a practical point of view, the MARC field 040$e asks which set of cataloging rules are being followed. The ability to enter a code for approved visual depiction cataloging rules would make dealing with the national utilities somewhat easier. Several of the photo archives that also catalog depictions have run into trouble with the national utilities and the cataloging communities over these same questions. The existence of an approved set of visual depiction cataloging guidelines would be a significant factor in increasing the stature of the profession of slide librarianship among our colleagues, the nonslide librarians. Slide librarians, photo archivists, and other art informatics professionals would be able to interpret MARC fields and tags consistently according to various data types, thus extending MARC into these areas.

RLG's BIBTECH Subcommittee on Bibliographic Standards is reviewing RLG standards as applied to visual materials. The subcommittee, while it has members drawn from the RLG community, does not have any slide librarians on it and will focus on the examination of existing published standards. To be counted in the review process, RLG slide librarians must make their views known to the appropriate RLG committee representatives.

MAPPING TO MARC

The Architecture Slide Library at the University of California at Berkeley has been planning to use a database management system that will run with a custom-written filtering program to translate local data records into MARC records. Numerous reasons support this decision. Earlier in this essay, I referred to MARC as just another logical system to learn, implying that it was not difficult. MARC has, however, its problems, especially for visual resources collections. Because it is a communications format, it lacks the efficiency of database management systems. For example, data is often entered in both the leader and the directory, and occasionally in several places in the directory. This redundancy slows down data entry time. In addition, MARC has hundreds of fields, more than the average small collection would use. MARC is also highly specialized, requiring particular knowledge, thus presenting problems for small nonbook collections.

Many of these problems are just beginning to disappear now that MARC is becoming available on personal computers. Nonetheless, one cannot go to a nearby computer store to buy MARC-compatible software. One cannot get help with MARC from a graduate student in art history or computer science. MARC user groups meet only twice a year at ALA, once a year at the Society of American Archivists, and at ARLIS. One cannot go to weekly and monthly MARC user group meetings on campus or downtown. Ordinarily, if an individual wanted to learn what new advances computer technology had in store, he or she would go to a MacWorld Fair, an IBM Fair, UNIFORM, or a computer store. Very little that is offered at such places will be useful for the MARC user. Currently, MARC exists solely in the library and archival world. Therefore, the cost savings of the mass market and the pressure to come out with newer, easier, cheaper, and faster ways of doing things do not apply to the world of MARC, with its mere thousands of users, in the same way it applies to the millions of users in the commercial world.

One of the most significant obstacles to widespread adoption of MARC has been technological: the imaging technology of bit-mapped workstations, developed in the commercial and engineering worlds, meets the needs of today's scholars and today's visual collections. No MARC-based system that can effectively merge visual depictions and the corresponding descriptive records exists yet, however. Furthermore, MARC has not been available on personal computers and workstations. In the past, it has required a dedicated machine, and dedicated, one-function machines are beyond the fiscal means of most small, specialized libraries and visual collections. At Berkeley, we wanted to utilize imaging functionality and couple it with the cost savings of a relational database management system.

The MARC record has a great deal of storage overhead in its layout. This means that a computer needs a lot more room to store the data for a MARC record than for a dbms record. In MARC most of the fields are defined, as are the subfields. The subfields are denoted by subfield delimiters, such as $a and $b. The subfield $a means something different for each field, and there is no simple mnemonic device to help you remember what the subfield delimiters stand for in MARC, even though the subfields are relatively consistent across all the MARC formats. In a dbms, you can name your own equivalents to the subfield delimiters, so they are easier to learn and remember.

How does one go about mapping a dbms to MARC? Very little has been written on this, and the few libraries that have done mappings have not published their experiences. Beware of asking nonlibrary computer programmers whether a dbms can be mapped to MARC; they always say, "Piece of cake." Most computer programmers have heard of MARC but have not studied it or used it. Be equally cautious asking a knowledgeable librarian whether a dbms can be mapped to MARC; you might hear an outright "No." The truth is somewhere in the middle, with the most accepted view being that a dbms can be mapped to MARC's wealth of fields and subfields if the dbms is adequately flexible.

To improve the art reference capabilities of the national bibliographic utilities as well as to take advantage of the shared cataloging enjoyed by the rest of the library world, a task force of slide librarians and photo archivists should begin the development of guidelines for the cataloging of visual depictions in MARC. In addition, any libraries with experience mapping between MARC and a dbms should publish their successes and their failures as a benefit to the library community.

ACKNOWLEDGMENTS

The author would like to acknowledge the generosity of spirit of James M. Bower, Vocabulary Control Group of the Getty Art History Information Program, Howard Besser of the University of California at Berkeley, Annette Melville and Jeannette Dixon with assistance on RLG matters, and the gracious and timely research support provided by the LAUC-B Research Grants for Librarians Program.

NOTES

1. Linda J. Evans and Maureen O'Brien Will, *MARC for Archival Visual Materials: A Compendium of Practice* (Chicago: Chicago Historical Society, 1988), 3.

2. The percentage of copy slides will vary from institution to institution and by subject matter. Architecture slide libraries will generally have a higher percentage of copy images than art slide libraries will because there is more demand for art images and because art museums are increasingly making their holdings available in slide format.

3. Elizabeth Bakewell and Marilyn Schmitt, *Object, Image, Inquiry: The Art Historian at Work* (Santa Monica: J. Paul Getty Trust, 1988).

4. California State Library. *California Library Networking Retreat, October 23-25, 1988.* "Summary and Outcomes," 8.

5. Betz has stated this position in telephone conversations with the author on several occasions.

6. Nancy B. Olson, *Cataloging of Audio-Visual Materials: A Manual Based on AACR 2.* (Mankato: Minnesota Scholarly Press, c. 1985), 48.

■ Can MARC Accommodate Archives and Museums? Technical and Political Challenges

David Bearman

The MARC formats have had a revolutionary and beneficial effect on the library community in their first twenty years. The formats, which are implementations of International Standards Organization (ISO) standard 2709 and American National Standards Institute (ANSI) standard Z39.2, are maintained by the Library of Congress. Maintaining them involves establishing and documenting their content designation so that they can be used by librarians to exchange information required by library practices. Over the past two decades, the demands of the library community for information exchange capabilities have grown and changed, and the MARC formats have evolved to meet these needs.

Not surprisingly, allied communities of culture curators (archivists, slide librarians, and museum curators, to name only a few) have looked with some envy on the experience and wondered whether they can partake in it or replicate it. Six years ago, the Society of American Archivists' National Information Systems Task Force designed an ANSI Z39.2 format content designation akin to MARC and negotiated with the library community to accept it, with modifications, as a MARC format for Archives and Manuscript Control (MARC AMC).[1] Archivists joined the MARC community to take advantage of the benefit of having the Library of Congress maintain the content designations and of having the library community accept archival description practices as a variant bibliographic approach available to libraries, but their continued involvement in MARC cannot be taken for granted. In using the MARC AMC format, archivists have further defined their needs for information exchange and have discovered requirements that go beyond the current limitations of the MARC content designations for bibliographic description and the library-based concept of authority control.[2]

Like archivists, the museum community has observed the development of MARC over the past twenty years with a mixture of admiration and fear. The benefits of information exchange to libraries were as self-evident as the limitations of the formats. It was obvious to museum professionals that libraries held artifacts and specimens and that librarians would eventually try to describe these holdings in MARC, and it was equally apparent that the model for description of museum holdings that librarians possessed was inadequate to meet the needs of museums either to describe their holdings or to achieve the benefits of inter-institutional information exchange.

This essay explores the nature of archival and museum needs for information exchange and the potential impact of those needs on MARC. It raises the possibility of the use of different ANSI Z39.2 formats by different curatorial communities. Its focus is on the technical and political obstacles facing archives and museums in the use of MARC. The purpose of exploring these is to discover what the archives and museum communities will need to do to take advantage of MARC, to examine the costs of achieving the same benefits using Z39.2, and to alert the library community to the political adjustments it will need to make to bring all cultural information exchange under the umbrella of MARC.

REALITY AND DESCRIPTIVE PRACTICES

Different professions of culture curators describe the evidence they collect regarding our world and its creations from different vantage points.

Library monographic catalogers describe their holdings with a focus on the physical item so they can effect content retrieval. The identity of the item is derived from the uniqueness of its title page. Another physical item with an identical title page is considered a duplicate and does not need to be uniquely cataloged by the holding institution if cataloging for it is available to copy. Based on this view of reality and the role of description, copy cataloging became the original economic driver for bibliographic networks and for MARC.

Library serials catalogers describe their holdings with a focus on issuance history and intent so they can manage past and future accessions. As physical issues are received, they inherit the attributes of logical series even though they differ slightly in title page, as long as their publisher clearly intends them to be part of the same issuance. Even changes in title are linked in records reflecting the publishers' intent. The practical reason for this focus is to be able to anticipate the arrival of the next issue of a periodical, claim a past issue, or bind a volume.

Archivists describe their holdings with a focus on provenance (the context of the creation of the records) and to manage records throughout their life cycle. The actual documents and materials within a body of records can physically change while the records retain the same description. The identity of the records derives from provenance, so the description is constant even in the face of life-cycle weeding, sampling, and destruction. The practical requirements of life-cycle management demand this continuity of focus on an abstract *record series* and *agency of origin*, rather than on the contents itself.

Curators in historical museums practice associational control, focusing on the life history of use with the effect of illuminating context and documenting use relationships. Associations may be made by producer or manufacturer, owner or context and function of use, individual or cultural group. Identical objects used by different individuals or cultures or in different ages or for different purposes will be uniquely, and variously, described. An ax used by George Washington may be described as such in a collection of artifacts belonging to him, but it also is an ax manufactured by a particular Delaware company and sold commercially through a particular network of hardware distributors on the East Coast. Identical axes will comprise other collections organized around these other views and will be differently described.

Science museums practice typological control, focusing on physical features to classify items. Distinguishable individuals may share a record while specimens serving the same ecological functions with different structures are uniquely described. A quartz crystal, oak leaf, or Tyrannosaurus rex tibia would be described according to its type. If a museum has numerous specimens of each, their differences are not in their basic description (except for physical size) but in the records documenting their collecting origin, managed according to the associational control practices of the historical museum, which emphasize the context of discovery and use. This view supports research on the natural world and its structure, making order out of what otherwise would be infinite variety.

All five methods of control are conceptual frameworks and can be applied to any holding. In fact, the same kinds of holdings will be controlled by different types of repositories, and the same objects can be described using several approaches even within one institution. Each of these perspectives answers different user needs.

FUNCTIONAL REQUIREMENTS FOR LOCAL SYSTEMS

The differences in descriptive practices identified above are a reflection of different requirements for effecting intellectual and physical control in each type of repository.

The requirements of the library catalog are to locate known items and items specified by their subject content or authorship. No specific copy of the item is expected. (Each copy produced with a given title page is considered identical.) What the patron expects to be retrieved is a physical object from the stacks – not information but a package. Library acquisition modules are intended simply to get an item that is not fully cataloged into the system. The method of acquisition and the source are irrelevant to our subsequent understanding and use of the object.

Library circulation systems are intended only to locate a specific copy of an item during the period of its use. They share with other library functions a disregard for the history and purposes of use, although they differ in considering the copy, or specific holding, relevant. Special features of some library circulation systems, such as undergraduate reading rooms and journal routing, do permit the reservation of items for future use but barely alter the underlying philosophy that all we need to know is what patron has an item while they have it.

The data architecture of the bibliographic utility, therefore, is built around a cataloging record that is in its function a bibliographic authority record vis-à-vis local cataloging. Specific items, or holdings, are located in individual libraries where they have occasional, transient links to stack locations or patron addresses.

The requirements of archival information systems resemble those of library systems in numerous superficial respects, but on closer examination the differences are more striking than the similarities. While physical items will be retrieved from the stacks in response to a query, the items retrieved will not usually be specified by the information system, only the general region in which they will be found. The source of the items is critical in an archival system because it is from provenance that archival records derive their identity.

Agency histories and personal biographies, therefore, not only record the context of records generation but also provide most of the access points to the likely contents of the records. Archival records scheduling is concerned with the uses of records during different phases of their life cycle and with both past and future actions that can fundamentally transform the physical items in hand, even while they retain their identity. Manuscript repositories and historical special collections also must track donors and members in ways that go far beyond any patron management features of library systems. And archival systems are likely to track users to provide future services to them, retaining links between users and uses that libraries reject.

Thus, the presumed data architecture of an archival system includes provenance authority records linked to descriptive records (at numerous levels of aggregation all internally linked) that have permanent links to internal processing action history and action schedules and to client records that incorporate information about the nature of the use.

The requirements of museum systems go beyond those of archives. The items in museums are frequently objects of study intended to establish what they are and how they came to be. Information used in this research concerns their sources and requires us to know, not just the static features of the context out of which they came, but also such dynamic features as the speed of the boat dragging a net and the size of the holes in the net or such rich context as the stratigraphic relationship of all other objects found on an archaeological site. The uses of museum artifacts in exhibits and interpretive programs require item itineraries, event records, and functions that support public attendance at events. Numerous kinds of patrons in a variety of individual and collective capacities make very different demands of museums requiring sophisticated means of constituency management. Other uses by curators include research on the items, which in turn enhances understanding of the items. At the same time, the kinds of collections management requirements envisioned for archives are equally valid for museums.

The anticipated data architecture of the museum system includes a host of different kinds of authority records for species, for objects of historical association, and for collecting activities, linked to items at numerous levels of aggregation (including both parts, or components, and pieces, or fragments). Source records reflect real time and space and rich context of finding, creation or habitat, events of startling complexity involving items and constituents in itineraries and schedules, fiscal and administrative relationships of all types, and substantial quantities of research and interpretive data.

Of course, these pure case differences do not adequately reflect the needs of any given institution – many hybrids exist in all camps – but they do illustrate why we can expect the information exchange requirements of other cultural institutions to stretch far beyond the need to exchange surrogate descriptions of bibliographic items.

FLAT IS BEAUTIFUL

As should be evident from the description of data architectures required to support management of these different kinds of cultural evidence, archives and museum information systems are likely to be implemented in relational databases with a number of tables, or record types. This realization has led many to despair that we will not be able to exchange museum data using MARC, which employs flat sequential records.

In circles discussing information exchange about complex objects, we confront the potentially crippling prejudice that the MARC format cannot hold information to be exchanged between relational databases because it is a flat file. Technically, the argument that flat files cannot specify complex three-dimensional relations has no merit at all. We need only observe that DNA, which is comprised of only four amino acids in different sequences, is a flat sequential file that specifies the structure of a most complex series of living creatures, including ourselves. We could also point out, since we are speaking of information exchange, that all data transmission is inherently sequential. Flat files are not very elegant ways to specify complex realities, but they are well suited to electronic communications precisely because they are easy to transmit and can so easily be defined in ways that are hardware and software independent.

To support the requirements of archives and museums, MARC, or whatever ANSI Z39.2 content designation is ultimately used, would have to support the definition of a number of record types. MARC already does this in differentiating among the bibliographic description formats, the authority format, and the holdings format, but it would need to go further. Presently, the bibliographic formats are the heart of MARC. Authority data are limited to "authorized headings" and other indexing information, and holdings data are limited to copy-specific information used largely for circulation and collections management.

At a minimum, archives and museums need to exchange information about several new entities. First, they need to exchange data, beyond those required for headings management purposes, about persons and organizations that were involved in the creation, discovery, and cultural use of their holdings. (Elsewhere, Richard Szary and I have referred to these data as reference files and have discussed how they differ from library name authorities.[3]) Second, they need to exchange data about persons and organizations involved in the management and use of their holdings, such as clients, visitors, students, patrons, shipping agents, and insurers. Third, they need to exchange information regarding projects and their execution: records retention schedules and dispositions, exhibit plans and exhibits, lecture schedules, and collections management activities such as preservation.[4]

Also, archives and museums need to exchange information in an environment that recognizes differences in practice and in ultimate purposes for information exchange rather than in one that assumes commonality of practice and intent. Some features of such an environment have been introduced into MARC with the MARC AMC format, but substantially more openness to differences in conventions, often involving field and subfield level designation of conventions, will need to be provided.

This last requirement is particularly irksome to librarians because it appears to them to erode the very purposes of information exchange. Why should they maintain a format within which participants are free to express themselves according their own conventions? I think the answer is because the library is an information service and desires to be an information center. If libraries maintain the vehicles for information exchange between other cultural repositories, they become the means by which researchers gain access to unpublished and artifactual scientific and humanistic information resources. Even though some communities will need to have distinctive conventions for one or more data elements and use them according to those standards, most access points into the shared database will be common to most records. Retrieval according to some discipline-specific views will be restricted to records created by curators in those disciplines, but many means of access will remain.

Librarians should also realize that multiple independent views of reality are also essential to support true scholarly information exchange and that we should be working toward methods of accessing distinctive views rather than distorting the underlying descriptions. Thus, chronological access to records of Renaissance music of Italy and of France would yield slightly different time frames based on different demarcations accepted by scholars in music history, and both would be different from retrievals for Renaissance political theory. Disciplines that use geo-ecological terminology would not be expected to employ geopolitical terms, or vice versa, but intelligent systems should be able to make paths between these vocabularies based on overlap in the spatial domains each represents.[5]

As we can see, the modification of content designation required to support archives and museum information exchange under the MARC umbrella is technically possible. But politically it may not fly. Can MARC, as we now know it, be made to carry information about so many different kinds of entities, when we have used it to date as the host for a narrow repertoire?

ISO 2709, ANSI Z39.2, AND THE POLITICS OF MARC

A decade from now, MARC may or may not accommodate the information exchange requirements of archives and museums, but if it does not, it will not be because of technical limitations. MARC is an instantiation of international and national technical standards that are quite adequate to support the exchange of a variety of records types required by archival and museum information systems; but it is itself not a technical standard but a content specification. The content specification is governed by the Library of

Congress and the library community as manifest in an ALA representative body, the Committee on Representation in Machine-Readable Form of Bibliographic Information (MARBI).

Within the next two years, the archives and museum communities will have formulated proposals for the exchange of more than one type of record using existing national bibliographic networks. The SAA Committee on Archival Information Exchange held a meeting of archival exchange experts in the spring of 1989 to map out these new directions.[6] The Museum Computer Network has organized a working group on the Computerized Interchange of Museum Information (CIMI), involving representatives of numerous museum professional associations, networks, and vendors, to define an interchange protocol for museum data consistent with ISO 2709/ANSI Z39.2.[7]

The resultant proposals will, most likely, be brought before MARBI. At the moment, it is not clear precisely what form they will take nor how MARBI might react, but it is clear that even if the library community does not want to expand the use of MARC, the ISO 2709/ANSI Z39.2 framework can support more than one body involved in content designation. If MARBI wishes, it can permit the kinds of changes to MARC content specifications and political accommodations that would open the way for the exchange of archives and museum data. If it chooses not to, archives and museums can, and I believe will, simply designate their own contents for ISO 2709/ANSI Z39.2 protocols and use the software, and possibly the networks, developed to exchange MARC records for their own ends. It is not at all clear that this outcome would be undesirable, although in principal it seems unnecessary. Over the next few years, I would expect this discussion to become more specific and the advantages and disadvantages of multiple communities of exchange under ANSI Z39.2 to be further explored.[8]

NOTES

1. David Bearman, *Towards National Information Systems for Archives and Manuscript Repositories: The NISTF Papers* (Chicago: Society of American Archivists, 1987).

2. David Bearman, "Archival and Bibliographic Information Networks," *Journal of Library Administration* 7 (Summer/Fall 1986): 99-110. See also David Bearman, "Archives and Manuscript Control with Bibliographic Utilities: Challenges and Opportunities," *American Archivist* 52 (Winter 1989): 26-39.

3. David Bearman and Richard Szary, "Beyond Authority Headings: Authorities as Reference Files in a Multi-Disciplinary Setting," in *Authority*

Control Symposium, ed. Karen Muller (Tucson, Ariz.: ARLIS/NA, 1987), 69-78.

4. David Bearman, *Functional Requirements for Collections Management Systems*, Archival Informatics Technical Report, no. 1 (Fall 1987).

5. David Bearman, "Considerations in the Design of Art Scholarly Databases," *Library Trends* 37 (Fall 1988): 206-19.

6. In addition to the national debate, an international discussion has recently been held under the auspices of the International Council on Archives, which is expected to become an ongoing forum. The first presentations are to be published as Proceedings of the ICA Meeting of Experts on Descriptive Standards (Ottawa, 1989).

7. For information about CIMI, contact Deirdre Stam, Executive Director, Museum Computer Network, Information Studies, Syracuse University, Syracuse, NY 13244-2340, (315) 443-5612.

8. The NHPRC has recently funded a project to bring archivists together to discuss standardization needs. A report on this Working Group on Standards for Archival Description and its preliminary findings can be obtained from Vicki Walch, Project Coordinator, 65 N. Westminster St., Iowa City, IA 52245.

■ MARC and the Promise of Artificial Intelligence for Subject Access: Current Limitations and Future Considerations

PAT MOLHOLT

The concept of artificial intelligence (AI) has been around a long time. Classical Greek mythology contains references to automata possessing human powers of judgment or reason. Through the ages, the concept was refined and elaborated upon until eventually attempts were made to build machines capable of "thinking." In the twentieth century, this effort focused first on the development of computer software, and later on specialized hardware, designed to apply reasoning and judgment to problem solving. Today the augmentation of human capability is accomplished by a range of means: from programs that operate on basic if-then logic on one end of the spectrum to complex multiworld logics, sophisticated heuristics, and elaborate explanation features on the other end.

The very phrase *artificial intelligence* is a confusing, oxymoronic concatenation. Sokolowski offers an explanation that is useful and interesting.[1] By drawing a distinction between two senses of *artificial*, he helps clarify the purpose and role of AI. *Artificial*, when it is used to describe silk flowers or fake fur, is meant to resemble the real, to serve as a useful but limited substitute for the real object. In another sense, as in artificial diamonds or artificial light, the implication is that the construct or artifact fully serves the function of the real object. Researchers in artificial intelligence categorize the intent of their work under the second sense. They are attempting to build systems that will fully substitute for human thought and reasoning. Such a goal, however, is still far from being realized.

Artificial intelligence is of obvious interest to information professionals. Librarians have already experimented with this new and challenging field in the creation of expert systems: software programs, typically running on personal computers, that give their users "expert" advice or guidance regarding which reference tools will answer particular types of questions, what journals or other serials may cover a given topic, how research should be done for a term paper, and so on. Tools or shells, the software programs used to build expert systems, are the most successful and readily available artificial intelligence products developed to date. The software ranges in sophistication from $49.95 packages that operate with a limited set of rules and methods of representing knowledge to systems costing between twenty and forty thousand dollars that require specialized equipment and highly knowledgeable programmers. In their most basic form, expert systems consist of an inference engine and a knowledge base. The inference engine is the logical foundation, the rules under which the system operates. The knowledge base is very much what its name implies, a database of knowledge – facts, statements, attributes, measurements, and so on – recorded in a structure that allows manipulations by the inference engine.

Expert systems have been accepted by librarians as a method of augmenting services and increasing productivity. Expert systems can be made available at times and in places inconvenient to traditional staffing patterns. Late into the evening and at remote sites, these AI programs can assist users in meeting their information needs. The National Agricultural Library created several small-scale microcomputer-based expert systems including AquaRef in 1987. In the same year, the National Archives engaged in an intense prototyping effort to determine the viability of expert systems in archival work. They concluded that expert systems are appropriate information handling tools for use by patrons and archivists but that the knowledge base required to operate a major system was beyond the Archives' ability to fully develop and maintain at this time. Even the prototype became unwieldy.

Information professionals need to integrate AI techniques into their work operations and service environments, particularly from the user's point of view. By all measures, whether book production, database size, or articles published, there is unprecedented growth in the quantity of information. This increased production and the consequent overwhelming availability of information often leave users awash. While librarians and others have developed cooperative techniques such as shared cataloging to deal with the rising tide of information, the user is essentially left alone to cope with the wealth of new, potentially relevant information resources. In addition, a variety of information media now exists to further compound and confound the prospective information seeker. CD-ROMs, videodiscs, user-accessible online databases, and combinations of these have joined the traditional print-on-paper, microform, and librarian-directed database searching. The result is a dense jungle of information growing at alarming rates and populated with exotic new access tools meant to carve a path but, in the end, often complicating matters as much as they help. Furthermore, as users have gained familiarity with, if not mastery of, electronically based information, they have begun to place unanticipated demands on systems. As an access mechanism, Boolean logic, already far from perfect, is useless when the information sought has no access point – that is, when the access point, or the term being searched, was not accounted for in the indexing process. The power of controlled vocabularies with rich lead-in terminology moves users well ahead of free-text searching yet leaves them stranded when only the literal meaning is recorded. In addition, no systematic methodology exists by which relationships between concepts can be identified and coded for use in retrieval. Broader Term and Narrower Term relationships are common to both information systems and AI systems, but they are inadequate in the face of the variety of information one finds in text. Language, even that found in the titles of articles and books, is rich in metaphor and analogy. Current systems do not begin to address these areas of language use.

While I am not prepared to claim that artificial intelligence techniques will perfectly answer the problems discussed above, it will go a considerable distance in addressing them. Software tools are being developed to guide users productively through masses of information without overwhelming them. Techniques exist to organize and structure information into knowledge bases capable of supporting inference-based reasoning. Also, the full power of controlled thesauri is being augmented with lexicons, resulting in full-text systems capable of ascertaining parts of speech, scope of meaning, and relationships among concepts. To reap benefits from these advances, the information profession must rethink both its traditional tools and its methods.

MARC, the core of standards-based information systems, is a starting point. While some online catalogs have exploited the MARC record formats beyond the author, title, and subject fields (Rensselaer's being one), most retrieval systems, particularly those commercial systems used for typical online public access catalog (OPAC) applications, barely recognize the existence of information in other parts of the MARC record such as the fixed fields. In addition, searching with Boolean logic is tightly constrained, often by a series of tedious menu-driven steps. When we speak of extending MARC and creating user-driven systems assisted by AI, then, it is necessary to keep in mind that many current systems fail to take full advantage of the existing MARC formats and full Boolean search capabilities and that systems designers may find it difficult to consider implementing even more complex systems. The rationale and justification, however, must be service to the user. Systems designers who do wish to be more creative in utilizing the full MARC record should find increasing support from librarians and users. Both groups are finally moving away from the view that there must be a close correspondence between the paper-based catalog and the online information system. Few libraries, however, are presently staffed with systems programmers who are given free reign over the OPAC software. The view taken on staffing patterns by a group of librarians in the Council on Library Resources Senior Fellows Program suggests changes in this area.[2] They predict that libraries will employ an increasing number of technically skilled individuals and will take a far more active role in the design of information systems both for the library and for its broader community, whether that be academe, business, or government.

TODAY'S SYSTEMS

In "Human Intelligence as a Precondition for the Machine Processing of Knowledge," Mater provides an excellent analysis of problems with traditional information retrieval systems.[3] He amply illustrates his thesis that AI will not, in and of itself, solve information retrieval problems. AI is not faster clock time, more memory, or moving from 16- to 64-bit processors. AI requires that we understand what it is we wish to accomplish and also understand the limitations of machine-based term matching that, to date, requires essentially perfect correspondence between the indexing terminology and query language for any result.

Mater makes a second point that clarifies the importance of AI in information handling. He says that it is problematic to consider the word as the smallest unit of information and suggests that words cannot be used without consideration of their context. What is minimally required is an intellectual process of abstraction where descriptors are derived from the content of a text, not plucked out simply on the basis of a word-matching process. The reference to context reaches beyond accounting for syntagmatic information. There are issues of modifiers and their nouns and of relationships among terms. Paradigmatic information must also be accounted for.

On one level it is critical to know which adjective modifies what noun, the key to avoiding false hits. When a modifier is bound to the term it modifies, which is sometimes the case in the processing of subject fields by automated systems, one avoids crossover between modifiers and the concepts being modified. RED DRESS and LEATHER BELT will not, in such bound systems, yield RED BELT or LEATHER DRESS. In the case of unbound subject phrases, such false drops are common and frustrating. When one moves to dealing with full-text systems, only syntactic parsing of the text can avoid such errors. Working in the context of full text, it is time consuming and costly.

Beyond this concern is that of retaining information on the relationships among concepts and on the idiosyncratic use of concepts in the form of metaphors. When a researcher examines a text, or even the physical cards in a catalog, he or she brings knowledge and a particular point of view to the search for information. When the same individual is faced with isolated key words, or single terms drawn from a text or a catalog entry with no way to relate them to each other, the task of bringing his or her knowledge to bear is significantly complicated. Relationships and context are the key to intelligible information processing by humans and machines.

By relationships between concepts, I am suggesting linkages such as those proposed by Neelameghan and Rau,[4] and others:

> x performs y.
> x is typically used for y.
> x is characterized by y.
> x is caused by y.
> x is produced by y.
> x resembles y

Linking concepts describing the subject content of a document with a consistent and agreed-upon set of relationships should significantly enhance the precision as well as the relevance of recall.

Subject headings, whether in the traditional 650 field or the new 654 field, serve to encapsulate the major concepts in the document being described. The next necessary and logical step is to encode relationships between those concepts and to provide the user with options that employ this same information. For example, if the user needs information on WASTE PLASTIC–that is, the plastic remaining as a waste product from extrusion–or some other forming process, it will be difficult, in conventional systems, to avoid false hits from materials dealing with PLASTIC WASTE, meaning fast food wrappers, and the like. Yet one is a form of plastic, the by-product of a manufacturing process, and the other is a type of waste, occurring at the intersection of convenience and consumerism. Using hierarchically structured thesauri built on single concept terms will not solve this problem because both PLASTIC WASTE and WASTE PLASTIC are compound concepts and would not be included. While this particular example would be much informed by the inclusion of simple syntactic information on nouns and adjectives, a more powerful tool would be an agreement on a core set of concept relationships and a methodology to include relationship coding in the indexing process.

Subject indexing systems have long employed a related term structure to assist the user in finding relevant information. Broader Term and Narrower Term references, along with other nonspecified references, were mixed together in the "see also" suggestions of older editions of the *Library of Congress Subject Headings (LCSH)*.[5] The most recent edition, the twelfth (1989), has removed some ambiguity by dividing references into BTs and NTs. There is no attempt within the vocabulary itself, nor any mechanism in conventional applications, to clarify or identify the relationships between concepts.

MARC AND AI

Two questions arise: (1) Can the MARC record be expanded to hold information on the relationships between concepts or the roles terms may play? (2) Is it appropriate to consider MARC as the vehicle for such information? Let us begin with work already accomplished. The enhancement of the 6xx field by the addition of the 654 field was an attempt to preserve the context of terms. In a hierarchically structured vocabulary, one can retain in the 654 subfield $c information giving the location of the term in the hierarchic structure of the vocabulary. This provides a sense of context for the term. In the new coding the subject heading HOUSING – UNITED STATES is represented as "654bbcobaHousing-czbUnited States$2aat." In this example, drawn from the *Art and Architecture Thesaurus*, the subfield $c tells the user that the term HOUSING comes from the objects facet of the vocabulary.[6] The fact that a system to accommodate some context information could be devised within the MARC record structure indicates that the idea of encoding relational data as well may be feasible.

In AI, the concept of semantic networks serves to link, by particular types of relations and associations, terms that operate together or that contribute to a larger process or to understanding of an event. Relating the term Grow, for example, to Alive, and Requires Food, begins to define *grow* and provide a context for using it appropriately. *Alive* and *food* would be part of the semantic network associated with the word *grow*. In a thesaurus, typically composed of nouns rather than verbs, CARROTS may be related to FOOD, or more specifically to VEGETABLES in a hierarchic sense, and to VITAMIN A or FARMING in the senses of "is a source of vitamin A" or "is the product of farming." The two universally accepted relationships used extensively in AI work are those of genus/species and whole/part. As we move toward defining others, such as process/product, agent/counteragent, we need ways to record this information in our retrieval systems. To accommodate semantic relationships in a MARC record would require considerable expansion for MARC as well as an agreed-upon method for their assignment. To the extent that a relationship is idiosyncratic or forms the basis for a metaphor, its use would be problematic. Humphrey's work, noted below, illustrates how role indicators can be a part of a record structure and can be used to encourage, if not control, correct use of terminology.

In addition to context information, a second needed feature is part-of-speech information recorded in a consistent and traceable way. Syntactic parsing is not a viable approach to subject entries because it would be highly redundant between applications and because subject entries are incomplete noun phrases. Retaining part-of-speech information is valuable as it is a useful way to address the confusion between Dress as a noun and as an adjective–for example, Red Dress and Dress Uniform in systems where modifiers are unbound and terms are searched individually.

This discussion leaves aside two questions, namely, who will code such data and by what methodology? These are especially interesting questions in view of the fact that any particular user's system could be a decade away from implementing enhancements based on the relationship data. When we look back at the history of cooperative cataloging using MARC, we see a remarkable event. Libraries joined utilities such as OCLC in droves and committed themselves to the complicated task of doing original cataloging according to a standard that required information well beyond their need for printed cards. There was an unquestioned sense of eventual benefit at a point where no one was entirely sure just how systems could and would make use of the full MARC record. Can this happen again? Will there be the visionary leadership of someone like Henriette Avram to convince librarians this is the way of the future, even the uncharted future?

The two features discussed above, part-of-speech and context information, relieve systems designers of a considerable amount of work. It has been said by Edward Feigenbaum that one of the most perplexing roadblocks to building large and robust (accurate, effective, consistent) expert systems is the building of the knowledge base–that is, the gathering and structuring of knowledge. Every move the information science community makes in standardizing vocabularies and organizing hierarchies has a direct payoff in the AI environment because this contributes to the building of knowledge bases. Creating hierarchies of terminology is, in fact, a form of knowledge structuring. In addition, a system that contains part-of-speech information begins to obviate the need for a separate lexicon.

Lexicons have long played a role in AI systems, and considerable research has been undertaken to parse machine-readable dictionaries so as to derive needed information.[7,8] More recently, some researchers in the combined fields of Information Science (IS) and Computer Science (CS) have begun to build their own lexicons, deciding that the software design work involved in building a system to accurately parse even machine-readable dictionaries has an insufficient payback. Including the relevant part of speech in an authority record represents a move in the right direction.

Similarly, the amount of time and effort that has gone into the machine-generation of thesauri is being questioned. To date, the general IS and CS communities have not experimented with hierarchically structured vocabularies. The majority of work has been done with alphabetic lists or free text. Thesauri that have been "automatically" generated are simple word lists with some Broader Terms and Narrower Terms provided. A next step in the enhancement of thesauri composed of single concept terms is to develop and code rules for combining terms. In AI-related lexicons, frames or structures are developed where properties such as "transitive" and "requires animate object" are recorded. The *MeSH* vocabulary has rules controlling term combinations or co-occurrences. They do not operate on a term-by-term basis but on a term-to-category/hierarchy basis. For example:

> etiology (C, F3) - Used with diseases for causative agents including microorganisms; includes environmental and social factors and personal habits as contributing factors; includes pathogenesis.[9]

The parenthetical information notifies the indexer that the subdivision Etiology can only be used with terms in hierarchy C, Chemicals and Drugs, and terms in section 3 of hierarchy F, Psychiatry and Psychology. Such building-block information is needed to build systems that, as Suzanne Humphrey proposes, can intelligently support indexing functions but also underpin the logic of AI information retrieval systems.[10]

The techniques of artificial intelligence–structuring knowledge, inheritance, logic, and, more specifically, inference-based reasoning–are applied subject domain by subject domain. The task of the so-called knowledge engineer is to extract knowledge from a variety of sources, including experts in the field, and structure that knowledge in ways intelligible to computers. What has been ignored to date is the amount of directly related work already done by those creating controlled vocabularies. First, gathering the most relevant and accurate terminology for a field, including variant spellings, alternate forms, and, in some cases, singular and plural forms of the term, has already been achieved. Admittedly, lexicographers use a different set of words to describe the structure of the vocabulary, namely USE and USE FORs, Preferred and Nonpreferred Terms, and so on, but the result, is nonetheless of direct value to knowledge engineers. Second, use of the related term structure, inadequate as it assuredly is, provides a context for terms. The information conveyed in the syndetic structure begins to address information in a paradigmatic or topographical manner that is a critical addition to the syntagmatic information of a sentence. More needs to be done, but what will the return be for the work?

FUTURE BENEFITS

Stated in its simplest form, the more inclusive and complete the conceptual mapping of knowledge is, the more accurate the information retrieval will be.

If we can enhance the schemes we use to code information in a way that includes term/concept relationships and context identifiers, we will provide the means for more complete and more accurate retrieval of information. The PRECIS indexing system, developed by Derek Austin, has elements of concept relations.[11] His four Grammatical Relations – predicative, possessive, active, and locative – are an attempt to disambiguate the relationships between concepts in an indexing string. The first two correlate exactly to the genus/species and whole/part relationships used both in AI work and in the structuring of hierarchical-based vocabularies. In the same vein, the classification scheme used in ICONCLASS allows precise identification of the iconography of visual images and the relationship between objects represented, such as a woman on a horse versus a woman walking a horse. Unfortunately, the method for building classification numbers does not always identify relationships. Often, especially in the case of the more complex themes in a painting, a colon is employed to join notations. The colon is deliberately void of information about the relationship between the notations being joined.

It is clear that the information science profession has attempted to address the need for more complete representation of concepts, including the relationships between concepts. The examples above make that point but they do not go far enough. Several questions linger: Can a core set of relationships be identified and agreed upon? How might such information be coded in the indexing process for use in retrieval? How much relationship information is an inherent part of a term or concept, and how much is dependent on the particular environment in which a concept is found? Once again, we have the matter of metaphor and analogy as well as the problem of idiosyncratic use of language. These questions point to areas of needed research. The benefits, while needing validation and refinement, seem reasonably clear. If users can employ more of the knowledge they bring to the information searching process, the relevance of the retrieved information should increase, reducing false hits. In today's retrieval systems, we consciously strip away extraneous information, such as concept relationships, brought to the search and instead require users to work around the problems our system's limitations impose. In the WASTE PLASTIC and PLASTIC WASTE example, users may be forced to use the NOT logic in Boolean searching in an attempt to exclude terms such as FOOD, PACKAGING, and BIODEGRADABLE so as to get at the industrial sense of the concept.

There is a popular concept making its way around the AI and IS communities. John Sculley, CEO of Apple, calls it a Knowledge Navigator. Robert Kahn, head of the Corporation for National Research Initiatives, refers to it as a Knowbot. Vanevar Bush called it the Memex fifty years ago. The essence of the concept is the suggestion that humans' information search activities will be assisted by intelligent, interactive, even humanlike software programs. Knowbots or Navigators will seek out needed information from complex information bases, or knowledge bases, negotiating differences in storage techniques, representation methods, and the networks that link such resources. These are not ordinary "front-end" software packages but, rather, highly individualized servantlike software-based agents ready to do one's information bidding.

For information professionals, there is a tremendously challenging opportunity to bring our work into the mainstream of AI. The work of organizing and structuring information needs to be augmented with a tighter control on fully representing concepts and the relationships between concepts. The challenging aspects to the Knowbot idea is neither the hardware nor the software but the intellectual effort required to bring such systems into productive reality.

NOTES

1. Robert Sokolowski, "Natural and Artificial Intelligence," *Daedalus, Journal of the American Academy of Arts and Sciences* (Winter 1988): 45-64.

2. Anne Woodsworth, Nancy Allen, Irene Hoadley, June Lester, Pat Molholt, Danuta Nitecki, and Lou Wetherbee, "The Model Research Library: Planning for the Future," *Journal of Academic Librarianship* 15, no. 3 (July 1988): 132-38.

3. Erick Mater, "Human Intelligence as a Precondition for the Machine Processing of Knowledge," *International Classification* 15, no. 3 (1988): 125-32.

4. A. Neelameghan and J. K. Ravichandra Rao, "Nonhierarchical Associative Relationships: Their Types and Computer-Generation of RT Links," *Library Science with a Slant toward Documentation* 13 (1976): 24-34.

5. Library of Congress, Subject Cataloging Division, *Library of Congress Subject Headings*, 12th ed. (Washington, D.C.: Cataloging Distribution Service, Library of Congress, 1989).

6. *Art and Architecture Thesaurus* (New York: Oxford University Press, 1990).

7. Nicoletta Calzolari, "The Dictionary and the Thesaurus Can Be Combined," in *Relational Model of the Lexicon: Representing Knowledge in Semantic Networks,* ed. Martha Walton Evens (Cambridge, Cambridge University Press, 1988).

8. Thomas Ahlswede and Martha Evens, "Generating a Relational Lexicon from a Machine-Readable Dictionary," *International Journal of Lexicography* (1988). Special Issue.

9. U.S. Department of Health and Human Services, National Library of Medicine, *National Library of Medicine Medical Subject Headings* (Bethesda, Md.: National Institutes of Health, 1990), I-ll.

10. Suzanne Humphrey, "A Knowledge-based Expert System for Computer-assisted Indexing," *IEEE Expert* 4, no. 3 (Fall 1989): 25-38.

11. Derek Austin, *PRECIS*, 2d ed. (London: British Library, 1984).

■ Contributors

Patricia Barnett is museum librarian for systems at the Thomas J. Watson Library at the Metropolitan Museum of Art. She serves as project coordinator for the Art Museum Library Consortium and is director of the Clearinghouse on Art Documentation and Computerization Project. She is a past chair of the ARLIS/AAT Advisory Committee and serves as a consultant and publishes in the areas of art libraries and research support projects on authority control and online catalogs.

David Bearman is founder and president of Archives & Museum Informatics and is editor of its newsletter and technical reports. He was deputy director of the Office of Information Resource Management at the Smithsonian Institution and director of the National Information Systems Task Force of the Society of American Archivists. He has been president of the Museum Computer Network and chair of the Arts & Humanities Special Interest Group of the American Society of Information Science. He publishes and lectures widely on archival and information science topics.

Howard Besser is assistant professor of library science at the University of Pittsburgh. From 1974 to 1989, he worked with visual collections at the University of California at Berkeley as information manager for the University Art Museum, and later as image database specialist for the central campus Computer Center's Advanced Technology Planning group. As image database specialist, he served as a consultant on collection management and automation issues to a wide variety of the campus's collections: geography, anthropology, art, architecture, and manuscripts. He has been involved with the UC Berkeley Image Database Project since its inception. He has published articles on automation of image collections and is a frequent speaker at professional conferences.

Jackie M. Dooley is special collections librarian at the University of California, San Diego, where she is a cataloger of rare books, manuscripts, archives, graphics, and other special collections materials. She is chair of the

Standards Committee of ALA's Rare Books and Manuscripts Section and has been a committee member since 1984. She previously worked as a cataloger in the Prints and Photographs Division of the Library of Congress.

Linda J. Evans is associate curator of archives and manuscripts at the Chicago Historical Society, where her work with a curatorial committee on computerization has included the preparation of sample MARC records for two-dimensional and three-dimensional artifacts and art as part of the staff's exploration of cataloging formats and software. She is the coauthor with Maureen O'Brien Will of *MARC for Archival Visual Materials: A Compendium of Practice.*

Christine Hennessey is coordinator of the Inventories of American Paintings and Sculpture in the Office of Research Support, National Museum of American Art, Smithsonian Institution. In 1985, she served on a resource committee formed by the Library of Congress Network Development and MARC Standards Office to assist in redefining the Visual Materials format to accommodate three-dimensional artifacts and realia. More recently, she participated in a national conference on the use of MARC records for Archival Visual Materials, which resulted in the production of a *Compendium of Practice.* She is also an active member of the standards committee for the Smithsonian Institution Bibliographic Information System and has published in *Art Documentation, Visual Resources,* and the *Archives of American Art Journal.*

Jeanne M. Keefe is the graphics curator at Rensselaer Polytechnic Institute in Troy, New York. She previously held the position of assistant archivist with the Armenian Architectural Photographic Archives Project, a multivolume inventory in microfiche form of the history of Armenian architecture. Her professional area of interest is in the interpretation and documentation of the built environment.

Pat Molholt is associate director of libraries at Rensselaer Polytechnic Institute, where she has been responsible for the development and implementation of a range of automated information services. In addition, she serves as affirmative action advisor to Rensselaer's president. Her B.S. and M.L.S. degrees were completed at the University of Wisconsin-Madison, along with a specialist certificate focusing on automation in libraries. She is currently a doctoral student at Rensselaer, working on the role of concept relationships in both lexicography and artificial intelligence. Along with Toni Petersen, Molholt was one of the cofounders of the *Art and Architecture Thesaurus* in 1979 and remained with the project until 1986. She has held positions at the University of Wisconsin-Madison, and the University of Wyoming. A past president of the Special Libraries Association, she was awarded its John Cotton Dana Award in 1989.

Alden Monroe worked with the Cincinnati Historical Society from 1977 to 1984, serving as manuscripts curator at the time he left in 1984 to accept a position with the Alabama Department of Archives and History (ADAH) where he now is head of the Archival Services Division. He is a member of numerous state and national archival organizations and currently serves on the Government Records Project Steering Committee (RLG); on the Steering Committee for the Archives, Manuscripts, and Special Collections Program Committee (RLG); and as chair of the Description Section.

Toni Petersen is director of the *Art and Architecture Thesaurus* and one of the original founders of this project to build a comprehensive, hierarchically structured thesaurus for the fields of art and architecture. She was previously director of the Bennington College Library (1980-1986) and executive editor of *RILA* (*International Repertory of the Literature of Art*) (1972-1980). Her background is as a library cataloger, having worked at Harvard University and Boston University prior to going to *RILA*. She lectures and publishes on authority control and on the *AAT* and currently serves on the NISO Committee to revise the American National Standard for Thesaurus Construction, the Subject Analysis Committee of the American Library Association, the Advisory Board of the Clearinghouse Project on Art Documentation and Computerization and on the Subcommittee on *AAT* Implementation of the Research Libraries Group's Art and Architecture Program Committee. She is a past-president of the Art Libraries Society of North America.

Kathleen Roe is associate archivist in the Collections Management Unit of the New York State Archives and Records Administration. In that capacity, she supervises the arrangement and description of state government records and is responsible for participation in automated bibliographic systems including the national database, RLIN and CMS, a local online public access catalog. She is a member of numerous state and national archival organizations, serving as an instructor for the Society of American Archivists' workshop on the MARC AMC Format, and is SAA's liaison to the American Library Association's MARBI Committee.

Maryly Snow has been working in academic libraries for almost twenty years, in reference, interlibrary loan, bibliographic instruction, and special libraries, with a concentration on visual materials. Currently, she is the librarian of the Architecture Slide and Photograph Library, College of Environmental Design, at the University of California at Berkeley. She is active in ARLIS/NA's (Art Libraries Society of North America) Visual Resources Division and the Visual Resources Association.

Deirdre Corcoran Stam has most recently been executive director of the Museum Computer Network. She began her formal education in art information with a B.A. in Fine Arts from Harvard University and an M.A. from the Institute of Fine Arts, New York University. Other degrees earned include an M.Ed. from The Johns Hopkins University, an M.L.S. from Catholic University, and a D.L.S. from Columbia University. Beginning professional life in a curatorial position at the Art Institute of Chicago, Stam moved on to library posts at SUNY/Purchase and The Cooper-Hewitt Museum, with occasional forays back to the museum world as curator. In recent years, she has taught at the School of Library Service, Columbia University, and the School of Information Studies, Syracuse University. Her research has centered on user studies and art historical material, authority work in the automated environment, and, most recently, the development of a MARC-based structure for communicating museum information.

Cathleen Whitehead is currently user services coordinator at the *Art and Architecture Thesaurus*, responsible for liaison with and training of *AAT* users.

Martha Yee has been cataloging supervisor of the Film and Television Archive at the University of California, Los Angeles, since 1983. Prior to that, she cataloged audiovisual materials at the UCLA Biomedical Library. She is active in the American Library Association, Resources and Technical Services Division, and is currently a member of the RTSD/LITA/RASD Representation in Machine-Readable Form of Bibliographic Information Committee (MARBI), which is charged with reviewing and evaluating proposals to change the MARC format. She is a member of the National Moving Image Database Standards Committee and, in that capacity, compiled *Moving Image Materials: Genre Terms* on behalf of the committee. She has published articles on nonbook cataloging, cataloging history, and online public access catalogs.

Brad Young is music technical services librarian of the Otto E. Albrecht Music Library at the University of Pennsylvania in Philadelphia. A graduate of McGill University in Montreal, he holds a master's degree in musicology and library science and is completing a Ph.D. dissertation in music bibliography at the University of Illinois. Formerly chair of the Music Library Association Subcommittee on Subject Access, he now chairs the MLA Bibliographic Control Committee and also chaired its Working Group on a Music Thesaurus. He is a member and current chair of the American Library Association Subject Analysis Committee (ALCTS/CCS). Recently he undertook a comparison of PRECIS and *LCSH* for the retrieval of printed music.

Helena Zinkham is a cataloger in the Library of Congress Prints and Photographs Division. She and Elisabeth Betz Parker are the cocompilers of *Descriptive Terms for Graphic Materials: Genre and Physical Characteristics Headings.*

■ Name Index

AACR 2, 13, 17, 118, 187, 191
AAM (American Association of
Museums), 122
AAPC (Art and Architecture
Program Committee), 19, 20
AASLH (American Association for
State and Local History), 138
AAT *(Art and Architecture
Thesaurus)*, 2-3, 37, 65, 68, 72, 94,
128, 137, 168, 183
    Document Types hierarchy, 55
    Drawings hierarchy, 52
    facets, 13, 17, 20, 21, 58, 93, 138
    Functions hierarchy, 166-67
    and LCSH, 45, 63, 66, 81-83, 92
    Location field (851), 147
    mapping, 86, 93
    and MARC-based systems, 19,
       40
    and NUCMC, 54, 55
    Object Genres hierarchies, 58
    and pre- and postcoordinated
       system, 103
    and RLG, 166
    Styles and Periods hierarchy,
       29, 38
    system, 85
    and uniterms, 84
ACRL (Association of College and
Research Libraries), 73
AFI (American Film Institute)
    and subject access, 107
Allen, Nancy, 19

AMC (Archives and Manuscripts
Control) format, 47, 53, 72, 147,
157-59, 165
Anderson, James, 19
ANSI (American National Standards
Institute), 12, 72
    thesaurus standard, 69, 82
Archives and Museum Informatics,
137
ARLIS (Art Libraries Society of
North America), 12, 138
Arms, William, 137
ASIS (American Society of
Information Science), 19, 138
Austin, Derek, 15, 176
*Avery Index to Architectural
Periodicals*, 13, 81

BCM *(British Catalogue of Music)*
(1957), 172
    classification, 174, 176
    PRECIS, 175-76
Bearman, David, 165
Bentley Historical Library, 166
Boolean logic, 53, 55, 59, 67, 71, 84,
101, 104, 131
Boston Museum of Fine Arts Library,
19
British Library, 15, 98
    Bibliographic Services Division,
       175
British Museums Association, 124
BSI (British Standards Institute), 12,
82, 90

UCLA (University of California at
  Los Angeles), 183
    and AFI catalogs, 107
    Film and Television Archive, 98
    and GMD, 110
    and LCSH, 106, 109
    MELVYL online union
      catalog, 68
    ORION system 68, 102
    and online public access
      catalog, 102
UNESCO Division of Culture, 126
    and Harmonization, 134
UCSD (University of California, San
  Diego), 68
UCSC (University of California at
  Santa Cruz) (Tansey), 26
University of Leicester, 127
University of Miami, Florida, 123

Vance, David, 123, 125, 128
    and Museum of Modern Art,
      126

Wajenberg, Arnold, 174
Watson Library, 138
Weihs, Jean, 110
Weinberg, Susan Kalb, 129

Yale Center for British Art, 126, 129

■ Subject Index

aboutness, 99-101
AI (artificial intelligence), 247-56
    and MARC, 252
archival cataloging,
    contrasted with library
       cataloging, 238-39
    contrasted with museum
       cataloging, 239
archival information systems,
    contrasted with library
       information systems, 240-41
    contrasted with museum
       information systems, 241
    information exchange
       requirements, 242-44
art object cataloging, 117-39
    data elements, 124
artifact cataloging, 188-200
authority control. *See* vocabulary
    control.

biographical databases, 136
    cataloging. *See* art object
       cataloging; artifact
       cataloging; descriptive
       cataloging; museum
       cataloging; rare book
       cataloging; subject
       cataloging
    classification, distinct from
       subject cataloging, 8

classifications,
    faceted, 172-74
    for music, 171-74
co-occurrence rules,/ 102-4
compound terms, 90
concept relationships, 250-52, 254-56
depicted work. *See* represented work
descriptive cataloging,
    distinct from subject cataloging,
       7-8, 44
    of moving images, 109-10
    of sculpture, 146-48
expert systems,
    in libraries, 248

faceted classification,
    for music, 172-74
    use in online retrieval, 174-75
faceted indexing, 15, 21, 85, 175-79,
    198
    in MARC, 21
facets,
    definition, 15
    AAT, 12-13, 20, 96
fields, data. *See* specific field names
    under MARC
flat files, 242
function,
    archivists' definition, 159
    as an access point, 157, 160-69

genre and form of material access,